Colin Wilson was born in Leicester in 1931. He left school at sixteen and spent several years working in a wool warehouse, a laboratory, a plastics factory and a coffee bar before *The Outsider* was published in 1956 to outstanding critical acclaim. Since then he has written many books on philosophy, the occult, crime and sexual deviance, plus a number of successful novels. His work includes *The Mammoth Book of True Crime*, *The Mammoth Book of the Supernatural*, *The Mind Parasites*, *New Pathways in Psychology*, and *The Occult*. Mr Wilson is well known as a lecturer and radio and television personality. He lives in Cornwall.

Colin Wilson's True Crime File

MURDER

in the 1940s

Edited by Colin and Damon Wilson

Robinson Publishing
London

For Denis Hocking
last of the great pathologists

––––––––––––––––

Robinson Publishing
7 Kensington Court
London W8 4SP

First published by Robinson Publishing 1993

Selection and all introductory material
copyright © by Colin Wilson 1993

A copy of the British Library Cataloguing in Publication
Data for this title is available from the British Library.

ISBN 1 85487 155 2

Typeset by Hewer Text Composition Services, Edinburgh

Printed by Harper Collins, Glasgow

10 9 8 7 6 5 4 3 2 1

Contents

Acknowledgements

The publishers would like to extend their grateful thanks to the following, authors, publishers and others for kindly granting them permission to reproduce the copyrighted material included in this book. Every effort has been made to secure and clear copyrights and the publishers trust that their apologies will be accepted for any errors or omissions.

"The Blackout Ripper" is an extract from *Cherrill of the Yard* by Fred Cherrill, Harrap, 1954. Copyright © 1954 Fred Cherrill. Reprinted by permission of the Harrap Publishing Group Ltd.

"The Blackburn Child Murder" is an extract from *Memories of Murder* by Tony Fletcher, Weidenfeld & Nicholson, 1986. Copyright © 1986 Tony Fletcher. Reprinted by permission of Weidenfeld & Nicholson Ltd.

"The Porthole Murder" is an extract from *Bodies and Crimes* by Denis Hocking, The Book Guild Ltd, 1992. Copyright © 1992 Denis Hocking. Reprinted by permission of the author and publishers.

"The Body in the Sack" is an extract from *Cavalcade of Murder* by T.C.H. Jacobs, Stanley Paul, 1955. Copyright © 1955 T.C.H. Jacobs. Reprinted by permission of Century Hutchinson Ltd, a division of Random Century.

"I Always Wanted to Torture a Girl" by George Vedder Jones. Originally published in *Master Detective*. Copyright © 1986 *Master Detective* magazine and George Vedder Jones. Reprinted by permission.

"Murder for Profit" is an extract from *Murder in France* by Alister Kershaw, Constable, 1955. Copyright © 1955 Alister Kershaw. Reprinted by permission of the publishers.

"The Wigwam Murder" is an extract from *Evidence for the Crown* by Molly Lefebure, William Heinemann Ltd, 1955. Copyright © 1955 Molly Lefebure. Reprinted by permission of the publishers.

"The Cleft Chin Murder" is from *Murder and the Trial* by Edgar Lustgarten, Consul Books, 1960. Copyright © 1960 Edgar Lustgarten. Reprinted by permission of the author's estate.

"The Black Dahlia" is an extract from *Famous American Crimes* by David Rowan, Frederick Muller, 1957. Copyright © 1957 David Rowan. Reprinted by permission of Century Hutchinson Ltd, a division of Random Century.

"Harry Dobkin: The Skeleton in the Cellar" is an extract from *Forty Years of Murder* by Keith Simpson, Harrap, 1978. Copyright © 1978 the Estate of Keith Simpson. Reprinted by permission of the author's estate and Harrap Publishing Group Ltd.

"The Heirens Case" is an extract from *The Serial Killers* by Colin Wilson and Donald Seaman. Copyright © 1990 Colin Wilson and Donald Seaman.

John Haigh: "The Vampire Murderer" is an extract from *Written in Blood* by Colin Wilson. Copyright © 1989 Colin Wilson.

"The Lonely Hearts Murders". Copyright © 1992 Colin Wilson.

All introductory material copyright © 1992 Colin Wilson.

Introduction

Criminologists of the future will see the 1940s as the first clear evidence that the "age of sex crime" had arrived.

It is natural for us to assume that there has been "sex crime" throughout the ages. This is untrue. The kind of rape that occurred in the past was essentially "opportunist"; invading armies regarded women as the spoils of war; so did the bands of robbers who attacked remote farmhouses. But the notion of a rapist deliberately *making* his opportunities – pursuing women as a hunter pursues game – was completely foreign to our ancestors. Of course, kings and emperors frequently used their position to treat their subjects as a kind of harem; but that applied to "good" rulers like Augustus and Peter the Great as much as to paranoiacs like Tiberius and Ivan the Terrible.

Sex crime – as I have pointed out elsewhere[1] – was a development of the pornography industry of the early 19th century. I say a development rather than a consequence, because it was not a case of cause and effect. Both were the effects of some deeper cause, connected with the frustrations of the Industrial Revolution. In other words, sex crime was one of the most unpleasant consequences of modern civilisation. Zoologists have made the same observation about apes; that in zoos sex is a non-stop preoccupation, while in the wild it is a mere "sideshow." When thousands of human being were cooped up in industrial slums, sex was only one of the natural instincts that reached bursting point.

The first sex crimes – in our modern sense of the word – occurred in the late 19th century: in England, the murders of Jack the Ripper, in France, those of Joseph Vacher the "disemboweller", while in America, a sinister crook who called himself H.H. Holmes built himself a "castle"

1 See "A Short History of Sex Crime" in *The Serial Killers*.

in which he could commit rape and murder like some mediaeval despot – his victims are believed to number at least twenty-seven.

In the 20th century, however, the Age of Sex Crime got off to a slow start. Between 1912 and 1914, a Hungarian Lothario named Bela Kiss murdered a dozen or so women and stored some of their bodies in oil drums; but although Kiss (who was never caught) was undoubtedly sex-mad, the motive of the murders was their savings. A Berlin pedlar named Georg Grossmann killed girls during the First World War and sold their carcases for meat. In Hanover soon after the war, a butcher named Fritz Haarmann – a homosexual – did the same to young men. Meanwhile, in America, a curious pervert named Albert Fish had already embarked on a career of child murder that would end in the electric chair in 1936. And during 1926 and 1927, a travelling rapist named Earle Nelson killed twenty-two women in America and Canada. These men were all sex criminals; and yet there is a sense in which every one of them was an "exception". Kiss, Grossmann and Haarmann were all partly motivated by greed; Fish "heard voices" and was undoubtedly insane. Earle Nelson had been subnormal since childhood, when he was knocked down by a street car and suffered a hole in the skull that rendered him unconscious for six days. Only the sadist Peter Kurten, who kept Dusseldorf in a state of terror in 1929 with his murderous attacks, can be truly classified as a sex killer. (Kurten was obsessed with blood, and said that his dearest wish was to hear his own blood flowing into the basket when he was beheaded.)

Oddly enough, the 1930s can offer no examples of sex crime that compare with those of Jack the Ripper or Peter Kurten. Perhaps the political violence of the time offered an outlet for the kind of pent-up emotions that lead to "lust murder". Whatever the reason, sexual violence marked time during the 1930s. By 1940, a historian with a taste for criminology might have concluded that the Age of Sex Crime had run its course.

The following decade was to show that it was only just beginning. Before I began selecting cases for this book, I made a "preliminary list" of killers, taken mostly from my

Encyclopedia of Murder (1961). Out of thirty-four cases, twelve were sex murders – more than a third. In other words, the whole of this book could, in theory, be devoted to sex crime – Cummins, Heath, Camb, Heys, Griffiths, Ludke, Ogorzov, Fearn and Heirens, to name only the best known (although, as we shall see, there are some interesting doubts in the case of Heirens). Even Christie, who will be represented in the volume covering the 1950s, committed his first rape murder as early as 1943, when he lured a colleague from work, Muriel Eadie, to his home during his wife's absence, persuaded her to bury her nose in a jar of Friar's Balsam – a catarrh remedy – then allowed coal gas to bubble into the jar until she lost consciousness.

Such a collection would be not only unrepresentative but absurd – who would want a volume on murder in the 1940s that excluded all mention of Haigh, Petiot, Fernandez and Beck (the "Lonely Hearts" killers) and the assassination of Leon Trotsky, not to mention such minor classics of detection as the cases of Harry Dobkin, August Sangret and Bertie Manton, or such strange unsolved mysteries as the Black Dahlia and the Texarcana Moonlight Murderer? Somehow a collection like this must strive to maintain an adequate balance, even if it means leaving out some of my own favourite examples of crime detection.

Now before we proceed, it is worth asking: why should there have been an outbreak of sex crime during the Second World War? The answer, though obvious enough, has some extremely disturbing implications. In a stable society, sex crime tends to be restricted to the mentally disturbed. But when society experiences a violent upheaval, normal human inhibitions are also undermined. Social instability has the same effect as alcohol, and a man who would usually feel "I couldn't possibly do that" suddenly asks himself: "Why not?"

This is clearly what happened in the case of the man who became known as "the S-Bahn rapist" of Berlin in 1940. The first victim, a gym teacher named Frieda Lausche was travelling on the S-Bahn (short for Schnell–Bahn, or fast railway) on the evening of September 20, 1940, when the man sitting opposite her in the dimly-lit carriage suddenly flung open the door and hurled her out. Because she was supple and in good training, she succeeded in falling safely, and hurried to the police. They were frankly incredulous. Why should a man simply fling a woman from a moving train, with no attempt either at assault or robbery? And why was she not scratched and bruised? They agreed to look into the case, then quietly shelved it.

Three weeks later they had to revise their opinion. On October 11, 1940, a secretary named Ingeborg Goetz was travelling on the elevated railway between Rummelsberg and Karlshorst around midnight when a man in the carriage struck her on the head with some sort of club, then slashed her stomach with a knife. After this he opened the door and threw her out. She recovered in hospital, but was unable to describe her attacker, except to say he wore a peaked cap and some kind of uniform with brass buttons.

Now the police were inclined to wonder if the attacker might have been responsible for a murder that had happened a week before the attack on Ingeborg Goetz; a war widow named Gerda Dietrich had been found stabbed to death in her cottage near the S-Bahn, in the suburb of Sommerland. It had been assumed she was the victim of a burglar, but wounds in the stomach – similar to those of Frau Goetz – suggested the madman who hurled women from trains.

Three weeks later, on December 3, the corpse of a girl was found near the S-Bahn station at Rummelberg; she was identified as 22-year-old Matilda Hollesch, and she had been clubbed to death with a blow on the back of the head, and then raped. A few hours after this attack, another woman was found by the S-Bahn track nearby; she had been struck violently on the head and hurled from the train. This victim, twenty-year-old postal clerk Irmgard Frank, had not been raped.

The following day, a passenger found the murder weapon down the back of a seat: a two foot piece of lead-covered cable, stained with blood and human hairs. Forensic tests established that it had been used to kill both women.

Nearly three weeks later, at 7 o'clock in the morning on December 22, the killer bludgeoned and hurled from the train a housewife named Maria Bahr, again killing her.

Now Detective Wilhelm Ludtke, one of Berlin's leading investigators, decided to try placing decoys on the trains – armed policewomen or volunteers. He also decided that "official guides" would escort young women who had to travel home late at night. But only two weeks later, on January 3, 1941, a man who had claimed to be an official guide pushed a cinema usher out of the train; fortunately, she was only scratched and bruised. But forty-eight hours later, a twenty-three-year-old telephone operator named Sonia Marke died when she was hurled from a train.

The skill shown by the S-Bahn rapist in avoiding traps suggested either a policeman or a railway employee: the description of survivors suggested the latter. But soon after the last murder one of the women "decoys" almost succeeded in arresting the killer. Alone in a carriage with an S-Bahn employee, she became suspicious of his sudden movements and his evident desire to make her nervous, and announced that she was a policewoman and that he was under arrest. The man leapt from the train as it pulled into a platform and disappeared.

On February 11, another woman, Martha Zernowski, was killed as she was clubbed and hurled from a train. On February 20, Lisa Novak, a thirty-year-old factory worker was raped, clubbed and hurled to her death from the train.

This time an arrest was made – a known sex offender named Richard Bauer, whose footprint was found in the girl's blood. He insisted that he had merely stumbled over her in the dark, but was kept in custody as a suspect.

Another possible suspect – among many – was a 28-year-old railway worker named Paul Ogorzov, a married man with two children. The Rummelsberg station master admitted that he was friendly with Ogorzov, and often told him what measures the police were planning. But Ogorzov was at work at the time of many of the murders, and workmates vouched for him; he was also dropped as suspect.

The attacks now ceased until July 3, 1941, when a woman named Olga Opell was found dead beside the tracks. Since Bauer was in prison, he was automatically exonerated and released.

But investigators now learned that Paul Ogorzov had slipped away from his job as a telegraph operator at about the time of the murder of Olga Opell – he had been seen climbing over a fence. Under interrogation, Ogorzov admitted this, and explained that he had a girlfriend who lived nearby. This proved to be true; moreover, the girl declared that Ogorzov had been with her at the time Olga Opell was attacked. But when traces of blood were found on Ogorzov's tunic, the questioning was renewed. He explained that one of his children had cut his finger. But Ludtke now took a long look at the map showing where attacks had taken place, and observed that most of them were along the route between the Rummelbberg station and Ogorzov's home. This seemed too much of a coincidence, so he began pressing Ogorzov about reports from women that a man had shone his torch in their eyes. Ogorzov finally admitted that he had done this on two occasions. Pressed to name precisely where this had happened, Ogorzov became confused, then mentioned a location where, in fact, a rape had occurred.

The victims who had escaped were brought in to confront Ogorzov; one positively identified him, and mentioned that he had worn a coat with a very wide collar; when police found such a coat in Ogorzov's home, he admitted to attempted assault on four women. Asked to pinpoint the places, he mentioned Sommerland, where Gerda Dietrich had been stabbed to death in her cottage. His state of confusion was now so great that he admitted that Gerda Dietrich had been one of the women he had beaten with his fists. This left Ludtke in no doubt that there had been so many victims that he was mixing them up.

Finally, shock tactics worked where long questioning had failed; when Ludtke showed him the smashed skulls of several victims, the harassed Ogorzov suddenly broke down, and admitted that he was the S-Bahn killer. He also admitted that he had also been guilty of a number of sexual attacks on women since 1939, mostly in the course of attempts to pick them up.

The incident that had turned him into a killer had occurred a few weeks before he threw the first victim – the gym teacher – from the moving train. He had accosted a woman near the

Rummelberg station, and she had screamed, bringing her menfolk from a nearby house. They beat up Ogorzov so badly that he had to spend a week in bed. He emerged vengeful and ruthless. Women would pay for this affront to his dignity . . .

And so the first two victims were hurled from the train, an act that he confessed gave him sadistic pleasure – his voice became hoarse as he described the sensation of opening the door and throwing them out into the darkness. But he quickly progressed to rape and murder, killing most victims with a tremendous blow from the lead-covered cable.

Perhaps because Ogorzov was a member of the Nazi Party, and the authorities wished to avoid embarrassment, his trial (on July 21, 1941) was rushed through in one day, and he was beheaded the following day.

I have described the Ogorzov case at length because it is virtually unknown outside Germany, and because Ogorzov is typical of the sex-killer of the 1940s. In effect, he was an opportunist predator, like a fox who has found a hole in the fence of a poultry farm. The same is true of many sex killers in this book – Cummins, Heath, Heys, Floyd, Cook, and the unknown Texarcana murderer. What is so disturbing is that the return of peace in 1945 did nothing to bring this era of sex crime to an end. On the contrary, the number of sex attacks on women has continued to rise steadily ever since, until in the 1990s, rape has become one of the commonest crimes.

This may be seen as a highly dangerous sign for our civilisation. In *Civilisation and Its Discontents*, Freud argued that man is basically a predator who is held in check by the artificial bonds of society. At the time he wrote it (1931), this seemed unnecessarily pessimistic. But the rise of the Nazis, and the increase in sex crime during the Second World War, suggested that he was basically correct. Zoologically speaking, the dominant male is intended to impregnate as many females as possible – in other words, man is born promiscuous. In nature, this natural promiscuity is kept in check by the fact that females are interesting only when on heat. Man has by-passed this limitation and is always ready for sex. For many centuries, society imposed its own natural restraints – in fact, most religion had always demanded fidelity from husband and wife. In the 19th century the social restraints began to dissolve, as increasing wealth and leisure allowed an increasing number of males to turn their attention to full-time seduction and adultery. The development of human imagination – accelerated by the universal popularity of the novel – made women seem more desirable than ever before. In the 18th century, most rapes had involved some drunken workman and a bedraggled street girl; by the late 19th century, "gentlemen" like "Walter", the anonymous author of *My Secret Life*, prowled the streets in search of the "forbidden". Every woman had become an object of feverish desire, and the hero of Barbusse's novel *Hell* declares: "It is not a woman I want; it is *all* women." It was literally as if a monster had been unchained. Bela Kiss, the Hungarian Lothario, was a "satyr" who had to possess women after woman, and who was capable of sex with several women a day.

Sixty years later, Georges Simenon, the creator of Inspector Maigret, claimed that he had slept with ten thousand women (mostly prostitutes) and admitted that the first thing he did in a strange city was to make his way to the nearest brothel. The confession aroused some outrage; yet it was clear that Simenon felt that he was merely confessing to being a normal male. He possessed the money – and the time – to spend his life in pursuit of sex; most dominant males would probably be happy to do the same. And the last quarter of the 20th century has seen the rise of the serial killer who treats his "objects of desire" (whether male or female) as mere throwaways to be raped and killed, and whose victims often far outnumber those of Ogorzov, Kurten and Christie. It is difficult to see the end of this process; for although new techniques of criminal investigation and forensic detection have shortened the odds against the sex killer[1], the basic *conditions* that produce sex murder are likely to remain with us into the foreseeable future.

1 See *The Serial Killer* by Colin Wilson and Donald Seaman

This, then, seems to me the major significance of the 1940s as a decade of murder. It is an ominous reflection, but one it would be pointless – and possibly dangerous – to ignore.

Colin Wilson

1940

By the Light of the Moon

Although psychologists do not know the answer, police will tell you that whenever there is a full moon, there is a sharp increase in police activity. Neighbors suddenly quarrel, cranks keep stationhouse telephone wires busy with complaints, and certain criminals are galvanized into action.

To police, such people are known as "mooners", those who react to the influence of a full moon. The ancient Romans, who observed this phenomenon, coined the word "lunatic" to indicate their belief that the moon had something to do with people going insane. Some psychiatrists scoff at the theory, but police psychiatrists who have to handle mooners are prone to wonder.

There was a full moon on the night of February 24th, when a drama class at the Los Angeles City College was getting ready to stage a public performance in the school auditorium. Most of the young hopefuls were chattering nervously backstage as curtain time neared when the director noticed that one member of the cast, Anya Sosoyeva, an attractive, slender blonde, was not among them. He asked Wally Myar, another cast member, to look for her.

Myar stepped out to the back, expecting to find Anya nervously pacing the walk and puffing furiously on a cigaret, a habit she had before show time, but the pretty Russian-born girl was not in sight. Although there was a full moon, the gravel walks were mainly in shadows cast by the stately trees on the campus.

As Myar moved along a path he heard a stumbling sound in front of him and hurried forward. He finally saw the girl walking with a lurching gait. "Anya, what is it?" he called out as he ran to her side.

He found the girl bleeding from the head, her sweater torn, her clothes dirt-stained. Her eyes were closed, her

1

fingernails torn, and she was groping for bushes lining the path.

"He hit me," she said, and then collapsed. Myar picked up the injured girl and carried her to a dressing room. By the time a physician arrived, the girl was in a coma from which she never recovered. The other young players went on with their roles, keeping the news of the tragedy from the audience.

The police investigation was headed by Captain Dalton R. Patton of the Homicide Squad. Officers found the murder scene only a few yards from the backstage entrance. The ground was badly churned up showing that she had put up a desperate fight. A blood-stained short length of a 2×4 was found in a nearby bush along with a man's blood-stained gray coat and a pair of gray gloves. From scuff marks in the gravel, detectives were able to follow the trail of the girl after the attack. She had staggered to a bench where she sat down and then had continued on her way only a short distance when Myar found her.

The victim's purse was missing. An examination of the gloves showed lipstick smudges, indicating that the killer had clapped his hand over her mouth in a surprise attack from behind.

One of the early officials to arrive was Dr J. Paul de River, police psychiatrist, who frequently was able to give investigators much helpful information about a killer just by studying the scene.

Dr de River cocked his head up toward the full moon overhead. "He may be a mooner," he informed Captain Patton, "one of those men who commit crimes, particularly attacks on women, during the time of the full moon. These attacks will continue until he is caught."

A thorough search was made of the campus without turning up any suspect.

Meanwhile, the routine mechanics of a police investigation went on. Members of the cast were interviewed after the show. Officials wanted to know if the murdered girl had any enemies, the names of her boy friends, and any information

2

about the background of the victim that might give them a lead.

Ruth Alderman, a pretty drama student, reported that the previous October she had been crossing the campus when a man leaped at her from behind some bushes. She said she screamed and fought him off and he became frightened and ran away. She could only offer a vague description of the man and said she had not informed police at the time partly because she feared the man might come back and seek her out.

Investigators learned that Anya, who had played several bit roles in motion pictures, had been a stage dancer originally, working to earn money to further her ambition to become a dramatic actress.

Some years earlier she had been married to a young radio writer and lived with him in San Francisco. After several years she left him because she had learned that he was carrying on with other women and she returned to the stage, going to New York. Her husband then started living with a divorcee. One night police were summoned to his apartment and found his mistress dead on the living room couch. The man first told police that she had committed suicide, but when detectives pointed out that the direction of the shot made it impossible, he then said he had shot her accidentally while playing with a gun. Anya returned from New York to be with him during the trial. When two juries failed to reach a verdict, he was discharged and Anya again left him. Detectives hurriedly checked into his whereabouts and learned he'd died of natural causes.

Los Angeles is overrun with bizarre groups and cults and police learned that Anya had been a member of a campus society known as the "Purple Cult" or Thelemites. The members called themselves votaries of the "purple passion of exotic prayer." Most of the members were graduate students and their high priestess was a woman instructor at the college. Meetings were held in a candlelighted room known as the Temple of Thelema.

Wondering if the murder could have stemmed from the "purple passion of exotic prayer," authorities conducted

3

a thorough investigation of the organization but finally decided the mystic rites and mumbo-jumbo that went on during the ceremonies were considered by most members as good-natured fun rather than anything serious.

One month later, on March 28th, Dr de River's prediction came true. Delia Bogard, a pretty 17-year-old actress, who had been a child star in the movies, was walking on North Wilton Street, hurrying home from a late movie on Sunset Boulevard, when a man suddenly sprang at her in front of a darkened house.

He placed a gloved hand over her mouth and began beating her with a stick. The young actress fought back vigorously, lashing out with her high heels, while he continued to rain blows down on her head. She managed to break loose and began to scream, before he seized her again.

Mrs Laura Lee, in front of whose home the attack was taking place, heard the screams. She seized one of her husband's golf clubs and dashed out. By this time the attacker had knocked down the girl and was bending over her. Running up silently on the lawn, Mrs Lee struck the man with the golf club. He turned with the stick in his hand and Mrs Lee brought it down again. By this time other neighbors had come out of their homes and were running toward them. The man tossed away his weapon, vaulted a high bush and disappeared in the darkness.

Miss Bogard was rushed to the hospital in a critical condition with severe skull injuries. Once again a short length of lumber had been used, and once again the victim's purse was missing.

Police were further disturbed by the third similarity, that Miss Bogard also was an actress and they wondered whether there wasn't some connection between the two crimes. Dr de River suggested that they would be wasting time pursuing that tangent. He pointed out that Los Angeles was filled with young actresses, so more than likely it was just a coincidence. What did alarm the psychiatrist was the fact that the same moonlight conditions existed at the time of both attacks.

"There's no doubt about it now that the man is a mooner,"

Dr de River said. "Unless we get him and get him fast, these attacks will continue every month."

The psychiatrist told the officers to concentrate their search on a young and agile man who derived a sadistic pleasure out of his attacks on helpless women, and to whom the thefts were not as important as the thrill of committing them. Such a person might not even bother to dispose of his loot.

"We're going to have more," was his gloomy prophecy.

Detectives found one possible clue at the scene, a foot print of a rubber-soled shoe that was in the soft earth behind the bush the man had leaped over.

Alarmed by the psychiatrist's warning, police began a roundup of all known perverts and sex deviates in Los Angeles, a task that required many days, but all were released after checking their alibis.

Miss Bogard recovered sufficiently from her injuries to be questioned. She described her attacker as a tall, slender man and said he was unshaven. She was certain that she had never seen him before the attack.

In late June, police thought the man had killed again when Mrs Margaret Campbell, a noted character actress in the silent screen days, was found battered to death in the room she shared with her son. She had been killed with a hammer and her nude body was streaked with blood. Adding an eerie touch to the death scene was a whistle, a book, and a candle, the tip daubed with red lipstick, arranged in a symbolic pattern near the body.

Several days later detectives located Campbell McDonald, the victim's son, and he confessed that he had murdered his mother because she wanted to place him in an institution.

"I put those objects beside her body because the dead should be buried with bell, book and candle," he explained. "I used a whistle instead of a bell." He was committed to an institution.

Meanwhile, although the attacks on women had ceased, police now were being confronted with a series of unsolved burglaries. After studying the records, Dr de River pointed out that these were occurring on fully moonlit nights and he said the killer probably had switched his activity because of the intense search for him.

On August 23rd, the attacker struck again, this time entering a house and beating a young maid who had been baby-sitting. She was found unconscious on the floor, her clothes torn from her. Nearby was a bloody piece of wood.

The following night, all police leaves were canceled and hundreds of extra patrolmen were placed on the streets, while radio-equipped cruiser cars were stationed at strategic spots throughout the city so that they could close in and seal off any district.

Shortly before midnight, a couple was returning to their home on Oakwood Avenue when they spotted a man in the backyard. The husband quietly put in a call to police headquarters and within a minute several cars rolled up the street and officers surrounded the house. Several of them, with guns drawn, dashed into the back yard. They caught a glimpse of a man racing for the fence and fired several warning shots in the air.

The figure stopped and put up his hands. The prisoner was a tall, slender youth dressed in dungarees and sneakers. At headquarters he gave his name as DeWitt Clinton Cook, 20 years old, but refused to answer any questions.

Detectives went to his home and found a pair of shoes, the soles of which matched the footprint left by the attacker of Miss Bogard. They also found a large cache of loot hidden in his home. When they learned that he had a car, they cruised the neighborhood where he had been picked up and located the machine. On the front seat was a short length of 2×4.

Confronted by evidence found in his home, the prisoner admitted to some 300 burglaries, but he vehemently denied being the moonlight assaulter.

After examining the suspect, Dr de River, who had a flair for well-rounded phrases, told the officers. "This fellow's mind is like a house with the shutters drawn, concealing in its shadows the mystery of what goes on behind the curtain. Wiry, catlike, he is of sadistic tendencies, but legally sane and knows right from wrong. He is the lone-wolf type – a

6

nocturnal prowler who likes to wander in lonely places at night."

In more prosaic language he added that he was certain that the prisoner was the moon man. Guided by this opinion, police resumed their questioning of Cook and he finally admitted the attacks.

"I didn't start out to hurt anybody," he said. "I always started after the girls to snatch their purses, but then impulse would get me and I beat them."

He said he had been lurking on the campus for some time and although several girls had passed, he had not molested anybody until the shapely Anya Sosoyeva went by. "I thought I saw a pretty good customer," he remarked.

He had seen Delia Bogard at the movie and had followed her. His attack on the maid occurred just after he had burglarized a home further down the street.

"I saw the maid sitting near a window, doing some embroidery. I don't know what came over me. I saw a hunk of wood in a woodpile near the back of the house, and I picked it up and climbed in through the window. The girl's back was toward me. I swung the club and she started to get up. So I hit her twice more. She sort of collapsed slowly. As the girl lay there I took off her clothes."

The following day Cook re-enacted the murder of Anya Sosoyeva in front of a movie camera.

When Cook was placed on trial in October, the film was shown to the jury. Dr de River testified that the prisoner was sane. Cook was convicted of first degree murder.

On January 31, 1941, the moonlight murderer was put to death in San Quentin Prison.

Edward Radin

Gordon Cummins:
The Blackout Ripper

Inevitably, the pattern of murder in the first half
of the 1940s is dominated by the war. And
wars, as pointed out in the Introduction, seem
to incubate sex crimes. So it seems appropriate
to continue with the curious case of Gordon
Cummins. Unfortunately, we know very little
about the psychology of the "blackout ripper".
In the account that follows – by Chief Superintendent Fred Cherrill, one of Scotland Yard's
best fingerprint experts – we learn that he was
born of "respectable parents", had an upper class
accent, and liked to pose as "the Hon. Gordon
Cummins". Yet Cherrill also mentions that he lost
a succession of jobs, and finally joined the RAF
in peace time; this seems to suggest a working
class background. He always killed for money –
sometimes fairly small sums. But he was also "a
sexual maniac" (the description of Sir Bernard
Spilsbury's biographers Browne and Tullett) who
mutilated his victims, in one case tearing open
the lower half of the body with a tin opener. His
crime rampage during the blackout lasted only a
few days; it if had stretched over months, like
the career of Jack the Ripper, or years, like
that of the Yorkshire Ripper, he would have
caused widespread panic and been extensively
chronicled. In fact, he was caught by his own
carelessness – the same carelessness he displayed
in leaving bloody fingerprints on the mirror of one
of his victims – and promptly executed. It seems
logical to infer that he was a sadist, like Neville

Heath (who will be found later in this volume), with that touch of the confidence trickster that is often found in multiple killers. But his execution – at the age of 28 – means we shall never know.

Spilsbury, who performed a post mortem on the second victim, also performed one on Gordon Cummins.

This account is taken from Fred Cherrill's autobiography *Cherrill of the Yard*.

In the pitch-like darkness of the blackout which enveloped London in February 1942 terror stalked through the blitz-shattered streets of our city. It was not just the terror that rained from the sky as Hitler's Luftwaffe flew overhead to wreak his mission of hate upon Britain. It was the terror created by a ghoulish slayer, who within four days strangled and mutilated four hapless women and attempted to murder two others.

Not since those panic-ridden days in 1888, when Jack the Ripper was abroad in the East End, had London known such a reign of terror as that which existed in this war-time February, when, night after night, death – fiendish, revolting, and gruesome – came to four unsuspecting women in the heart of the Metropolis.

There was no inkling of the orgy of murder which was to follow when, in the early hours of February 9, 1942, the body of Miss Evelyn Hamilton, a woman of irreproachable character, was found strangled in an air-raid shelter in Montagu Place, Marylebone. It was one of those ordinary surface shelters which lined the streets in those days, brick-built, with a seat along one side.

The dead woman was a chemist's assistant who had not long before resigned her post as manageress of a shop at Hornchurch, Essex, and had come to live in the Marylebone area of London.

When I arrived at Montagu Place it looked to me as though the body had been hurriedly pushed through the narrow door of the shelter after strangulation. It lay upon the floor against the seat, face upward. Round the mouth and nose the murderer had wound tightly the woman's own silk scarf as a gag. Her clothes were disarranged, and a hat lay near by. At her side were a matchbox and a powder-compact, which had been turned out of her handbag. A foot or two away was an electric torch, which she doubtless carried to light her on her way through the blackout.

What interested me most, however, were marks on the victim's throat. In the dim light of the shelter they appeared to have been made by the fingers of the murderer. From their position I rapidly made another deduction, and said to myself, "*This seems to have been a left-handed job.*"

Under a powerful light and with the aid of my hand-lens I made a close and minute examination of the marks in the hope that the murderer might have left some trace of his fingers – no matter how small – that would assist in deciding whose hands had choked the life out of this poor victim.

Luck was against me in this respect, for the marks were only bruises. But they enabled me to confirm my first impression that they had been made by the left hand of the strangler, whoever he might be. I was no more fortunate with the handbag and its contents, for the only finger-marks upon them were those of the dead woman.

I had only just reached my office at the Yard the next morning, February 10, when a message came over the 'phone asking me to go at once to a flat in Wardour Street, where a Mrs Evelyn Oatley (also known at Nita Ward) had been found murdered.

On my arrival I entered the bedroom. Lying across a bed, consisting of nothing but a flock mattress, with not even a sheet as covering, was the almost nude body of a woman. She was a ghastly sight. She had been the victim of a sadistic attack of the most horrible and revolting nature.

There were scarcely any signs of disorder in the room itself, articles on a table beside the bed being undisturbed. Some stockings hung upon a rail at the head of the bed, and, but for the still, dead figure of the murdered woman, there was little to show that anything untoward had taken place in that room.

It was only when one turned one's eyes to the bed that one realized the enormity of the crime which had been committed. Near the body of the dead woman lay a pair of curling-tongs and a blood-stained tin-opener. The latter was evidently the weapon with which the murderer had so wantonly mutilated his victim. At one side of the room was a couch, on which I found a woman's handbag. It was open, as if the contents had fallen out, but inside was a piece of mirror.

After a minute examination of the room and its contents I took possession of the tin-opener and the piece of mirror. To me these were very interesting exhibits, for upon that bit of looking-glass, into which the dead woman had doubtless looked a hundred times in the process of beautifying herself, I detected what I knew to be a thumbprint. I soon ascertained that it had not been made by the dead woman, and I assumed that it had been made by the murderer when he was turning out the handbag.

On the handle of the tin-opener I also discovered faint impressions of fingers.

They had been made by a left hand, and were not in such a position that they could have come there by the innocent use of this utensil. Indeed, they were so arranged that I decided this improvised weapon had been grasped in the *left* hand of the murderer during his attack on the woman. Moreover, certain aspects of the print on the mirror indicated to me that it had been made by a left thumb.

Were there any records in our files of corresponding prints? If so, it need be a matter only of minutes, perhaps, before a nation-wide search for the man who had made it could be set in motion. Alas, once more the fates were against us. The killer of Mrs Oatley had no criminal record. He had never been in the hands of the police.

Two days went by – two days during which Yard men followed up every slender clue in their possession in an effort to find the strangler of Evelyn Hamilton and the sadistic "ripper" who had murdered Mrs Oatley.

The husband of the latter was traced to Blackpool, and was able to prove that he and his wife had separated by mutual agreement some time before, and were living apart. A woman in the next room to Mrs Oatley described how she saw the latter enter the house with a man about 11.15 p.m., and heard voices and the wireless.

Evelyn Oatley had once been a promising young actress on the London stage, but, with the outbreak of war, engagements became few, and she drifted into the life which was destined to end in tragedy.

Already the reports of these two crimes, coming so quickly one upon the other, had aroused a feeling of alarm among the people of London. As women passed through the lightless streets at nights on the way to their regular air-raid shelters they looked apprehensively around them, wondering whether the silent and elusive murderer might be lurking in some door or alleyway ready to pounce upon another victim.

Nor was this alarm lessened when the evening papers of February 13 came out with the startling news that another woman had been found strangled and mutilated in a flat at Gosfield Street, just off the Tottenham Court Road.

The discovery was made by a neighbour of the dead woman. The victim was Mrs Margaret Lowe, a handsome and finely built woman who was known locally as "Pearl." The neighbour noticed that a parcel lying outside the door of the flat had not been taken in, and therefore notified the police. The door of the flat was forced, and the tragedy revealed in all its stark and vivid horror.

In a scantily furnished room, almost bare except for a single bed set lengthwise against a wall, an occasional table, a small carpet, a rug, and a chair or two, death had come to Margaret Lowe.

At first sight on entering the room there was no sign of the gruesome work which had been carried out by the sex-mad murderer. On the black eiderdown near the foot of the bed lay a woman's coat, skirt, and jumper, where they had been hurriedly flung down by their owner. Lying on the floor was a gay little hat with a feather, while on the mantelpiece stood a glass candlestick and a tumbler containing a liquid which looked like beer.

A sinister hump in the eiderdown gave an inkling of what lay beneath. There was an unnatural stillness about it. When the bedclothes were pulled back the nude dead body of Margaret Lowe was revealed. Round her neck was tightly knotted a much-darned silk stocking.

But it was not these things which attracted my eye so much as the vicious mutilations which had been wreaked upon the dead woman, and which were even more shocking than those inflicted upon Mrs Oatley. This, and the small armoury of weapons with which the mutilations had been inflicted.

A rapid survey of the room showed me that a candle had been wrenched from the glass candlestick on the mantelpiece. This candle appeared incongruous against the collection of sinister-looking implements surrounding the body. Yet that innocent-looking object was destined to lead to the identification of the murderer of Mrs Lowe, for it directed my attention to the candlestick from which it had been torn.

There were finger-impressions upon the base of it.

After examining the room where the body lay I went to the kitchen at the rear of the premises, where I found a bottle of stout. Some of the contents had been drunk. There were fingermarks on the bottle, and I came to the conclusion that the beer in the glass on the bedroom mantelpiece had been poured from this bottle.

I took possession of the glass candlestick, together with the tumbler and bottle. The marks on the candlestick were of particular interest to me, as they were prints of the fingers of a *right* hand. By means of a rapidly conducted experiment, placing myself in the position of the murderer, I was satisfied that a *right*-handed person, in snatching the candle from the candlestick, would naturally place his *left* hand on the base, using his right hand to grasp the candle. The process would be reversed in the case of a *left*-handed person, so that once more it appeared that a left-handed person had been at work.

If this deduction proved correct, in view of the similarity in the mode of killing and the nature of the injuries inflicted, it appeared likely – in fact, almost certain – that the two murders, those of Mrs Oatley and Mrs Lowe, were the work of one and the same left-handed man. It also struck me at this time that the same person might have strangled Miss Evelyn Hamilton, the victim of the air-raid shelter crime, on whose throat I had detected the finger-marks of a left hand.

In view of these premises, it may appear something of a paradox that I should make another check-up on the newly discovered prints, for were not the impressions found in the flat of Mrs Oatley available for comparison with those which I had now obtained from articles in Mrs Lowe's flat? Would not such a comparison either confirm or disprove my suspicions? They might do, but, on the other hand, they might not. A comparison of the prints in both places would not settle the matter one way or the other, for the simple reason that although they might well be the prints of the same man, they might be the marks of *different fingers*.

That is why I carried out a further search in our records for any prints corresponding to those found in Mrs Lowe's flat, only to come up against the same apparently impenetrable barrier. The search proved negative.

It now seemed pretty certain that a killer was abroad who murdered not only for gain – in each case the handbags of the murdered women had been rifled – but in order to indulge a wicked and insensate lust to perpetrate the most diabolical injuries upon the women he killed.

It was at 6.30 on the evening of February 13 that I went to Mrs Lowe's flat in Gosfield Street, the murder having actually taken place on the 12th. Having completed my fingerprint investigations there, I returned to the Yard. The time was then about 10.30 p.m., and I was just preparing to go home when the telephone-bell in my office rang again.

I lifted the receiver. "Fingerprint Office," I said, in what sounded to me a rather tired voice. And then came this: "Will you go at once to Sussex Gardens, Paddington? Another woman has been found murdered."

It only needs a message like this to snap one out of all sense of weariness. In a matter of minutes I was on my way to carry out a second murder investigation, within a few hours of the other, and both on the same day.

The victim was a Mrs Doris Jouannet. She was the wife of a London hotel manager, and he usually slept at the hotel, but saw his wife daily at their flat in Sussex Gardens. On the night of the tragedy he had supper with his wife, and she accompanied him to Paddington Station. But let Mr Jouannet tell his own story.

"She wished me good-night very sweetly, and her last words to me were, 'Don't be late to-morrow, darling,'" he said.

"I returned to the flat at seven o'clock on Friday night, and was surprised to see that the milk had not been taken in. When I got into the flat I shouted out 'Doris,' but there was no reply. On going into the sitting-room I found that the supper-things from the night before were still on the table, and the curtains had not been drawn. I was worried, and when I found the bedroom door locked I knew something was amiss. I could not get any reply, so I went to the housekeeper, and we sent for the police."

Mr Jouannet described how the police burst open the door, and how a kindly constable held him back from entering the room of death with a gentle, "Don't go in, sir," and then broke the news that his wife was dead.

Thus it was only an hour or two after the body of Doris Jouannet was discovered that I was in the flat where she lay.

One glance was sufficient to tell me that the strangling "ripper" had struck again. There was no doubt about it. He had left his signature to the atrocities as surely as if he had written his name.

Around the neck of the woman was a tightly knotted scarf. Her body, clad only in a dressing-gown, which had been dragged open in the frenzied lust of the murderer, was lying across a bed, the clothes of which had been flung back in haste by the killer after he had completed his crime. The body had been savagely slashed.

There had been no struggle. The murderer had worked swiftly and surely. The woman's clothes lay in a heap on a chair at the foot of the bed. A clock standing on a bedside table had stopped. It registered the time – 4.45.

I made an intensive search for fingerprints. On the door of a cupboard close to the bed I found several. I detected others on a hand-mirror lying on the dressing-table. From the dust on the latter I could see that some articles had recently been removed from it. On the door of the bedroom itself I found other impressions.

I took possession of the mirror, and had the cupboard and bedroom doors removed and brought to the Yard for a more detailed and exhaustive examination of the articles. This time, however, the murderer had left behind no fingerprints of any value. All those which were identifiable belonged to the dead woman.

Such was the position on February 14, when the whole resources of Scotland Yard were mobilized to run this wholesale murderer to earth. At that time we were not absolutely certain that Evelyn Hamilton had met her death at the hands of the same person, although, as you will remember, I was convinced that her strangler was left-handed.

Women police in ordinary clothes – always under the alert and watchful eyes of Yard men – strolled about the streets of the West End in the hope of being accosted by the unknown killer. So great was the terror which swept like a wave over the square mile in which these crimes had been committed that the regular street-walkers who haunted the area were too scared to venture out. Small wonder, for nobody knew when or where the killer would strike next. That he *would* strike again seemed certain, for the lust of killing appeared to have seized him in a merciless grip. And he *did* strike again! Though not with such fatal results.

On the night of February 12 – within a few hours of the murders of Mrs Lowe and Mrs Jouannet – a young woman, Mrs H——, was having a quiet drink in a public-house near Piccadilly when an Air Force cadet entered. He got into conversation with her, flourishing a wad of Treasury notes. He made a certain suggestion, which she rejected.

When she left he followed her into the darkened street, and, having caught up with her, pushed her into a doorway. "You must let me kiss you good-night," he said.

He placed his gas-respirator on the ground, and made as though to put his arm round her. Instead he seized her by the throat, maintaining his grip until she lost consciousness. One can only imagine what might then have happened but for the approach of a passer-by, who heard scuffling and saw a man disappear into the shadows. He then noticed

Mrs H—— lying on the ground. She was just regaining her senses. The stranger helped her to her feet, and when she had gasped out the story of the attack upon her he escorted her to the police-station.

At once police officers went to the scene of the attack. There they found the woman's handbag rifled of its contents, while in the doorway lay the respirator belonging to her assailant, which he had left behind in his haste to get away.

Meanwhile the young airman had happened on another woman, Mrs M——. The lust for blood must still have been upon him, for he persuaded her to enter a taxi-cab with him, and together they drove to her flat in Southwick Street, Paddington, less than a stone's throw from Sussex Gardens, where lay the undiscovered body of Doris Jouannet, for it was not till the following day, February 13, that her husband returned to the flat to find her dead.

While the airman was in the room with Mrs M—— the electric light failed, and it was at this propitious moment that her companion seized her by the throat and tried to strangle her.

The frightened woman fought and kicked with such violence, however, that she managed to free herself from the hand that was choking her, and gave vent to piercing screams, which aroused the household. Her would-be murderer fled the scene, but in his anxiety to get away left behind the belt belonging to his uniform.

So well within the space of forty-eight hours the mysterious murderer had slain and mutilated two women and had attempted to murder another two. He had gone straight from one crime to another almost without pause. I still felt that he was the man who had also killed Miss Hamilton.

But now he was no longer a mystery man. There was a definite clue to his identity – the respirator which he had left in the doorway when interrupted in his attack upon Mrs H——.

On this respirator was his Air Force number, 525987, and to trace its owner was just a matter of routine inquiry. A scrutiny of R.A.F. records was sufficient to establish that the owner of the gas-mask found in the doorway in Haymarket, and also of the belt left behind in the flat of Mrs M——, was a twenty-eight-year-old R.A.F. cadet, one Gordon Frederick Cummins. He was soon tracked down at his billet in North London, and put up for identification by the two women whom he had tried to strangle.

Mrs H—— had no difficulty in picking him out as the man who had attacked her. Mrs M—— could only say that his eyes were the same as those of her assailant, who was in R.A.F. uniform.

Cummins was charged with the murders of Mrs Oatley, Mrs Lowe, and Mrs Jouannet, and with the attempted murder of Mrs H—— and Mrs M——.

At that time there was not sufficient evidence on which to charge him with the murder of Miss Hamilton, although there was now little doubt that the accused was responsible for her death.

On his arrest he made a statement. In it he described how, on the night of February 9 – the night of the Hamilton murder – he and another cadet named Johnson spent the evening in the West End visiting various bars. About 11 p.m. they met two women and separated, arranging to meet later. Cummins insisted that they *did* meet, and that they were so drunk when they reached their billet that other airmen had to put them to bed.

When Johnson was interviewed he stated that after waiting for some time at the appointed rendezvous, and Cummins not putting in an appearance, he (Johnson) went off with another woman, and did not return to the billet until 6 a.m., when he found Cummins in bed. So the latter's story of his movements on that fatal night was obviously false.

When Cummins was brought up at Bow Street Police Court and formally charged I took his fingerprints. As is usual on these occasions, he was asked to sign the fingerprint form. He made no demur, and – *signed with his left hand.*

Meanwhile his respirator had been minutely examined. Adhering to the fabric were found particles of dust. On comparison with dust taken from the air-raid shelter where Miss Hamilton's body was found, these particles were found to be identical in colour and in form with mortar-dust taken from the shelter. Thus was forged the first direct link in the chain connecting Cummins with the murder of Evelyn Hamilton.

There was another link, for when his billet was searched a fountain-pen which had belonged to the dead woman was discovered among his possessions, together with a cigarette-case which was subsequently identified as the property of Mrs Lowe.

The strands of evidence connecting Cummins with the crimes which had created a reign of terror throughout the West End of London were gradually being woven into a noose. But still the final strand had yet to be included which would place that noose around the neck of this multi-murderer.

I was not idle after taking the accused man's fingerprints at Bow Street Police Court. On comparing these prints with those on the tin-opener found on the bed where lay the body of Mrs Oatley I was able to establish that the clearest mark was made by the left little finger of the accused, while the print on the mirror taken from the handbag of the dead woman was that of his left thumb. So much for Mrs Oatley.

The finger-marks on the base of the candlestick taken from the flat of Mrs Lowe were made by the fingers of the right hand of Cummins. Those on the tumbler and beer-bottle found in the flat of Mrs Lowe were also made by the same hand. The accused had been in that flat, and had undoubtedly joined his victim in her last drink on earth before killing and mutilating her.

As I have already stated, there were no prints of any value in connexion with the murder of Mrs Jouannet, and, apart from the left-hand marks on the throat of Evelyn Hamilton, none that helped in the inquiries into the deaths of these two women.

Cummins was brought to trial at the Old Bailey in April 1942. And it was there, while I was in the witness-box giving fingerprint evidence, that I was instrumental in stopping a trial for murder – a dramatic and almost unheard-of thing.

I should explain that Cummins was tried on *one* charge of murder only – that of Mrs Evelyn Oatley. This is the usual practice when a person has been committed for trial on more than one murder charge, and is an example of the scrupulous fairness with which justice is administered in our criminal courts.

It is necessary that you should know this in order to understand how I came to stop the trial of Cummins.

During my evidence I had just reached the point where I was about to describe to the jury how I had come to my conclusions regarding the print on the tin-opener and the mark on the bit of mirror when the fingerprint exhibits were put in. These were photographic enlargements of the marks on the articles side by side with the corresponding prints taken by me from Cummins, and copies were handed to the jury, so that they could follow what I was about to say. Mr G. B. McClure, counsel for the Crown, was just about to ask me to describe the similarities when, out of the corner of my eye, I observed that the jury had been handed copies of the fingerprints in *another* case on which Cummins had been indicted, but was not being tried.

Even from that distance, between witness-box and the box where the jury sat, just to my right, I could detect the difference in the prints before me and those they were gazing at. I stood for a moment, not a little perplexed. I realized that somehow a mistake had been made, and I had to think quickly. There was only one course to take. I turned to Mr Justice Asquith, the presiding judge.

"I think the jury has been handed a wrong exhibit," I said quietly.

Puzzled looks appeared on the faces of the jurors, and the copies with which they had been provided were hastily recovered. But the damage had been done, and the whole essence of that justice to which I have referred would have been vitiated if those same jurors had been allowed to continue the hearing of the case.

They were asked to retire while the legal position was discussed. On their return Mr Justice Asquith discharged them, explaining that "It is possible, and very probable, that from the exhibit before you you might have drawn certain inferences which would have made it impossible for you to try this action properly. I know I can rely on you not to mention anything that has come to your knowledge from this exhibit."

The judge also appealed to the Press to "treat this with every discretion," adding, "The full truth will be published later, but not until this trial is over."

It was the first time in the history of the Old Bailey that a trial had ever been stopped for such a reason.

On the following Monday the trial was reopened with another jury. I gave evidence, and was rigorously cross-examined by Mr John Flowers, K.C., counsel for the defence. How rigorously will be seen later. Cummins was found guilty and sentenced to death.

You may wonder what manner of man was this who, night after night, set out to murder and mutilate women with such wanton savagery.

Born of highly respectable parents, he was given every chance as regards education, but his school record was described as "poor". He fared no better when he took up work in the leather-tanning industry, being dismissed from one job after another as being "unsatisfactory", "irresponsible", and fond of the company of women.

In 1935 he joined the R.A.F. as a flight-rigger, and continued in the Service until his arrest. In 1936 he married, his wife continuing work as secretary to a theatrical producer.

Possessed of a vain streak, Cummins loved to pose as the son of a nobleman, and because of his cultured speech and polished manner became known as "The Count" or "The Duke" among his comrades. He was boastful of his conquests with women, and was doubtless helped in his amorous escapades by his masquerade as "the Hon. Gordon Cummins".

There are many such men, I am afraid, who love to swagger about assuming titles to which they have no right, and imposing on credulous women. But there are not many who resort to the murder of those who fall victims to their plausible tongues. One is left perplexed and horrified at the vicious cruelty which animated Cummins in his lust to kill.

Cummins appealed, and while seated between two warders in the dock at the Court of Criminal Appeal he listened to Mr D. N. Pritt, K.C., urging his case before the Lord Chief Justice, Mr Justice Humphreys, and Mr Justice Tucker. He laughed and appeared to be joking with his guardians. Now and again he looked across the court and smiled at his wife.

It was Mr Justice Humphreys who delivered judgment. In dealing with the ground that the "verdict was against the weight of evidence" he was at great pains to emphasize the fingerprint evidence which I had given in the court below.

"There was no scamping the evidence in this case," he said. "Superintendent Cherrill was examined fairly fully in chief; he was cross-examined most properly in the most minute detail by the learned counsel who appeared for the accused, and in order to make his points quite clear to the jury, counsel obtained permission from the learned judge to leave his place and go close to the jury-box, in order that he might point with a pencil to his copy of the photograph, so that the jury might see what it was that he was referring to . . . Superintendent Cherrill was cross-examined as to dissimilarities. He said, 'I quite agree that there are some dissimilarities which you have discovered and put to me,' and he added, 'I can show you some more if you want them which I have discovered and you have not. But as to those dissimilarities, the same observation is to be made with regard to all of them, and that is this. They are dissimilarities which may well be caused either by the shape or the movement of the article at the time the fingerprint was made upon it, inasmuch as there was no movement of the paper upon which the fingerprints of the accused were taken for the purpose of this case.'"

Mr Justice Humphreys concluded his reference to the fingerprint evidence by pointing out that no witness had been called to combat my evidence, which he described as being "this peculiar but singularly conclusive form of evidence, because it was claimed nearly 600,000 persons have been identified without any error being known to have been made, and in no case have two people been found to have fingers or thumbs which make identical marks."

The appeal was dismissed, and on the morning of June 25, 1942, Cummins went to his death at the hands of the hangman.

Fred Cherrill

The Man Who Wanted Voices

Two months after the killing rampage of Gordon Cummins, another serviceman went on a murder spree, this time on the other side of the world. Inevitably, newspapers compared him to Jack the Ripper. The truth seems to be that the "brown-out killer" of Melbourne was an emotionally unstable mother's boy, whose attitude to his adored mother was ambiguous enough to make him kill middle-aged women who reminded him of her, then rip off their lower garments without actually committing rape. John Godwin's account, from *Killers in Paradise* (1962), gives some insight into Leonski's peculiar psychology.

F ive months after the attack on Pearl Harbour the Australian city of Melbourne was hourly expecting the first Japanese bombs to scream down on her own roofs. And in those five months of waiting the face, character and outlook of the Victorian capital had changed more radically than in the fifteen years that preceded them.

Melbourne had been nothing if not a conservative town. Her police were unarmed, high-buttoned and helmeted on the traditional English pattern; her one-and-a-quarter million people dressed drably, went to bed early, and took their schools almost as seriously as their cricket; her broad, well-swept main streets were laid out in rigidly planned chessboard fashion and through them the traffic flowed at a remarkably slow and disciplined pace. Book and film censorship was the strictest in Australia, there was no night life to speak of, and a "temporary Emergency Regulation" of the first World War that ordered public houses to shut at 6 p.m. was conveniently still in force at the outbreak of the second.

The fighting in Europe and Africa did not affect Melbourne, except that fewer young men were seen in the streets. But on December 7, 1941, Japan struck, and suddenly the war had reached Australia's doorstep.

The city was "browned-out", meaning that enough lights were turned off to make driving as well as walking hazardous occupations. The beautifully kept public parks developed rashes of slit trenches, housewives spent hours pasting strips of paper over window panes, while their menfolk dug family air raid shelters in the back garden. Searchlights swept the night sky, wardens practised sprinkling sand on incendiaries, and every afternoon the harbour batteries filled the air with white shrapnel puffs. The only thing that was missing was the bombs.

Few Melburnians doubted that they would come. Malaya, Singapore and the East Indies fell, the Japanese tide was licking across the hump-backed razor mountains of New Guinea, in the far north of Australia Port Darwin was virtually flattened. It was just a matter of days . . .

With the exception of air raids came a curious feeling of helpless rage and frustration. Everyone knew that over New Guinea the tiny Royal Australian Air Force was trying to fight Japanese Zeros with converted training planes. The country's trained manpower lay dead in the Libyan desert or rotted in Jap prison camps. At home the Government was scraping up a new conscript army, half-trained and a quarter armed. The country lay wide open and exposed, and the people knew it.

Into dimmed-out Melbourne, almost denuded of able-bodied males, poured a flood of foreign servicemen. Dutch and Indonesian troops, evacuated from the East Indies, Free Norwegians and Fighting French, British Navy personnel, Malays, Filipinos, and – above all – Americans. Tens of thousands of G.I.s used the city as a supply and assembly base before being shunted to the fighting zones in the North, meanwhile filling it with alien-sounding English, the smell of Lucky Strikes and the clink of immense pay packets, itching to be spent before their owners were killed.

With the civilian population in the grip of nervous apprehension, with the police force at rock-bottom strength through enlistments, with half the local wives minus husbands, and with an army camp on every sports ground, Melbourne's staunch moral fibre disintegrated and the town went – temporarily – haywire. Motivated by patriotism, profits, loneliness, unaccustomed freedom or long dormant erotic urges, respectable suburbanites held night-long bottle parties, hitherto scrupulous businessmen peddled black-market tyres and cigarettes, schoolgirls and middle-aged matrons smiled at anything resembling a uniform, and land-ladies and cinema usherettes closed both eyes at love scenes that would have sent them into screaming hysterics a year earlier.

This was the background against which three Melbourne women were murdered in identical circumstances and within less than three weeks.

Early factory workers of the inner seaside suburb of Albert Park found the first body, sprawling in a doorway on the chilly morning of May 3, 1942. It was a plump, middle-aged woman, her clothes hanging in shreds from her belted waist, her mouth gaping open as if frozen in a silent scream.

From the identity card in the dead woman's handbag police established that her name was Ivy Violet McLeod, that she was 40 years old, a "lady's domestic helper", and lived three miles from the spot where she was found. She had been lying on her back in the doorway, her eyes, knees and hands heavily bruised, her left temple fractured and her throat swollen. The police pathologist diagnosed that she had died of suffocation and a fractured skull. The doorway bore signs of a struggle, indicating that she had been murdered right there. Whoever did the killing had obviously first choked her into unconsciousness, then dropped her heavily on the ground, cracking her skull.

But whoever had killed her had also torn her clothes with maniacal force and with no apparent purpose. The woman had been neither robbed nor sexually assaulted, nor beaten up in the normal sense. Time of death was assumed to have been the late hours of the previous night, but even then the browned-out street was a fairly well frequented place. Had the victim screamed someone would have been bound to have heard her . . . but no one had. The attack, therefore, must have come as a complete surprise. Her throat must have been gripped so suddenly and powerfully that she couldn't utter a sound before blacking out. But since it had been gripped from the front the woman must have stood close to her assailant in the first place – probably in the doorway.

There was nothing in Mrs McLeod's character to indicate a semi-public cuddling session. She was a plain, motherly woman who would have looked most in place over a kitchen stove. Only these days nobody knew what sort of women were liable to get up to what escapades . . .

Melbourne's Criminal Investigation Branch were still probing into Mrs McLeod's past when – six days later – they were faced with another victim.

At four a.m. on Saturday morning a city night watchman found a lady's handbag on his beat. He delivered it to the nearest police station, and had barely returned to his rounds when he also found its owner. The second body lay on the steps of one of the hideously ornate lodging houses in Spring Street that Melbourne owes to her Victorian past. This time the woman was brunette, slender and pretty, but she had died in the same fashion as Mrs McLeod. Her neck showed bluish-red strangulation marks, her smart clothes were ripped to tatters, and the back of her head was fractured by a heavy fall.

The city police had no trouble identifying the dead woman as the owner of the bag – she was the wife of one of their colleagues.

She had been living on the fourth floor of the curli-cued apartment house on whose doorstep she was found. There she called herself Miss O'Brien. In reality she was Mrs Pauline Buchan Thompson, and her husband did duty as a police constable in the country town of Bendigo. Hazel-eyed and soft-voiced, Mrs Thompson had stage leanings not usually associated with policemen's wives. During the five years she lived with her husband in Bendigo she had become something of a local celebrity. She sang at troop concerts

26

and charity shows, worked as announcer at the town's broadcasting station, and conducted a weekly women's session on the air. The Thompsons had two children; a four-year-old daughter and an adopted son aged seven.

But in February, 1942, acting on an impulse Mrs Thompson left her husband in Bendigo and moved to Melbourne. First she worked for a machinery firm, then she got a telephonist's job with another radio station. At the same time she moved to her city address and – for reasons of her own – began calling herself Miss O'Brien.

Dr C. H. Mollison, who conducted her post-mortem examination, reported that death was due "to pressure on each side of the neck. Considerable force had been used, causing nervous paralysis rather than suffocation or strangulation".

Three homicide officers, Detective-Inspector Gray and Detective-Sergeants McGuffie and Lyon, gathered what clues there were. Mrs Thompson's pearl necklace had been broken and the pearls scattered over the steps. One of her shoes had slipped off and was found two steps below the body.

These signs made it obvious that – like Mrs McLeod – Pauline Thompson had died where she was found. Her handbag, however, was picked up several streets away. As it was most unlikely that she had dropped it herself, it must have been taken and later thrown away by her murderer. But why?

This last Why was only one of many the detectives were asking themselves. The two killings were so similar that there was little doubt of their having been the work of the same murderer. Both women had been strangled by hand, both had been half-stripped, both were attacked in semi-public places and neither had been sexually interfered with. What sort of freakish satisfaction had they afforded their killer? And how did he, on each occasion, prevent them from uttering even a single cry?

For Mrs Thompson had died as swiftly and silently as her predecessor. The proprietor of the lodging house and his wife were sleeping in a basement bedroom a few yards from the steps where the murder took place. They hadn't heard a sound; neither had the half-dozen tenants who were at home at the time. Spring Street was no suburban lane but a city thoroughfare that is never completely deserted. Yet no late pedestrian could be found who could recall hearing the slightest suspicious noise.

Had the killer been lurking on the steps? Most improbable. If attacked by a stranger in the darkness Mrs Thompson would have had time for at least one scream. It was much more likely that she had known her murderer, stood close to him before the sudden assault – exactly like Mrs McLeod.

Somehow the killer in both cases had managed to get at least on speaking terms with his victims; a fairly easy task for virtually any male in wartime Melbourne. But then the chances were good that someone had spotted him with them. The problem: find that someone.

The C.I.B. investigators had no trouble tracing Mrs Thompson's movements up to about six hours before her death. Her constable husband had come on escort duty to Melbourne on the same day, bringing their adopted son with him. Mrs Thompson had spent most of the afternoon with them and saw them off by the 5.40 p.m. train to Bendigo. Before parting she had told her husband that she was going to the Theatre Lovers' Club that Friday night. From then on her movements became shadowy with only one certain point – she had not gone to the Club she mentioned nor, apparently, had she ever intended to.

This the police discovered very quickly. Melbourne's main railway station – Flinders Street – has a row of train departure clocks above the entrance. Apart from informing people how fast they have to run for their trains the clocks also mark the city's most famous rendezvous position. "Meet you under the clocks at Flinders Street," is a time-honoured Melburnian phrase, indicating a dating spot no one can possibly miss. And beneath those clocks Mrs Thompson had waited for about half-an-hour; waited for someone who evidently didn't turn up. Witnesses had seen her waiting and finally walking off with every sign of disgust. This was at around seven o'clock – but where had she gone from there?

"Where do you go around seven in the evening when you

28

don't have a kitchen of your own?" reasoned Detective-Sergeant McGuffie. "You go and have a meal. Chances are that somebody's seen her eating in a city restaurant. Let's find him."

At Russell Street, Melbourne's police headquarters, laboratory men got busy with a window dummy. They dressed the figure in the dead woman's clothes, superimposed a photograph of her face on the dummy's head and distributed the finished picture to every newspaper and cinema in the town. The portrait with the blazing caption "*Have you seen this woman*?" reached an estimated million people within 48 hours.

Several of them stepped forward at once. The first was the man who had stood Mrs Thompson up under the Flinders Street clocks. He turned out to be a young American soldier who had dated her in haste, then found something better to do and didn't bother to inform her of his changed plans. He may not have been everyone's idea of a gallant escort, but he certainly had nothing to do with her murder. His alibi for the evening was water-tight.

But to the detective who interrogated him the broken date provided a clue that turned out to be vital: Mrs Thompson had liked "the Yanks".

Next in line were three people who had noticed the constable's wife later that night. She had been drinking in a hotel in Collins Place – and with her was another young G.I.

According to the strange ritual imposed by Melbourne's licensing laws the two had to use the hotel's dining-room to drink; the bar was shut. Different witnesses noticed them between eight o'clock and midnight, when they left. They were sitting close together and occasionally the woman had stroked the soldier's hair.

Mrs Thompson was murdered some time between midnight and two a.m., which made it more than likely that the young man with her was her killer . . . *the* killer.

"What did he look like? Try and remember some feature about him – anything!" McGuffie prodded the witnesses. Their replies were discouragingly vague. He was tall – he was young – he was fair. No, he had no outstanding features. Was he an officer? No . . . but he could have been an N.C.O.

No one appeared to have seen the couple after they left the hotel. Which left the C.I.B. with a physical description that amounted to virtually nothing. Tall . . . young . . . fair, a private or N.C.O. – all this could apply to something like 20,000 Americans stationed in or around Melbourne.

A week had passed since the murder, Russell Street was getting restless – and so was Melbourne's population. The story of the two killings, their striking similarity and utter senselessness, had leaped at newspapers readers from among the welter of war news that seemed to be getting worse every day. Never mind about the yellow tide in the North . . . there was a maniac loose right here in town!

A maniac; certainly, but obsessed by what sort of mania? The man did not rape, bite or mutilate, which ruled out the more common variety of sex pervert. He did not inflict injuries that caused blood or suffering, which eliminated the most widespread forms of sadism. He invariably ripped his victims' clothing, a feature that indicated a fetishist; but fetishists are usually non-violent, preferring to steal the garments they desire to gloat over them in solitude.

Then, if the killer really was a U.S. serviceman, his particular psychosis would have to lie deep below the surface of his personality. In 1942 America was not yet scraping the bottom of her manpower barrel, this was before the time when medical examiners were ordered "Don't check their eyes – count 'em".

The C.I.B. consulted Melbourne's leading psychiatrists and received in reply a series of shoulder-shrugs couched in exquisite medical terminology. The man may be planning his murders weeks ahead, or he may be acting on the impulse of the moment – he may be handsome and popular or a repressed introvert – he may suffer from psychotic amnesia, in which case he wouldn't even remember the deed an hour later. Only one of the mind specialists offered an observation that turned out to be uncannily relevant: "The witnesses described this fellow as a *young* man. Well, the women he picks on aren't so very young – maybe he has some sort of mother complex?"

Retrospective analysis is as cheap in criminology as else-where, but in few cases could it ever have been so infuriating for the harassed investigators. For while the undermanned, overworked C.I.B. spent days listing the names of 1,000 known Australian sex offenders and shadowing the move-ments of some 80 "possibilities", the man they were seeking had already half-confessed the murders to a friend. While they were still trying to establish some sort of motive he had already demanded to be locked up "because I'm too dangerous to run around loose". While they were trying to guess his nationality he was weeping into his pillow at night, beating the mattress with his fists and screaming in a voice that sent shivers down the spines of the listeners: "I killed! – I killed! – I killed! . . ."

But all this the Homicide Squad officers had no way of knowing. No one stepped forward to tell them because of the curious unwillingness of the human mind to accept that someone you know and like can be a monster. It is a failing by no means confined to laymen. The highly skilled police of the German city of Hanover, for instance, kept on employing the services of their favourite stool-pigeon, Fritz Haarmann, long after they realised there was something "dangerously peculiar" about him. Herr Haarmann, who was eventually convicted of 24 murders, turned out to be a cannibal as well as a mass-slayer and a homosexual. None of his colleagues informed on Dr Palmer of Rugeley, even after it became a standing joke around town that the good doctor was poisoning his patients wholesale.

The hunt for new witnesses, fresh leads, dragged on, with 50 detectives of Victoria's meagre force detailed for this chase alone. They had made no visible progress at all on the morning of May 19, when a pale-faced gardener raced out of Royal Park screaming on top of his voice: "Police! Call the police, somebody . . . there's been another murder!"

The third victim turned out to be a tiny, thin spinster, whose neck was so hideously bruised that she looked like a corpse taken from the gallows. She was lying face down in the yellow sticky mud that had been excavated from a freshly-dug air raid trench in the park, her clothes clawed in strips from her child-like body. The soft mud around her was like a swamp; detectives waded up to their ankles as they pieced together the evidence embedded in it.

Scattered in a radius of 20 feet were the dead woman's gloves, shoes and handbag. Her umbrella – still open and wet from last night's rain – rested on a grass walk near by. The oozing clay told its own story. It clearly marked the spot where the little woman had been dragged into the park, limp and unresisting after having been strangled somewhere out in the street. The contents of her bag described her as Miss Gladys Lillian Hosking, 41 years old, private secretary to a professor of chemistry at Melbourne University. Miss Hosking had lived in a boarding house only a few hundred feet from the spot where she was found. In private life she was an enthusiastic amateur theatrical and member of an organisation rather painfully entitled "The Merrymakers' Concert Party".

The headlines that stared at Melbourne's newspaper readers that evening were the most frightening since the fall of Singapore. The maniac had struck for the third time, and now it was certain that the city's dimmed, wintry streets were haunted by something far worse than the fear of air raids. Women were bluntly warned not to go out unescorted after dark – an almost impossible advice for thousands of wartime night-shift workers. The war, clothing coupons and petrol rations were forgotten; the sole conversation topic was the monster prowling somewhere in the darkness out there, choosing his next victim.

There was now no doubt in anyone's mind that the strangler would leave his trail of corpses until he was caught: "How many did Jack the Ripper kill? – Was it six . . . or a dozen?" Tell-tale signs of panic flickered in every part of the city. Women breathlessly phoned police stations, reporting that they were being "followed by someone", that their lodger was "acting strange", that they "felt" they were being watched. Pure fantasies in most cases; but ominous symptoms of mass hysteria to those whose business it was to keep a finger on the national pulse.

Hysteria was precisely what a hard-pressed wartime administration could least afford. From "higher up" – from State Government and City Hall – came urgent, tensely-nervous nudges to the police force: "Why don't you fellows get a move on? We can't have another killing . . . not at this time . . ."

All police leave in the Melbourne area was cancelled, the C.I.B. worked double shifts, every man who could possibly be spared from other duties was put on the case. Within the next 48 hours the district of Royal Park was flooded with police – uniformed constables, plain-clothes officers, military provosts – knocking on every door up and down four miles of streets, questioning 650 men, women and children who might have noticed something – anything – that would offer one more clue.

The police didn't need goading from the press, reminders from the Government, or jitters from the public to realise they were racing against time. Every night that fell increased the chances of yet another body being found somewhere. Six nights between the first murder and the second; nine between the second and the third . . . the hunters didn't have much time.

Throughout Melbourne casual pick-ups virtually ceased, the hip-swinging ladies who used to patrol St Kilda Road vanished as if by magic, wives stayed home alone by the fireside, and young soldiers out for a spree found themselves forced to spree with other young soldiers. As one member of the U.S. Marine Corps, shortly due to leave for the Solomons, put it: "Why the hell don't they catch that bastard so we can all get back to having a good time before we croak?"

Within two days of the murder the C.I.B. was no longer thrashing around in the dark. They were following a definite line, based on the topography of the scene of the crime. In due course the line was bound to lead them to the killer. The question was only whether it would lead them there quick enough to prevent him from striking again.

Miss Hosking had been murdered in Gatehouse Street, a residential thoroughfare adjoining Royal Park. Since the beginning of the emergency the actual parkland, criss-crossed by air raid trenches, had been divided into two separate portions. The one nearest to Gatehouse Street was known as Camp Pell and housed an American army establishment. The other was an Australian camp site. The entire area was guarded and the chances were that one of the sentries had spotted the murderer returning to one of the two camps. Long, painstaking questioning revealed that no Australian had entered his camp from the direction of Gatehouse Street. This left an American. An American who was tall, fair, and had exceptionally large and powerful hands. This description was still too general to be of much use; but there was another point – a point connected with the spot where the body had been dumped.

It was an Australian soldier on picket duty that night who spoke the words that electrified the plain-clothes men: "I called out to a Yank who was plastered all over in yellow mud."

Yellow mud! In the whole of Royal Park there was only one freshly-dug trench – only one spot where a man could get covered in the moist clay: the place where the body was found.

"What did he look like?"

"Big bloke," said the sentry. "He was a bit full, too. I yelled out to him: 'Where the hell have you been?' And he said something about falling over a pool of mud while he was going through the park. And then he said – I remember this – he said: 'Boy, you should have seen the girl I was with. I thought I could drink, but she drank me right under the table.'"

The detectives looked at each other. Barring a truly fantastic coincidence they had located the strangler.

The following morning homicide officers F. Adam and W. Mooney entered Camp Pell and slowly walked down the long rows of tents. They stopped before each one, running expert eyes over the canvas, passing on to the next. At the 29th tent they paused for good. Near the entrance opening was an unmistakable patch of dried yellow mud. The detectives entered the tent, scrutinising the two iron bedsteads. On the frame of one were several yellow smears. The first officer scraped them off with his pocket knife and carefully placed the sample in an envelope.

Mooney turned to the American officer who had accompanied them. "Whose bed is that?"

The officer consulted his list. "Private first-class Edward Joseph Leonski."

Adam and Mooney took their samples to police analyst Charles Taylor; probably the most dreaded "lab man" in the Southern Hemisphere. Taylor's findings left little doubt – the dried mud was identical with the clay from the Royal Park air raid trench. The traces on the bed had been left by someone clutching the iron frame with mud-smeared hands.

The detectives hurried back to Camp Pell. There a surprise was waiting for them. Leonski's tent-mate and closest "buddy" in the camp had talked to his company commander. He felt he couldn't keep quiet any longer. He had, in fact, kept quiet at least a fortnight too long. But who could possibly blame him? Leonski, when drunk, was noted for his irrational behaviour.

Leonski, he said, had twice returned to the tent blubbering incoherently before sinking into twitching, tossing sleep from which he awoke at intervals, screaming. He had also pored for hours over the newspaper reports of the stranglings, mumbling things like "doorstep, doorstep" until his friend told him to "pipe down".

One day he had asked his tent-mate whether he believed that a werewolf could only be killed with silver bullets.

"What the hell do I know about werewolves," was the reply.

"Well, do you know Mr Hyde and Dr Jekyll?" Leonski had asked in an urgent whisper. "That's what I'm like – one guy, two personalities." Later he added: "All you guys are wondering about these murders. Only I don't – I know!"

It was then that the G.I. for the first time began to wonder seriously about Leonski and the murders.

"You see," he explained, "I've never known anyone to change so much when he's drunk as this Leonski guy. He might just have been blowing off steam – he always does when he's had a few. Half the time he doesn't know what he's talking about then."

He had challenged Leonski on his suspicions and Leonski had grasped him by the shoulder, tears in his eyes. "You're generous," he said, "you're the most generous man I've ever met. I'm depending on your generosity."

The detectives listened, their jaws clenched bitterly. "All right," they said finally, "let's have a line-up."

The Australian sentry was brought to the camp and shown the rows of assembled Americans. Then he was told to pick out the man he had challenged on the night of the 19th. The sentry stopped in front of a broad-shouldered, snub-nosed youngster with wavy fair hair and candid blue eyes.

"That's him," he said. "That's the man!"

It was Edward Leonski.

The American was taken to the guard house for questioning, but a real interrogation turned out to be unnecessary. He confessed all three murders, there and then, with an eager haste that sounded almost like relief. Drawing at a cigarette he murmured contentedly: "I knew all along this was the end of the trail."

In the latter part of the 19th century the Italian mind-specialist Cesare Lombroso expounded a theory according to which criminals are born, not made. The professor maintained, among other things, that all criminals are branded with certain physical characteristics and that these would show what sort of delinquent a person was going to be – even if he hadn't yet committed any crime. Lombroso maintained that criminals are degenerate types of a special, recognisable kind and that an expert – like himself – could spot them by appearance alone.

Among the characteristics discovered by the professor were: receding forehead, huge jaws and frontal sinuses, jutting chin, large quantities of body hair, and outstanding ears. "A type," Lombroso announced, "sometimes resembling the negro, sometimes the gipsy, sometimes the Mongolian. We note the large pale face, the prominent eyebrows, the wild eye – which alone is often enough to betray a criminal nature".

Luckily for the underworld and unfortunately for a great many innocent people the learned professor wielded considerable influence over the police theories of his time. He died in Italy in 1909, and was thus deprived of ever meeting Edward Leonski face to face. If he had he might have eaten his text books.

For the soldier who had reached "the end of the trail"

at the early age of 24 was a living refutation of everything Lombroso and his followers had dreamt up.

Tall, fair, magnificently proportioned, with a round baby face, button nose, and an engaging grin, he could have stepped straight from the campus poster of an American college. Eddie Leonski's outstanding characteristics were his gentleness, his almost permanent good nature, and his tearful nostalgia for "Mom back home".

Home was New York City and Mom – by all accounts – a formidable personality. Born in Poland, she had been a professional weightlifter before migrating to the U.S. Eddie had inherited his physique from her and she taught him how to lift weights at a very early age. His strength became immense. While working as a grocery clerk he used to entertain customers by lifting 100 lb. sugar bags above his head with one hand. Nor was Eddie merely a hunk of handsome brawn. To his mother's delight he played the piano, drew passable sketches, sang in the local church choir, and finished high school as an honours student.

But if ever a human being had been cursed by heredity it was Leonski. His father – a Russian – drank himself to death. His mother married again but the marriage was not a success. Embittered by two unhappy marriages Mrs Leonski clung fiercely to her favourite son; and he to her. Eddie had no girl friends, a harsh word from his mother could make him cry, and as long as she was near his behaviour was, if anything, too genteel.

Came the war and a call-up notice for Eddie. He seems to have spent the early part of his army career in tears – he cried when he was sent to a Texas training camp, cried when he received the first letter from his mother, cried when writing his answer, and cried the day he was shipped overseas. But between bouts of weeping another, hitherto submerged, facet of his character began to show through.

Cut off from his mother, Leonski started drinking. His army buddies, noting his crying jags, his sexual timidity and effeminate giggles, had put him down as "queer". He undoubtedly was that – but not in the way they imagined. For under alcoholic stimulus a completely different Leonski appeared; a swaggering show-off who would do anything to attract attention, fight at the drop of a hat, and wander off into the night on weird adventures of his own.

"The first thing that always changed was his voice," one of his fellow doughboys testified. "It became kinda soft and purry, like a girl's. Then he'd start telling you all kinds of creepy stuff – about werewolves and split personalities and jazz like that. After that he'd either want to hug you or fight you – you never knew which. And he was a pretty hard man to handle in a brawl."

It was at the Texan base of San Antonio that Leonski first fell foul of the law. A local girl charged him with rape and he had to answer to an army enquiry. It was a strange accusation for the girl-shy mother's boy. Eddie was acquitted. He definitely had not raped the girl, but had given her a terrible and quite inexplicable beating.

Shortly afterwards a bitterly crying Leonski was shipped to Australia in a signals battalion. From that day on his army record rapidly went downhill. His leaves became uninterrupted drinking sessions during which he dumbfounded Melbourne hotel patrons by mixing beer, whisky, gin, ice cream, mustard and ketchup in one glass and swallowing the concoction in one gulp. He also walked up and down bar rooms on his hands and at regular intervals sent out the traditional offer to "lick any man in the house".

Leonski also began to pick up girls. Not the young slips his colleagues preferred, but mature, more matronly types who were sometimes delighted at getting such a desirable escort.

"I don't know why I go for them," he confided to his tent-mate. "Their voices remind me of mom, I reckon. I like it when they talk to me. Makes me feel less homesick."

In camp he became a problem soldier; a chronic shirker and A.W.L. regular who spent more time on guard duty and k.p. than any other private in the battalion. Had anyone compared his civilian record with his army behaviour he would have noticed at a glance that something was going seriously askew with Eddie Leonski. No one realised this more than himself. Once, when a captain caught him returning to camp after an illicit outing, Eddie pleaded: "Put me in the guardhouse and keep me there, sir. Keep me there all the time – I'm too dangerous to run around loose!"

Leonski himself couldn't remember the precise date when he started to become violent. He pin-pointed it at soon after his plea to the captain; but his memory covering the entire period that followed resembled a grey fog patch shot through occasionally with blinding shafts of clarity.

He remembered assaulting three girls in quick succession, half-strangling each one, but letting go before they went limp in his grip. He couldn't recall either the localities or the circumstances of the attacks. "It had something to do with their voices," he said. "I used to feel terribly lonely and they spoke to me and I felt if I grabbed them I'd somehow be able to keep their voices for good . . ."

Two of his three early victims reported him to the police. But their statements were so vague and made so long after the assaults that they were useless in the later manhunt.

Leonski was perfectly aware that his dark urges only overwhelmed him when he drank. But he seems to have made no effort to cut down his alcohol consumption. He had been drinking heavily on the cold evening of May 2. Walking down an Albert Park street he remembered thinking of his mother, and how far he was from home. Then he saw a woman standing in a doorway . . . a pleasant-faced woman, holding a curiously old-fashioned handbag.

"I said something about that handbag, then I walked up to her and felt it. It was soft – strange and soft and it made me feel all strange inside. She stepped further back in the doorway and I followed her and grabbed her. I grabbed her by the neck . . .

"I changed the position of my thumbs so that they were at her throat and I choked her. She fell down . . . I could hear her head hitting the wall. I fell on top of her and I started to rip her clothes. I ripped them and ripped them and ripped them, but I couldn't rip her belt. I let go for a moment, then I got back to it. I felt mad and I thought I *had* to rip that belt . . . so I ripped and ripped at it . . ."

These were the words of Leonski's statement to the police. He had done his best to give an accurate account of the murder, but could not remember either how or what time he got back to camp. The following day he read that he had killed Mrs McLeod. For several nights he cried himself to sleep.

Five nights later Pauline Thompson, the policeman's wife, was stood up by her U.S. Army date and went to a café for a solitary meal. In the restaurant sat another G.I., a tall, good-looking one.

Mrs Thompson saw him looking at her across the tables. The soldier was Eddie Leonski, and Eddie was sober.

He joined her table and they ate together. The café was unlicensed and he suggested they go to a nearby hotel for a few drinks. He suggested what was tantamount to her death sentence. They walked to Collins Place, Eddie chatting in his easy-going college-kid manner. They drank – whisky with beer chasers; round after round. Eddie's voice grew softer, his smile became vapid and infantile. The woman noticed it. "Baby face," she chortled, flattening his snub nose with her finger. "But underneath – underneath you're vicious."

Around eleven o'clock Leonski ran out of funds. He was high by then, but not yet at danger pitch. Mrs Thompson paid for more drinks, inexorably pushing him towards the shadow line where the campus boy passed out and Moloch took over.

They walked to her home in Spring Street together, arm in arm through the drizzling rain. Mrs Thompson, feeling alcoholically Bohemian, sang songs in his ears; sentimental pops from her stage repertoire. She crooned softly and affectionately . . .

". . . She was singing for me. She had a nice voice. We turned a corner and there was nobody around. All I heard was that voice of hers. I wanted that voice. We came to some long steps. Then I grabbed her. I don't know why, I just grabbed her. She stopped singing and I said to her: 'Keep singing – keep on singing'. But she wouldn't, she fell down instead. I got mad and I tore at her. I tore her apart. I kept on tearing until I heard someone coming up the street. I ducked behind the stone wall. My heart was pounding so I could hardly breathe. I thought I couldn't bear to look at her any more."

Nevertheless, Leonski remembered that he was out of

money. He took the dead woman's handbag and ran down the street. At the next corner he opened the bag, took two pound notes, and ran on. He hurled the bag away and hailed a taxi.

The next few days seem to have been a sort of waking nightmare for Leonski. He was quite conscious of what he had done – and he knew dimly that he would do it again. And he made what appeared to be an earnest effort to get caught.

No multiple slayer has ever surrendered voluntarily to the police, but a remarkable number seem to drop hints and scatter clues deliberately as if filled with an irrational desire to help fate along. Peter Kurten virtually confessed to his wife, Christie sublet the flat in which he had walled up his victims, Heath contacted the police under an assumed name, Manuel offered to investigate the deaths of a family he himself had wiped out. In the nine days between his second and his last murder Leonski literally goaded his comrades to inform on him.

He hinted that he was a "werewolf", a man with a split personality. He pencil-marked newspaper reports of his slayings and showed them to his friends, muttering "That's the doorway here." He talked and screamed in his sleep – always about women and killings, he clenched and unclenched his huge hands, gazing at them with such an expression of horror that one G.I. inquired: "What's the matter with your mitts, Eddie?"

No one informed on Eddie Leonski and like the inevitable third act of a Greek tragedy he found himself shuffling through the rain towards his last victim. The street was bleak and lonely and Leonski had been drinking all afternoon and most of the evening. He was on his way back to Camp Pell when he saw the umbrella in front of him and the small, slender figure of Gladys Hoskins underneath.

He caught up with her and smiled down from six feet. "May I walk along with you, mam? It's raining pretty hard."

Miss Hosking smiled back and nodded. She made comfortable small-talk to put the big, shy, lonely boy beside her at his ease. Her voice was soft and motherly . . . "It was a lovely voice," Leonski remembered.

They came to her home and he asked her to walk with him a little farther. "I don't know my way around here any too well." Miss Hosking nodded again.

"We came to the edge of Royal Park and she stopped and pointed and said: 'There's your camp, over there.' I knew she was going to leave then and I didn't want her to go. I wanted her voice with me. As she turned I took her by the throat. She didn't make a sound, didn't struggle, nothing. She just went limp . . . all soft. I pulled her by the armpits, pushed her under the fence. Then I climbed over and pulled her through from the other side. I carried her for a stretch but then I fell over and in the mud. She was making a kind of gurgling noise then and I said to myself 'I have to stop this'. So I pulled her dress over her face and I ripped some of her clothes."

Leonski made his three confessions willingly, halting only when his memory dimmed out. In the presence of his own officers and the detectives he signed the sheets in a curiously stilted schoolboy's hand.

From that moment he passed into the custody of the U.S. Army. Apart from presenting evidence the Australian police had nothing further to do with him. He was probably the most embarrassing accused ever to face an American Court Martial.

He had terrorised a civilian population on whose continued goodwill U.S. army operations largely depended and stretched their already hard-pressed police force almost to breaking point. He had been hunted down without the aid of American investigators and, worse, he had shown up his army's medical check as a complete farce – in spite of its vaunted accent on "psychological fitness".

Leonski was transferred to the City Watchhouse to await trial. Kept under constant observation by heavily-armed U.S. Provosts and barred from liquor he quickly regained his former good-natured placidity. Twice a day he did physical jerks "to keep in trim", he ate heartily, read whatever book or magazine was given to him, and spent happy hours sketching pretty, long-legged "Esquire Girls" on wrapping paper. Service and civilian psychiatrists eagerly scanned the drawings for some symbol of Leonski's mental kink. They found none. The sketches showed exactly the same types of chocolate-box cuties that were allegedly maintaining the morale of millions of normal Allied soldiers.

The U.S. Army authorities went to extraordinary lengths to keep their prisoner unlynched and unmolested. The location of the General Court Martial was made a top military secret – though anyone passing Melbourne's elaborate Horticultural Hall could see by the awesome concentration of armed men that something unusual was taking place there.

The incongruity that had always hung over the tear-stained mother's-boy-maniac persisted right to his end. The second-last act of his career was staged in surroundings intended for prize geraniums and seedling exhibitions.

Leonski had to plead Not Guilty, according to the Law. But since he never retracted his detailed confessions the trial became purely a matter of confirming them and deciding whether or not he was sane enough to be hanged. The question of his sanity was fascinating to the psychiatrists – for the officers sitting in judgment over him it was a source of acute embarrassment.

The fact that he had taken money from the purse of one of his victims, that he had tried to conceal the body of another, that he had felt remorse and horror for his deeds possibly made him "rational" in the strictly judicial sense. That he was utterly irrational in every other did not concern the Court Martial. But to those among us who prefer analysis – and therefore possible prevention – to legalise annihilation it is of some importance to try and fathom his motives.

The one Melbourne psychologist who had early recognised the pattern in Leonski's killings also offered the only explanation for them: "Leonski obviously adored his mother. Equally obviously he became a helpless reed when separated from her. He may have blamed her for his helplessness, bitterly resented how firmly she had tied him to her apron strings. With every middle-aged, kind-voiced woman he strangled he could have been strangling *her*."

Leonski seems to have been a creature of "Momism"

carried to its ultimate extreme – where it turns on and destroys the thing it loves. He was undoubtedly a fetishist; hence his preoccupation with clothes-tearing and soft handbags. He was also possibly a sadist; though of a rare "unbloody" kind who gains satisfaction not from the sights and sounds of suffering but from the *knowledge* that he has inflicted it. The only parallel to him in the history of crime would be Neill Cream, the Canadian doctor who haunted London in the 1890's killing prostitutes by means of poisoned "cough remedies". Cream was a sadist who didn't even have to be present when his victims died in agony. The realisation that the agony was happening somewhere was sufficient for him.

But all of Leonski's abberations didn't constitute insanity within the legal meaning. Even if they had it would have been very doubtful whether this could have saved his life. The pressure of public indignation on the Court Martial was tremendous; coupled with the anxiety of the U.S. Army authorities to eliminate that human blot on their escutcheon it could only result in one verdict.

After a trial lasting five days Leonski was found guilty and sentenced to death. Following the tradition of nearly all mass-murderers he took the sentence calmly. His composure lasted to the moment he died.

Back in New York his sister seemed stunned when she heard the news. "It can't be Eddie – it just can't be!" she cried. "He was the best in our family . . . the kindest, gentlest."

Old Mrs Leonski couldn't read English newspapers and was completely unaware of the fate of her favourite son. Her daughter managed to keep her so by switching off the radio whenever the news bulletins came through.

The sentence of the Court Martial had to be sent to Washington for confirmation by the President. This resulted in a delay of nearly four months; common in American legal practice but highly unusual by Anglo-Australian methods. After F.D. Roosevelt had signed his name on the document the confirmation was read out to Leonski in the death cell. He nodded pleasantly, as if in complete agreement with his President.

At six o'clock on the morning of November 9, 1942, Edward Joseph Leonski was hanged by the neck in Pentridge Gaol. He was the first foreigner ever executed there.

John Godwin

"I Always Wanted to Torture a Girl"

The next case, hardly known outside America (for example, it is not to be found in the otherwise comprehensive *Murderers' Who's Who* by J.H.H. Gaute and Robin Odell), seems to me among the most horrific murders ever committed. The only account I could find was in an old issue of *Master Detective*, written by George Vedder Jones. I mention this to explain phrases like "shocking crime" and "the vicious depravity of his nature", for true crime magazines have always – since they began to appear in the 1920s – displayed a tendency to reassure their readers by taking a tone of high moral indignation. If the writer fails to adopt it, then I suspect it is often inserted by the editor. This has been so since the Elizabethans began producing pamphlets about the crimes of notorious criminals, which were hawked among the crowd at public executions, and it can be found in 17th century volumes on the lives of famous highwaymen and in the classic *Newgate Calendar* of the late 18th century. In fact, it is only in the last few decades of the 20th century that historians of crime have felt able to adopt the tone of scientific detachment that is, after all, appropriate to the science of criminology. I hasten to add that, in general, Mr Vedder Jones writes with admirable precision and objectivity.

At exactly 9.25 on an evening in late April, 1942 three teenage student nurses stepped from a streetcar in suburban Pueblo, Colorado. Gathering clouds obscured the moon and a few large drops of rain were splashing into the street, driven by a raw wind from the mountains. The girls were returning home from an evening nursing class. "It'll be coming down in buckets in a few minutes," blonde-haired Margaret Driscoll said. "Better stay here at my house till the storm passes." She paused before the path leading to the home of her parents.

Pretty 17-year-old Alice Porter glanced up at the blackening sky. A flash of lightning stabbed down from the clouds. She shook her head. "I only have a few blocks to go. I can get home before the storm breaks."

"I'm going to wait here at Margaret's," Eileen Muhic said. "Better stay, too, Alice."

"No, I'm going on home," Alice insisted. "So long, girls. See you at school tomorrow."

She turned and started away, her high heels clicking along the pavement.

At 9.30 that evening, Ward Lennon, who lived two blocks down the street, was sitting across from his wife in their living-room when he heard a clap of thunder.

"Better close those front windows," his wife told him. "It'll be pouring in a minute."

Suddenly a scream rang out in the night.

"What was that?" exclaimed Mrs Lennon.

"It sounded like a woman." Lennon peered out into the darkness. In the street he saw what looked like a tan-coloured car picking up speed. He listened, but heard no further sound. "The scream must have come from that car that just drove away," he concluded.

Lennon wondered if he should telephone the police, but decided that it was probably only some high school youngsters out joyriding. He closed the windows and went back to his easy chair.

At 9.45, Marvin Porter, a retired Pueblo detective, put aside the newspaper he had been reading uneasily and looked out of his front door. The rain was coming down in solid sheets, driven by a strong wind.

"I'm worried about Alice," he told his wife. "I hope she isn't out in this rain."

"She probably stopped off at the Driscolls'," his wife reassured him.

The shower passed and the moon came out again. Still Alice did not return.

At 10.15, Porter said: "I'm going to call the Driscolls and see if she's there."

He returned to the living-room a moment later. "That's strange. The Driscolls say she left for here 50 minutes ago. It's only about a five-minutes walk," he said, obviously worried.

Porter put on his coat and hat and went out. He stopped at every house on the way to the Driscolls' to inquire about Alice. No one had seen her. Ward Lennon, however, told of hearing the scream and seeing the car drive rapidly away.

At the Driscolls' house, Porter asked Margaret Driscoll if she had noticed a tan-coloured car along the street when Alice started home.

Margaret did not recall such a car. "But I wasn't noticing cars particularly," she said. "We were worried about Alice getting home before the rain."

Then she added: "I remember now! I've seen a car like that other nights, though. Eileen Muhic and I remarked about it. We saw the same car with a man in it parked near the nursing home several nights in a row. Then one night last week, after we'd got on the streetcar, the driver started up and followed along behind us. Another night, I saw that same car parked not far from Alice's house. I thought it was kind of strange."

"Did you notice anything special about the car or the driver?" Porter asked. His fears were mounting.

"No, it was too dark. I'm not even certain that it was a tan car. All I know is that it was some light colour – might have been a light grey. But I saw that same car five or six times. The driver always acted as though he was waiting for someone."

"Waiting for someone," Porter echoed under his breath. Using the Driscolls' phone, he immediately notified the police.

Picking up Ward Lennon on the way, Porter hurried home, arriving there just as a police car with Captain

Robert Pratt and a patrolman pulled up. Porter had known Pratt when both worked together at the detective bureau. The two men exchanged sober greetings.

"She simply vanished off the street," Porter said. "There's no place I know where she could possibly be." He told the captain about the car seen near the nursing school which had followed the streetcar home. Lennon told of hearing a woman's scream and seeing a similar car drive away.

"I'm certain Alice was in that car," Porter said, "and I know she didn't get in willingly. Alice is barely 17. She's had a few dates with boys. But she'd never think of getting into a car with a stranger. And this is the first time since she started nursing school that she hasn't been home promptly at 9.30."

Captain Pratt telephoned Chief of Police Arthur Grady at his home. Agreeing that the girl's disappearance called for immediate action, Grady contacted Pueblo County Sheriff Thomas Murphy and asked that county patrols be alerted to halt any suspicious-looking cars on all highways leading out of Pueblo.

When Pratt asked if there was any reason why anyone should want to harm his daughter, Porter said hesitantly: "I can think of only one reason. You remember the Dorothy Drain murder, of course. While I was working on it as a detective, I received an anonymous letter threatening my daughter with the same fate as Dorothy if I didn't lay off the investigation."

Pratt well remembered the shocking rape-murder. On a warm evening in August, Riley Drain, a Pueblo County sheriff's deputy, returned home from a dance with his wife. His two pretty daughters, Dorothy, 16, and Barbara, 14, had been left asleep in a bedroom of their modest bungalow. The Drains were startled to find the front door standing open. On the blood-drenched double bed lay the nude body of Dorothy Drain. She had been brutally assaulted, then killed by a blow on the head with an axe. An unsuccessful attempt had been made to rape the younger girl, Barbara. She lay feebly whimpering, her skull also fractured by a blow.

Prompt emergency hospital treatment saved the younger

49

girl's life, although months passed before she was fully recovered.

While the manhunt for the killer was in progress, Porter received the threatening letter. Police eventually tracked down two men – Frank Aguilar and Joseph Arridy. Both were convicted on the strongest evidence, including the court testimony of Barbara Drain, and were executed in the gas chamber at Canon City. Presumably the threatening letter, which was never traced, was sent by a friend of one of the slayers.

"Friends of Frank Aguilar still live here in Pueblo, so we'll certainly check on them," Captain Pratt assured Porter. "But I think we ought first to find out what men Alice knew. The man in the car may not have been a stranger to Alice. She may have gone up to the car willingly, then screamed when he forced her inside. Teenage girls sometimes keep silent about friendships with men whom they think their parents wouldn't approve of."

By this time, other detectives were arriving. Police technicians brought floodlights and other equipment. The street near the Porter home was carefully searched for some clue to Alice's abductor. Nothing was found.

Meanwhile, Pratt searched the girl's bedroom. He learned nothing from a packet of letters found in a desk. Then he came upon a diary secreted behind some books in a bookcase. Kept in a painstaking feminine hand, the last entry was for the previous day. The entries were mostly a recapitulation of everyday events at the high school which Alice attended.

Then Pratt noted the entry: "Bob drove me home again today. I think he's cute." Looking back, Pratt saw one other entry: "Bob tried to tease me again today. I believe he likes me."

Pratt asked Porter whether Alice had ever mentioned anyone named Bob.

"Not that I can recall," Porter said.

"Did she ever drive home in the car of a young man?"

Porter consulted his wife. Neither remembered Alice ever being driven home from school.

Pratt left at last. Driving to the slum area of Pueblo, he

questioned friends of Frank Aguilar who lived there. He could find nothing to arouse his suspicion, and returned to headquarters.

Chief of Police Grady agreed to assign a detective to look further into the possibility that someone connected with Frank Aguilar was involved. The chief had already called out off-duty police and detectives to visit every garage and gas station in the area in an effort to trace the missing car.

"I just had a call from Sheriff Murphy," the police chief said. "Some of his deputies near Cedarwood picked up a man driving south from Pueblo in a tan sedan. They're bringing him here for questioning."

Pratt told Grady of the "Bob" mentioned in the girl's diary. "If she'd ridden with this Bob before, she might not have hesitated to accept a ride again. The way I see it, he may have known the time Alice came home from nursing school every night and was waiting for her in the car."

"That seems to make sense," Grady said. "We'd better check up on him right away. Some of Alice's friends must know who he is."

Margaret Driscoll said that there were two young men named Bob in the crowd she and Alice went with.

"But she must have meant Bob McShane in the diary," Margaret said.

"He drives a car and he's got a crush on Alice."

The girl supplied the address of McShane's parents and Pratt went there at once.

I remember Bob speaking of Alice," the youth's father said. "He'd taken quite a fancy to her."

"Where is Bob now?" Pratt asked.

"He went to a basketball game up in Colorado Springs. He should be back before long."

"Did he drive?"

"Yes, he took the family car." McShane said the car was a tan sedan, about two years old.

"Did anyone go with him to the game?"

"As far as I know, he went alone."

Pratt asked the officer who had come with him to wait until Robert McShane returned and then bring him to headquarters, Pratt returned there himself. He found technicians examining a light tan Chevrolet sedan which stood outside the building. In his office, Chief Grady was talking to a handsome, expensively dressed man in his 30s. The man's clothing was dishevelled and the collar on his shirt was torn.

When Pratt entered, Grady told him: "Bob, this is Albert Sterling. He's the one Sheriff Murphy phoned us about. His deputies found two bobby-pins and a woman's handkerchief in his car. His clothing was in that condition when he was picked up."

Sterling, sitting tensely in his chair, pleaded: "You fellows have got to believe me. I'm a salesman and I work all over southern Colorado. I have to be in Las Animas County tomorrow, so I left here this evening, meaning to stay overnight at Trinidad. Well, it's a lonely drive, so I stopped at the bus depot to see if I could give anybody a lift in that direction."

Pausing for breath, he continued: "I found a neat little brunette who looked about 20. I got talking to her and she said she was a waitress at a place near Cedarwood. She jumped at the chance of a ride. She was so friendly that I began getting ideas. When we were about halfway to Cedarwood, I pulled off the road and started to make a play for her.

"She said no. But you know how it is with some girls. They just like to play hard to get. If a fellow's determined enough, they finally give in and like him all the better for it.

"Not this chick, though. She fought like a pack of wildcats. When I saw I wasn't getting anywhere, I finally let her alone. She wanted to get out of the car then and there, but I said I'd drive her on to Cedarwood and no hard feelings. So I did. I'd just left there when those deputies nabbed me at the roadblock."

Chief Grady asked the waitress' name.

"Her first name was Kay," Sterling said. "She told me her last name, but it was a long name and I've forgotten it."

"Where did you let her out?"

"At the bus stop. She was going to stay overnight with her brother, who lives just out of town. I offered to drive her there, but she said no, she'd telephone her brother and he'd pick her up in his car."

"Then you've no idea how we could locate this girl?"

"No, but somebody in Cedarwood must know a waitress named Kay."

Sterling said that he himself lived in Denver, but came to Pueblo several times a month. He said he did not know Alice Porter and never had been in the part of town where she lived.

"We're going to have to hold you here until we can investigate this," Grady said. So Sterling was taken to a detention room, while Grady and Pratt went out to the suspect's car. A fingerprint man pointed to places where powder had adhered to the car's inner surfaces. "There are quite a lot of prints," he said, "but none so far that correspond with those we took from Alice Porter's room. Nothing else incriminating about the car, except that there was definitely a girl in it lately. You can notice a faint odour of perfume."

The handkerchief and the bobby-pins found in Sterling's car were shown to Mrs Porter, but they were of an ordinary type and she could not identify them.

Shortly after midnight, Robert McShane was brought into the chief's office. A sallow faced, blond youth, he appeared frightened. He told Grady that he had last seen Alice Porter at high school the previous afternoon.

"Did she ever ride in your car?" Grady asked.

"Yes, I took her home after school a few times."

"And she trusted you and got into your car willingly when you asked her?"

"Yes, she did."

"Where did you go when you left the house tonight?"

"To the basketball game at Colorado Springs, like my dad said."

Asked to give an account of the game, McShane said uneasily: "I didn't get there until it was half over. I ran into a regular cloud burst on the way to Colorado Springs and pulled off the road to wait. Then the car wouldn't start. I had to dry off the spark plugs and the wiring. Even then, I had trouble getting it started."

"Where were you at 9.30?"

"I must have been stuck there."

A technician examined McShane's car. "Alice Porter's prints are in it," he reported. "But it's hard to say whether they were made tonight. They look fresh."

It was decided to detain McShane for further questioning.

Grady now telephoned newspapers, urging them to publish a detailed description of the missing girl. Since kidnapping is a federal offence, he also notified the Denver office of the FBI. From then until morning, the chief remained at his desk.

Early the next morning, Sheriff Murphy stopped in at his office. "We've questioned more than 200 drivers during the night," he reported wearily. "We're holding four men till we check their alibis further, but there's no evidence against any of them. I wouldn't be surprised if the car we're looking for is right here in Pueblo, either in a public or a private garage."

A few hours later, however, Captain Pratt called in to say that the check of garages and filling stations had brought no results.

Ward Lennon viewed the cars of the two suspects, Albert Sterling and Robert McShane. He looked critically at both vehicles. "It might have been either one," he stated at last. "At that distance I couldn't see much, though I'd swear it was a tan car."

Chief Grady now called the motor vehicle bureau in Denver and asked them to list all the tan sedans registered from Pueblo County. Detectives then went from one Pueblo address another, patiently questioning car owners, while out in the county Sheriff Murphy's men conducted a similar check.

Meanwhile, sheriff's deputies in the southern part of the county located the waitress, Kay. She confirmed that she had ridden with Sterling and that he had tried to force his attentions on her. But she said he had behaved well later and she did not wish to see him prosecuted.

Grady then released Sterling, and also released Robert McShane into the charge of his parents, since there were

insufficient legal grounds for holding the youth. Despite
the near-certainty that Alice Porter had been kidnapped,
there was still no physical evidence that a crime had been
committed.

The search for the missing girl was into its third weary day
when, in midmorning, Grady received a call from Sheriff
Murphy.

"I'm at Johnson's Garage in Beulah, about 25 miles
southwest of Pueblo," Murphy said. "Can you get down
here right away?" We've found a man we think may have
seen the kidnap car."

Grady picked up Earl A. Morse, a special investigator for
the district attorney's office, and sped southwest along the
highway. At the garage he found Sheriff Murphy with Deputies Maurice Corrister, Walter Chrisman and Undersheriff
Riley Drain. The latter, father of the murdered Dorothy
Drain, was taking a strong interest in trying to solve the
Porter mystery.

"This is Harry Johnson, who owns the garage," Murphy
told the new arrivals. "Harry, tell these men what you
told us."

The elderly garage owner said that about 4 o'clock on
Thursday morning, the day after Alice's disappearance, a
man came to the garage on foot.

"I was asleep in my room at the rear," Johnson went on,
"and he woke me. He said that his car was bogged down in
mud on a back road about three miles from here and asked
me to haul him out.

"I asked him why he hadn't dozed in the car till daylight,
so we could see what we were doing. He said he was in a
hurry to get back to Pueblo. So I got out the wrecker and we
drove to a rutted, single-track road off the highway about a
mile from here. It leads to an old abandoned ranch back in
the hills. We bounced along a couple of miles and there was
his car, hub-deep in mud.

"Well, I got him out all right, but I couldn't figure what
he'd been doing in the night at that abandoned ranch. He
said he'd been looking for another road and took the wrong
turn. He acted very nervous and jumpy. And as soon as we
got back to the highway, he hurried away towards Pueblo."

"What colour was the car?" Grady asked.

"It was some light colour. I don't remember exactly. I do recall that it was covered with mud – including the licence plates."

"Could it have been a tan car?"

"It could have been. I can't be sure."

Johnson described the driver as tall, slightly-built, thin-faced and wearing steel-rimmed glasses. "He didn't say much, and I noticed he kept his face turned away from me."

"What do you think?" Murphy asked Grady. "Does he sound like a kidnapper? Or is he a moonshiner with a still somewhere back in the hills?"

"I think he's worth investigating," Grady said. "Let's have a look along that back road."

The ground had dried out since Wednesday night's rain, and the two cars negotiated without difficulty the twisting uphill road. At the top of the hill, surrounded by desolate, barren country, was an old ranch house of crumbling abode. Its windows were boarded up, but its front door was hanging half-off its rotted iron hinges.

Sheriff Murphy pointed to fresh tyre marks in front of the ranch house. "A car turned around here," he said. "And here's a fresh oil spot, where a car had been standing for some time. Obviously, it was made after Wednesday night's rain."

The officials entered the crumbling one-room ranch building. It was littered with broken furniture and debris.

Grady directed his attention to a heavy wooden table in the middle of the room and the surrounding floor. Accustomed as he was to gruesome sights, he gasped. The table was literally covered with freshly-dried blood, some of which had dripped onto the hard-packed earth floor. On the floor were a pair of scissors, pliers, several strands of baling wire and a shoemaker's awl. All of them bore traces of blood.

"Good God!" Murphy gasped.

One by one, further evidences of a gruesome crime revealed themselves to the shocked officials. In a rude fireplace at one side of the room were the charred remnants of a woman's dress, the frame of a handbag, metal holders for cosmetics, and a number of Pueblo street-car ticket tokens. While Murphy and his deputies searched the room, Grady and Morse went outside. At the rear of the house they spotted the wooden cover of a cistern.

They lifted it aside and shone their flashlights into the murky depths below.

"Murphy, come here!" Grady's voice was hoarse with shock. The others came running from the house. In the cistern lay the nude and mutilated body of Alice Porter.

Undersheriff Riley Drain, whose own daughter had been the victim of a brutal killer, muttered: "I'm going to find the monster responsible for this, if I have to devote the rest of my life to it."

The body was covered with a cloth and lifted gently into one of the cars. Drain and Corrister volunteered to remain on watch at the abandoned ranch, while the others drove back to Pueblo. The body was taken to the mortuary, where Marvin Porter made formal identification. Then he broke down completely.

The coroner examined the body prior to autopsy. He emerged from the examination room, pale and shaken. "I've never seen anything like it, never," he said hoarsely. "Alice was bound to the table, nude, then tortured by a sex-crazed fiend. Her killer apparently heated the baling wire and used it to brand her. He stabbed her repeatedly with the awl. Then he criminally assaulted her. She bled slowly through several hours of agony, before he struck her head with some heavy object, probably to stun her. Then he shot her twice through the head."

News of the atrocity spread rapidly. Evening newspapers throughout Colorado carried the story in blazing headlines. In Pueblo, the police were swamped with telephone calls from outraged citizens who demanded that the sex slayer be found before he could attack again.

Meanwhile, Chief Grady and the Pueblo police worked on virtually a round-the-clock schedule. Robert McShane was definitely eliminated as a suspect when the garage owner stated positively that he was not the person whose car he had towed out of the mud. Nothing further had been found to connect the slaying of Alice Porter with the Dorothy Drain case.

Left with no suspects at all, Chief Grady threw himself into the task of evaluating the fresh evidence that had been found. Plaster moulds were made of the tyre marks found at the scene of the crime. The articles found in the ranch house were examined by technicians, and clear, sharp fingerprints were found on the awl. Criminal files were searched, but the prints could not be identified.

Then Grady was struck by an idea. Ward Lennon, the man who had heard the scream and seen the murder car driven away, had said repeatedly that he believed the car was tan in colour. But Lennon had admittedly seen the car only briefly and in poor light. Harry Johnson, the garage owner, had got a much better view of the car, but had observed only that it was "some light colour." Johnson had emphasised that the car was covered with mud. Perhaps Lennon had seen a car of some other colour covered with mud. Margaret Driscoll had said that the car she saw might have been a light grey one.

Grady instructed Captain Pratt to widen his search to include all light-coloured sedans. "And if the murder car was covered with mud when it was seen by Johnson, it seems to me the first thing the killer would do would be to wash it. Check up to see if it was washed in a public garage.

Captain Pratt gave the new instructions to his men early on Sunday morning. Towards noon, a detective and a patrolman walked into a garage owned by Boyd Whaley on East Fourth Street in Pueblo.

"There haven't been any new tan-coloured sedans in here since the last time you came, or I'd have got in touch with you," Whaley said.

"We're looking for something else this trip," the detective told him. "A very muddy car of any light colour that was brought in for a wash job."

Whaley stared at him. "Why, I've got a car like that here right now! I don't usually wash cars on Sundays, but the fellow said he was in a hurry, so I told him I'd have it for him. He said he'd pick it up at 6 o'clock.

"Who was the man?"

"I don't know. Never saw him before."

The detective took one look at a mud-covered grey Ford sedan and telephoned Captain Pratt. The latter was particularly interested in the caked mud adhering to the rear hub caps and rear axle. It was a car that had recently been stuck in deep mud.

The two officers waited at the garage all afternoon.

Promptly at 6 o'clock, a thin-faced, bespectacled man in his 20s walked into the garage and asked for his car.

"It's over there by the door," Whaley told him. "You can drive it out yourself."

As the thin-faced man reached for the door handle of his car, firm hands seized him by the arms.

Brought before Chief Grady, the suspect gave his name as Donald H. Fearn. "But why have you brought me here?" he demanded. "I haven't done anything. I was just getting my car to visit my wife in the hospital. She had her second baby 10 days ago."

A telephone call to the hospital confirmed Fearn's statement.

Asked if he had known Alice Porter, Fearn shook his head. "So that's what it's all about?" he said. "Well, you've made a mistake. I certainly don't know her."

"Then, if you're in the clear, you won't mind giving us your fingerprints, will you?" Grady asked him.

Fearn hesitated briefly. Then he shrugged. "Go ahead and take them if you want. Why should I mind?"

About 15 minutes after his fingerprints were sent to the laboratory, Grady's phone rang.

"The prints of the right hand match the prints on the awl," a technician said. "There's not the slightest question of it."

Grady asked for the two sets of prints. He showed them to Fearn, indicating points of identity marked by the expert.

"You're guilty and you know it, Fearn!" the chief said sharply. "You'll tell us about it sooner or later. It may as well be now."

Fearn stared numbly at the identical prints, then down at the floor. "I killed her," he mumbled.

A stenographer was summoned. For the next two hours,

the officers listened to an incredible tale of horror and depravity.

"I always wanted to torture a girl," Fearn said unemotionally. "I'd planned it several times before. I picked out the place for it and made a number of trips there to be sure it was all right. It was. No matter how much she screamed, I was sure no one would hear.

"I hung around that nursing class to pick out my victim. I'd follow the streetcar and watch where each girl lived. I decided on Alice Porter because she lived in a lonely block.

"I waited till my wife was in the hospital, so she wouldn't get suspicious if I was out all night. On Wednesday night I parked just down the street from the Porter house. When Alice came along, I drew up beside her, stepped out and pulled my gun on her. I ordered her into the car. But she screamed. I grabbed her, threw her inside and drove off."

Fearn told the officials in lurid detail of the depravity he had committed at the ranch house. After six hours of unbelievable torture, he snuffed out her life.

"I didn't want to kill her particularly," he said. "But I knew I'd have to, so she wouldn't identify me. I struck her over the head with a hammer I had in the car. Then I shot her twice and threw her body in the cistern."

News leaked out that an arrest had been made in the Alice Porter case, and reporters were soon swarming outside Grady's office, waiting for a statement. Grady knew what the temper of the public would be when the headlines hit the newsstands. To avoid any possibility of a lynching, he had Fearn driven secretly to the state penitentiary at Canon City.

Further proof of Fearn's guilt was provided when the tyres on his car were matched to the tread marks found at the scene of the crime. Alice Porter's fingerprints were also found inside his car.

Fearn was indicted for first-degree murder, tried and convicted. On October 23rd, 1942, he paid the penalty for his shocking crime in the gas chamber at Canon City.

So cleverly had Fearn hidden the vicious depravity of his nature from his family that they refused to believe the police chief's report of his confession. Not until that confession was read at the trial did they reluctantly give up their belief in his innocence.

George Vedder Jones

Harry Dobkin: The Skeleton in the Cellar

The case of Harry Dobkin is one of the classics of forensic detection, and Professor Keith Simpson's work on it ranks with that of Spilsbury on the Crippen case and Glaister on the double murder committed by Buck Ruxton. This version is told in Simpson's own words from his autobiography *Forty Years of Murder* (1978). I was acquainted with Simpson who, in spite of the rather cold and forbidding look of his photographs – that vast, egg-shaped head reminds one of Sherlock Holmes –, was a friendly man. When he sent me his book, I was excited by it, and suggested that we work together in turning it into a television series. He was enthusiastic about the idea; but alas, televison companies take years to make up their minds, and by the time things began to look promising, Simpson had died.

I was only thirty-five when I had the sort of case every young pathologist dreams of, "the case of a lifetime", Molly Lefebure called it. It certainly had all the ingredients, and, but for the heavy shadow of a war that still hung desperately in the balance, it would have hit the news headlines as Crippen did in Spilsbury's younger days.

On 17th July 1942, a workman helping to demolish a bombed Baptist church premises in Vauxhall Road, South London, drove his pick under a heavy stone slab set on the floor of a cellar under the vestry and prised it up. Underneath lay a skeleton with a few tags of flesh clinging to it, which he assumed to be the remains of another victim of the Blitz. He put his shovel under the skeleton and lifted it out. The head stayed on the ground.

Detective Inspectors Hatton and Keeling, who were called in to investigate, wrapped the bones in a brown paper parcel and took them to the public mortuary at Southwark, where I inspected them the next morning. The sight of a dried-up womb tucked down in the remains of the trunk established the sex. There was a yellowish deposit on the head and neck. Fire had blackened parts of the skull, the hip, and the knees.

Could she have been the victim of a bomb explosion? Hardly likely, considering she had been lying neatly buried under a slab of stone, neatly set in the floor of a cellar; this was no bomb crater. The detectives told me there had been an ancient cemetery on the site: could the body have been there fifty years? I shook my head. Soft tissues do not last so long. I thought the body was only about twelve to eighteen months dead. The church had been blitzed in August 1940, almost two years before.

Who was it? How had it got there? Was it murder? These questions were obviously going to take a lot of answering, and neither the cellar nor an old-fashioned mortuary was a suitable place for a scientific reconstruction. I asked the Coroner, Hervey Wyatt, for permission to take it to my laboratory at Guy's to sort it out in the only way possible – a slow step-by-step laboratory reconstruction.

The head had not broken off when the workman had shovelled up the skeleton, as he had thought. It had been cut off. Further, both arms had been cut off at the elbow, and both legs at the knee. Bomb blast could do strange things, I knew from experience, but not as strange as that. Someone had dismembered the body.

Pieces of the limbs were missing, and the first job was to try to find them. I spent two afternoons with the police sifting nearly three tons of earth from under the floor of the cellar. We found animal bones but nothing human. However, I noted two interesting things in the cellar: a yellowish powder on the earth where the body had been buried, and a wooden chest slightly less than five feet long.

John Ryffel, the Home Office analyst and Head of the

Department of Clinical Chemistry at Guy's, analysed both the powder from the cellar and the yellowish deposit on the body, and reported that she had been buried in slaked lime.

I reassembled the body and measured it. After making due allowance for missing bones and soft tissues, I calculated the height as 5 feet 1/2 inch. I checked this by reference to the well-known "Pearson's formulae" and also the less reliable Rollet's tables, both of which give estimates of height based on one of the long bones of the limbs. I had one long bone, the left humerus. Pearson and Rollet differed slightly, but the mean was 5 feet 1/2 inch.

The woman's neck was bent at a fairly sharp angle upon the trunk, and if she had been like that in life she would have been a conspicuous figure. I had X-ray photographs taken to see if there had been any disease to cause curvature of the spine. Nothing was found, and I concluded the neck had been bent after death. Why? Perhaps, at some stage, to cram the body into a space that was a little too small for it. As it was, it would have just fitted into the wooden chest. I examined this for bloodstains, but all the tests were negative.

How old was she? I had X-ray photographs taken of the skull plates, which join together at pretty constant periods between the 'teens and old age. Her brow plates were completely fused, fusion was in progress between the top plates, and there was no fusion between the two groups. That put her age between forty and fifty.

The person who had dismembered the body had evidently tried to make her utterly unidentifiable. The scalp and hair, face, eyes, hands and feet had all gone. No, not quite all: I found a fragment of hair sticking to the back of her skull. It was dark brown, going grey.

The uterus was enlarged. Another X-ray photograph, in case there was a pregnancy. No foetal bones. Instead, the swelling proved to be a fibroid tumour, three to four inches in diameter, for which she might well have sought medical attention.

Teeth? Her lower jaw had gone completely, but in the upper jaw I found as much dental information as a portrait, if her dentist could ever be found. Three molars on the right, two of them filled; the first molar on the left also filled. Marks from the metal claws of a dental plate. A high palate, and considerable thickening of the bone in the region of the back teeth. It was a mine of information. "If you trace her dentist, and he has kept proper records, you'll identify her beyond doubt," I told the police.

Inspector Keeling thought he might have found her. Working through the lists of missing persons, he discovered that Rachel Dobkin, the wife of the fire-watcher to the bombed Baptist Church premises, had disappeared after setting out to visit him to collect arrears of maintenance fifteen months previously. Her sister, Polly Dubinski, had reported her disappearance to the police.

Rachel was forty-seven, Polly said. Height about 5 feet to 5 feet 1 inch, "the same height as me". Dark hair going grey. She had been going to hospital about "something internal". Her dentist was Mr Kopkin – a strangely close spelling! – of Stoke Newington. Polly gave the police a photograph of Rachel.

Yes, said Dr Marie Watson, of the Mildmay Mission Hospital, Bethnal Green, she had examined Mrs Rachel Dobkin in October 1939, and found fibroid growths of the uterus. Yes, confirmed another doctor, at the London Hospital, fibroid growths of the uterus: an operation had been advised, but Mrs Dobkin had refused.

Yes, said Barnett Kopkin, the dental surgeon, recognizing Rachel Dobkin from the photograph – yes, she had been his patient for six years. From April 1934 to March 1940, to be precise; and Kopkin could be very precise, for his record cards were the most comprehensive that Inspector Keeling had ever seen.

"From these cards", he asked, "could you draw a picture of her upper jaw as it was when you saw her last?"

Kopkin sat down in his consulting room and drew the diagram. At Keeling's request he signed and dated it: 3rd August 1942, at 11 a.m. Then Keeling brought him to my laboratory at Guy's, where the skull of Rachel Dobkin lay upside down on the bench.

"That's my patient!" he burst out excitedly, before I had

time to greet him. "That's Mrs Dobkin! Those are my fillings!"

It was as dramatic a moment as I can remember. Molly Lefebure nearly fell off her lab stool.

Inspector Keeling produced the diagram the dental surgeon had made. It was an exact replica of the upper jaw from the cellar – teeth in the right positions, fillings just so, gap for the denture, claw marks – but also a couple of possible extra: tiny fragments of the roots of the first and second pre-molars on the left side that Kopkin thought he might have left in the jaw when extracting those teeth in April 1934. These did not appear on our X-ray photographs.

We had the jaw X-rayed again, this time by Guy's own senior dental surgeon, the famous Sir William Kelsey Fry. He found the fragments.

Meanwhile I had been feeling my way in photography myself, with the help of Mary Newman, who was in charge of the Photographic Department of Guy's. Now that we had a photograph of the missing woman, a full-face portrait, I wanted to try to superimpose it on a similar photograph of the skull. This identification technique had been used first in 1936, by Professors Glaister and Brash, in the famous case of Buck Ruxton, the Indian doctor who had murdered his wife and her maid and thrown their dismembered bodies into a ravine. Having the jumbled remains of two bodies, Glaister and Brash had been concerned with sorting out the pieces. I had only one head and one photograph, and I wanted to see how far they matched.

Miss Newman photographed the skull and photographed the portrait, and enlarged the latter to the same size. Then she made fresh photographs on X-ray film, a negative of the skull and a positive of the portrait, and placed them together superimposed. We found no dissimilarities whatever. The portrait fitted the skull like a mask.

Keeling was so pleased you would think he had caught the murderer. And in a sense he had; at least, he had him half in the bag.

Murderer? It is all very well to say you do not find yourself in several pieces under a slab of stone in the floor of a Baptist Church cellar unless something sinister has been going on, but that is not enough for a charge of murder. What evidence was there that she had been killed?

Probably there would have been none, but for a very important contribution by the murderer himself. In sprinkling slaked lime over the body he had no doubt intended to keep down the smell of decomposition and perhaps to destroy the soft tissues. Lime has a reputation for burning human flesh. But slaked lime has little or no destructive action; on the contrary, by killing maggots and beetles it acts as a preservative. Thanks to the lime, certain injuries to the throat, in part to the voice box, had been preserved in this way.

It was another dramatic moment, late in the evening, when I was alone in my laboratory and dissected out the voice box and saw that the upper horn of the thyroid cartilage on the right side was fractured. There was a little blood clot round it, so the workmen had not done the damage with their picks and shovels. It had occurred in life.

Now this little bone never gets broken, alone, except when the neck is gripped tight by a strangling hand. It is the pressure of a finger tip or thumb that does it.

"Are you quite sure, doctor?" Could I really say it was strangling without the classic signs, the imprint of fingers, the asphyxia? Both Hatton and Keeling were very tense.

"I'm certain. This means strangling. This little bone gets broken in no other way. I am quite prepared to say so in court. And if any other pathologist wants to confirm the injury for himself, well, there it is. We'll keep it and I'll have microscopic sections made to confirm the bruising."

I found another possible bruise on the back of the head. It could have followed upon the throat being gripped and the head bashed against the ground, but it might equally have followed upon a fall. This was a much less significant injury, and as there were no tissues left for microscopical examination I could not be so sure it had occurred before death.

My work was done. I had, I thought, enough evidence to convince a jury that the skeleton was Rachel Dobkin, and that she had been murdered by strangling some fifteen months previously. It was for the police to show who had killed her.

Rachel Dubinski had married the future fire-watcher in September 1920. The union had been arranged, according to Jewish custom, by a marriage-broker, and it was an immediate failure. The couple separated after three days; but nine months later a child was born, a boy. In 1923 Mrs Dobkin obtained a maintenance order. Dobkin was most irregular with payments, from 1923 to 1940 or so, and several times he served a term of imprisonment in default. Rachel had been reduced to waylaying him in the street to obtain some payment, and he had come to regard her as a pestering nuisance. On four separate occasions she summoned him for assault, but each time the magistrate dismissed the charge.

On 11th April 1941, Good Friday, the couple had tea together in a café in Dalston. They left at about 6.30 p.m., and Rachel was never seen again. Next day at 3 p.m. her sister Polly reported her disappearance to the police, saying she suspected Harry of foul play. But London was at war, the police were undermanned and overworked, and Harry was not interviewed until 16th April. Meanwhile, on the night of 14th-15th April, a mysterious fire had occurred on the Baptist Church premises.

It was mysterious because there had been no enemy action that night, and no inflammable material was kept in the cellar behind the church where the fire apparently began. Another mystery was that Harry Dobkin, the fire-watcher, did not give the alarm. The fire was first noticed by a patrolling constable, at 3.20 a.m. He summoned the Fire Brigade and went into the premises, where he met Dobkin. "I'm glad you've come, gentlemen," the fire-watcher greeted him. "It's a terrible blaze, isn't it?"

The fire was put out, and the minister, the Rev. Herbert Burgess, went round taking stock of the damage. In the cellar he saw the charred remains of a straw mattress; it appeared to have been ripped open, and straw from it had been scattered in heaps over the floor. Mr Burgess sought out Dobkin and asked him what he knew about it. The fire-watcher said he had tried to put out the fire and then called the Fire Brigade. Mr Burgess felt very strongly that the fire had been deliberately caused and he made an entry to that effect in his diary.

The next day, 16th April, there was what was officially called an "incident" at Kennington Oval, less that 250 yards from the church, killing 23 persons and injuring more than twice as many. Enemy planes had dropped a land mine. When such disasters were considered only incidental, it is not surprising that a small fire in an unoccupied cellar was just put out and forgotten. The police did not mention it when they asked Harry Dobkin that day about the disappearance of his wife. He told them he had not seen her since they had tea together on 11th April.

The police circulated a description of Rachel and inquired at hospitals and the other usual places, including the Central Air Raid Casualty Bureau. The police found out nothing more, but evidently had suspicions, for on 28th April, and again on 1st and 2nd May, they searched the Church premises, dug up the floor of the crypt, and discovered a freshly dug hole some 6 feet long by 2 feet wide. It was empty. The police finally published Rachel's photograph in the *Police Gazette* and then filed the case away.

All of which made very interesting reading for Hatton and Keeling more than a year later.

Dobkin had left his job as fire-watcher in May 1942 and was living in Dalston when his wife's remains were unearthed. Three weeks later a constable who knew him by sight saw him enter the Baptist Church premises at about 6 a.m. The constable, who was on a bicycle, stopped and watched, and presently saw Dobkin look out of an upstairs window.

Not a word about the skeleton had yet leaked into the press, Hatton waited until 26th August before asking Dobkin himself to "assist the police in their inquiries". Hatton took

Dobkin to the cellar and showed him where his wife's strangled body had been found.

"I wouldn't strangle a woman," he said. "I wouldn't hit a woman. Some men might, but I wouldn't. I didn't know the cellar was here, and I've certainly never been down here in my life." He also said he had not been back to the premises since leaving his job in May.

"I have information," Hatton told him, "that a policeman saw you going into the house on 4th August."

"Show him to me, the liar!" demanded Dobkin excitedly. "Show him to me!"

The officer, P.C. Wakeley, magically appeared. "That's the man," he said. "I've spoken to him several times at Kennington Lane about lights he has shown. I know him well."

"That's a lie!" shouted Dobkin. "I've never seen him before and I wasn't there. He's lying, he's lying!"

Inspector Hatton then formally charged him with the murder of his wife.

The trial of Harry Dobkin opened at the Old Bailey on 17th November 1942. F.H. Lawton, not yet a K.C. but later to become Mr Justice Lawton, appeared for the defence, which consulted my friend Eric Gardner on the medico-legal aspects of the case. Gardner told me later that he had advised them not to challenge the identification evidence, but Lawton chose to fight identity step by step.

"Anybody with a neck with that curvature would be a very obvious sight in life, would they not?" he asked me.

"If it was present in life."

"It would be obvious?"

"Very obvious indeed."

"If it was present in life, it could not be Mrs Dobkin, could it?"

"It was not present in life."

"That is not quite the question which I asked you: if it was present in life it could not be Mrs Dobkin?"

"But I am not prepared to consider the question whether it was present in life, because I found evidence to show it was not."

With forensic skill and remarkable medical knowledge he challenged my opinion about the dead woman's age and teeth (and gave Kopkin, who followed me, an even harder time). He also questioned me, but with an ominous lack of scepticism, about the dead woman's height.

"Taking a combination of all three methods of calculating stature, what do you say are the outside limits of stature, both up and down?"

"Working from the average height I expressed of 5 feet ½ inch, I think the possible limits are really an inch in either direction."

"So the maximum height would be what?"

"Five feet one and a half inches."

"So if Mrs Dobkin in life was 5 feet 3 inches, then this body cannot be that of Mrs Dobkin?"

"Yes." It was the only possible answer. But what was the point of the question? Counsel had something up his sleeve; he had asked Polly Dubinski at the beginning of the trial if her sister could have been 5 feet 3 inches. Why that figure? And why did counsel seem so pleased with my reply?

He left it at that for the time being, and went on to challenge the evidence of the superimposed photographs, quoting from Glaister and Brash's book on the Buck Ruxton case.

"And you are saying in this case that the photograph and the photograph of the skull together help you to make a decision as to identity?" he asked lightly, casually, as if he was not going to bother me much longer on the subject.

"Yes," I said.

"And a positive decision?"

"Yes."

The trap had closed. "Now may I turn," counsel using his heaviest voice, "to a passage on page 161 of Professor Glaister's book and see what you say about it." I waited uneasily. "'Owing to the novelty of the method and the uncertainty of some parts of the technique, a positive identification of the skulls, no matter how close a correspondence of skulls and portraits was obtained, would have been open to very grave objection.'" I had expected worse; I was relieved. "Do you agree with that?" counsel asked earnestly.

"I think it has an element of truth: it is open to objection," I said at once. "It is being used to give assistance in identification, not to prove identification."

"It is just part of the circumstantial evidence?"

"It is not circumstantial."

"You say it is direct?"

"It is scientific evidence."

"You do not agree with the words at the end of the sentence which I read to you, that this method is 'open to very grave objection'?"

"I think it is open to objection."

"But not very grave objection?"

"I should not have used those words myself."

"Now let us see why it is open to objection", and again this young barrister showed a disconcerting grasp of scientific data and technique. But I had disarmed him by conceding the limited value of the evidence.

As I had expected, counsel saved his heaviest guns for the evidence of strangling.

He asked me to imagine somebody standing in the road, or on a piece of waste land with a lot of rubble about, parts of bricks and so on, when a bomb exploded and the blast throws him violently forward so that in falling he catches his voice box on a kerb or a piece of brick or masonry or something like that. "Is it not possible – I do not put it any higher than that – that a fall under those circumstances might break the horn of the right thyroid?"

"I have seen injuries under those circumstances on many occasions," I said, "and the injuries have never been confined to a fracture of the horn, as present here."

I said I had seen the whole thyroid crushed, with fractures of both horns and both wings; I had seen only one wing and one horn broken together. But never only the horn. "In fifteen years I have personally examined over 11,000 cases, and I have never seen this injury except in manual strangulation."

"Do you say it is impossible?"

"I say that I have never seen it; and I have seen many falls and many strangulations."

72

Counsel asked me how many of my 11,000 cases showed any fracture of the thyroid.

"I can obtain such figures from my records, if necessary. I cannot say off-hand."

"Of course you cannot. I was wondering if I might suggest to you, then we can have a round figure" – counsel clearly hadn't consulted Eric Gardner about this – "that the number was well under fifty."

"No."

"More than that?"

"It would run into several hundreds."

It was Lawton's only slip, and at the end of the trial he gave us a bad few minutes. Harry Dobkin had spent more than a day in the witness box, largely to his own detriment, and now Counsel for the Defence was asking for one of the Crown witnesses to be recalled. "My lord, about twenty minutes ago a document came into my possession, and I wish to ask Miss Polly Dubinski a question on it. It is a matter of very great importance," he urged, looking young and guileless, "and, as I say, until twenty minutes ago I had no knowledge of it."

The document was a copy of the *News of the World* of 4th May 1941. The "Missing from Home" column included a description and photograph of Rachel Dobkin, both of which had been supplied to the newspaper by her sister Polly. Counsel began to read it out: "Height, about 5 feet 3 inches."

And he had got me to say that if Mrs Dobkin had been 5 feet 3 inches, the body from the cellar was not Mrs Dobkin!

But Polly denied she had told the newspaper 5 feet 3 inches. "I gave my evidence of 5 feet 1 inch. She was almost my own height."

Everybody was looking her up and down, literally, trying to guess her height. Dobkin would certainly be acquitted if Polly was 5 feet 3 inches. But neither the Crown nor the Defence suggested she should be measured then and there. Every pair of eyes followed her as she left the witness box and walked out of court.

Three more witnesses were called for the defence. Then Lawton: "My lord, that is the case for the defence."

L.A. Byrne, the Crown counsel, was on his feet. "Your Lordship will recall that Miss Dubinski . . . Since she was recalled I have had her measured . . ."

The judge gave permission for Byrne to call the police officer who had measured her. No witness was listened to more attentively.

What is your name . . . What are you? . . . Did you take the height measurement . . . (On and on went the preliminaries.) Is *that* the woman? . . . Was that at Snow Hill Police Station? . . .

And then, at last:

"What did you find her height to be?"

"Height without shoes, 4 feet 11¾ inches; height with shoes, 5 feet 1 inch."

And that was that. The jury took only twenty minutes to find Dobkin guilty of murder. He was executed at Wandsworth, where I had the lugubrious duty of performing the routine post-mortem that the law demanded, if only to show that the sentence had been "expeditiously carried out". It had.

Keith Simpson

The Wigwam Murder

In 1942, Simpson acquired himself a secretary, an attractive blonde journalist named Molly Lefebure; when she left him to get married five years later, she wrote a book about her experiences called *Evidence for the Crown* (1955), one of the liveliest books ever written about murder. She tells the story of the Wigwam Murder in the chapter that follows immediately on her account of the Dobkin case.

We must now go back to the beginning of October 1942 and those days when D.D.I. Hatton was in the throes of arresting Dobkin, and was receiving all those wordy notes, "Divisional Inspector, Dear Sir . . ."

That was in Southwark, among sooty warehouses and grey old streets. In Surrey, against a background of autumn-tinted trees and windy heathland slopes, another outstanding murder drama came to light.

On October 7th C.K.S. got a call from the Surrey police, saying that a body had been found buried on Hankley Common, near Godalming, and they were anxious for Dr Simpson to come at once. We cancelled all other appointments and by midday we were driving fast in the direction of Godalming.

Hankley Common was a former beauty spot, all heathery slopes, broken with graceful spinneys of birch and oak, and surrounded by wide vistas of wooded countryside and windswept sky. The Army, noting its loveliness, had of course taken it over as a battle-training ground. Camps had been built in the neighbouring woods and every day young men were taken out and toughened up amidst a welter of anti-tank obstacles, mortar ranges, field telephones and trip-wires.

We arrived at Hankley Common to find a large party of policemen, headed by the Chief Constable of Surrey and Supt. Roberts, and fortified by Dr Eric Gardner, the pathologist, awaiting us in a muddy hollow. Greetings were exchanged and then off we set to climb a windy ridge which reared itself, rain-swept and dismal, ahead of us.

(It is odd how it invariably begins to rain when one reaches the scene of a crime. Up till that time, for instance, it had been quite a bright sunny day.

As we struggled up the ridge, Supt. Roberts told us how the body was found. The previous day two marines, busy training, had discovered an arm sticking out of a mound of earth on the top of the ridge and had immediately reported this to the police. The body had been left buried until the pathologists should arrive.

The top of the ridge was gained and there was the mound of earth with a withered arm sticking out from the side of it. Rats had gnawed away parts of the fingers. We stood contemplating it, shivering a little in the wet wind, and trying to warm ourselves with cigarettes, while the Chief Constable, Dr Gardner, Dr Simpson and Supt. Roberts held a quick consultation. Below us a party of soldiers were busy at mortar practice, their shells whirling and whining over our heads every few minutes.

The two pathologists now took shovels and began very carefully uncovering the rest of the body. They had not been long at the job before a great stench of rotting flesh set everybody else busily judging the direction of the wind and then moving accordingly. The pathologists continued to dig, oblivious of everything but their task, and I was obliged to stay beside them, taking from them specimens of beetles, maggots, earth and heather, which I placed in the famous buff envelopes. And so the work went slowly on, until there lay exposed the sprawling, badly decomposed body of a girl.

The body was clothed in a green and white summer dress, light summer underwear, woollen ankle-socks, and a headscarf which lay loosely round the neck. The head had been battered in by some heavy, blunt implement.

76

It was decided to move the body to Guy's, and there was some discussion as to whether C.K.S. and I should travel back to London in a van with the body or by police-car. Much to my relief the police-car was finally chosen.

The body soon arrived at Guy's and C.K.S. had it placed in a large carbolic tank so that he might study it at his leisure, or, if you prefer it, in his "spare time".

"Spare time" mostly came at tea-time, so, for the next few weeks, C.K.S. arranged for us to take our tea beside the carbolic tank and its gruesome contents. This, I thought, was a very unattractive idea, for the smell of the body combined with the carbolic was enough to put the most insensitive off anchovy-toast and tea-cakes. However, it was not my place to complain, so there I sat with my tea-tray and memo-pad, jotting the notes which C.K.S. dictated to me as he stooped, all concentration, over the body.

Dr Gardner frequently came up to Guy's to assist with the examination of the body. The two pathologists discovered that the girl had received stabbing wounds to the left side of the top of the head, accompanied by similar wounds to the right arm and hand; these last resulting from the victim putting up her arm in an attempt to ward off the attack.

The pathologists came to a very interesting conclusion about these stab wounds. Because of certain characteristics it was clear they must have been inflicted with a hook-pointed knife. Neither Dr Simpson nor Dr Gardner had ever seen such a knife, but the nature of the wounds convinced them that such a knife must have been used.

Secondly, there were injuries to the mouth in keeping with the girl having fallen heavily on to her face, knocking out her front teeth.

Thirdly, there had been a single very heavy, blunt blow to the back of the head. Dr Simpson and I spent a whole afternoon wiring together all the fragments of shattered skull; it was like doing an exceptionally thrilling and elaborate jigsaw puzzle. When we had finished we found there was a vast depressed fracture of the skull, five inches in length and one-and-three-quarters in breadth, across the back of the head, as from a blow with a stake, or bough, or rounded bar. Such a blow would have killed the girl immediately.

A crush fracture of the right cheek-bone showed that she had been lying face downwards on the ground at the time she received this blow.

Lastly there were dragging wounds to the right leg, which had occurred after death, and which indicated that her body had been dragged over rough, open ground before burial.

So, from these tea-time sessions beside the carbolic tank, C. K. S. was able to tell the police that the girl had been stabbed at with a strange hook-pointed knife, had fallen on her face, knocking out three teeth, and while lying thus had been dealt a tremendously heavy murderous blow to the back of her head with a round, blunt instrument such as a bar, or stake, and finally, being dead, had been dragged over rough ground to the top of the ridge.

Meantime things had not been standing still in Surrey, either.

The Surrey police had decided to call in Scotland Yard, and Mr Greeno, now a Chief Inspector, had gone down to Godalming, on what was to prove one of his most exciting investigations.

It did not take the police long to identify the dead girl, through the clothes she was wearing and a portion of scalp with bleached blonde hair. A blonde girl in her late teens, wearing a green and white frock and a head-scarf, was already known to the local police; she had for some time past caused them concern by her mode of life, for she lived rough like a tramp and consorted with soldiers. She was not, the police thought, a really bad girl, but she had run away from her home, and was in need of proper care and protection, or she would, they surmised, rapidly come to grief.

Her name was Joan Pearl Wolfe, she was a Roman Catholic with a strong religious conviction and, alas, poor girl, she surely came to grief.

She had last been seen alive on September 13th, which tallied with Dr Simpson's estimate of the time which must have elapsed since death.

Mr Greeno on his arrival set his men to searching the ground round Hankley Common ridge. Day in, day out, they searched.

Bit by bit they collected clues. First they found the girl's shoes, lying some distance apart from one another, and some way from the body's burial-place. Then a bag with a rosary in it was found near one of the shoes, close by a small stream where there was a military trip-wire. Sixteen yards away was found a heavy birch stake. Clinging to this stake were a number of long blonde hairs.

Later, in a small dell up the hillside above the stream, Joan Pearl Wolfe's identity card was found, with a religious tract, and a document which was issued by the Canadian Army to men applying for permission to marry. There was also a green purse, an elephant charm, and a letter from Joan to a Canadian private called August Sangret, telling him she was pregnant by him and hoping he would marry her.

Mr Greeno learned that Joan, since July, had been living in the neighbourhood in rough huts, or "wigwams", which August Sangret had built for her, and where he had spent his leaves with her.

A deserted cricket pavilion which had also been a favourite rendezvous for Joan and Sangret was visited by the detective. Inside, Joan had drawn and scribbled all over the walls. She had drawn a wild rose, writing under it, "Wild Rose of England for ever – September 1942." And there was another sketch of a cabin, "My little grey home in the West." And a prayer written in pencil:

"O holy Virgin in the midst of all thy glory we
implore thee not to forget the sorrows of this world . . ."

There was also pencilled the address of Private A. Sangret, of Canada, and the address of Joan's mother in Kent.

The girl, at one stage, it was discovered, had been admitted to a local hospital, where she kept a photograph of Sangret, her "fiancé", on her bedside locker. From hospital she had written to tell him she was pregnant; pathetic letters explaining that the nuns at the convent where she had been brought up had taught her that an illegitimate baby was a terrible sin, but, she naïvely added, when she and Sangret were married and happy together with the baby everything would be all right.

She bought layette patterns, and people who saw this

girl-tramp in the woods in the weeks before she was murdered noticed she was knitting baby-clothes . . .

Chief Inspector Greeno now went to the nearby Canadian Army camp where Sangret was stationed. Sangret was a young man half French-Canadian, half Cree Indian. He had recently asked his C.O. for a marriage application form, but had not returned it filled in. He admitted to Mr Greeno that he had associated with Joan, but added he had not seen her since September 14th, when she had failed to keep a date with him. He had reported her "disappearance" to his provost sergeant, saying, "If she should be found, and anything has happened to her, I don't want to be mixed up in it." He had told a friend that he had sent Joan home, as she had no clothes, and he told another friend that she was in hospital. These friends of Sangret admitted to Mr Greeno that they thought Sangret's behaviour over Joan's disappearance "very strange". First he had said one thing, then he said another, and seemed very much on edge over the whole business.

While Sangret was waiting in the guard-room for this first interview with Mr Greeno he excused himself and went to the wash-house. Nobody thought anything of it, at the time . . .

Mr Greeno, after this interview, came hurrying up to Guy's. He arrived in a van, in the back of which he had what appeared to be a section of Hankley Common. There were furze and bracken, hummocks of grass, and a small tree. These were to be examined for bloodstains. There was, in addition, a Canadian Army blanket, and a battle-dress, and the birch stake that had been found by the stream.

Dr Simpson and Mr Greeno spread the blanket and battle-dress out on a table in the lab. and examined them. Both belonged to Sangret and both had recently, but not very effectively, been washed. (Sangret apparently could not, or would not, explain why he had washed them.) On the blanket, despite the washing, were faded bloodstains, distributed exactly in keeping with a person bleeding from the head and right hand that had been wrapped in the blanket. Dr Simpson decided that the body, prior to burial, had been wrapped in this blanket – and probably concealed among bushes. This would explain the very heavy maggot infestation of the body, which had clearly not been buried immediately after death.

The bloodstains on the battle-dress no doubt occurred during Sangret's attack on the girl.

The hairs on the birch stake were examined, compared with the hank of the dead girl's hair already in our possession, and proved beyond doubt to be hairs from the head of Joan Pearl Wolfe. The birch stake, too, exactly fitted the huge fracture at the back of the reconstructed skull. This was certainly the weapon with which the girl had been murdered.

"Now all we want is to find the knife," said Mr Greeno. And returned, accordingly, to searching the ground that had already been searched and searched. For it is infinite patience which so often wins the detective's day. But the knife was not lying amongst the grass and bracken of Hankley Common. Very dramatically it turned up in quite a different place . . .

In mid-November, long after all the leaves had blown down from the trees of Surrey, and Mr Greeno's investigations were plugging doggedly, but not very rapidly, along, up at the Canadian Army camp the waste-pipe of one of the wash-house basins was cleared of an obstruction which had been blocking it for the past five weeks. This obstruction turned out to be a clasp-knife; not a Canadian Army issue, but an unusual-looking knife with a hooked point; a point like a parrot's beak. And it was immediately recalled that Sangret had excused himself and gone into the wash-house while waiting for that first interview with Mr Greeno, five weeks previously. Was this Sangret's knife, and had he dropped it down the pipe in an attempt to hide it from Mr Greeno, knowing what a vital clue it would be to the detective?

It was Sangret's knife all right. One of his fellow soldiers recognised it as such. This soldier had found the knife, he said, during summer stuck in the trunk of a tree by one of the shacks Sangret had built for Joan. The soldier had pulled it out of the tree and shown it to Sangret, who had immediately claimed it as his own.

The knife was now brought to Guy's and shown to Dr Simpson. Its peculiar hook-tipped blade was, of course, precisely the sort of thing the pathologists had described after examining the stabbing wounds.

The last lap of the investigations had now been reached. C. K. S. travelled down to Surrey again and there, with Chief Inspector Greeno, made a final reconstruction of the murder at the actual scene.

It was clear now what had happened on that September afternoon when Sangret and Joan had their last date. They had quarrelled in the dell up the hillside; probably over the marriage application form which Joan was so anxious for Sangret to fill in and sign, and which he was so loath to complete. Sangret attacked the girl with his knife. She managed to escape him and, terrified, wounded and bleeding, ran down the hill away from him, but at the bottom, by the stream, she fell over the military trip-wire, landing heavily on her face, smashing her teeth. As she lay there, stunned by the fall, Sangret overtook her and murdered her by a crashing blow on the head with the birch stake, which he afterwards flung away. He then wrapped her body in an army blanket and hid it under the bushes for twenty-four hours or so, after which he dragged his victim to the top of the ridge, a distance of some four hundred yards, and buried her.

This reconstruction of the murder must have fitted the actual circumstances very closely, for at the trial Sangret's Counsel never questioned it.

It seemed odd, perhaps, that Sangret should have troubled to drag the body up a fairly steep hill for burial, but perhaps, almost unconsciously, he was following the ritual of his Indian ancestors, who always buried their vanquished enemies upon a height.

Sangret was charged with the murder on December 16th in the presence of Mr Greeno. He said, "No, sir, I did not do it. No, sir. Somebody did it and I'll have to take the rap." He added, uselessly, "She might have killed herself."

The trial was held at Kingston Assizes at the end of the following February. Dr Simpson took the skull along with him to court. We arrived just before the court adjourned for tea. Dr Grierson, then the Chief Medical Officer at Brixton prison, asked C. K. S. if he would care to take some tea down in the gaoler's room, beneath the dock. C. K. S. accepted the invitation, and I was invited too. So into the dock we climbed and thence down the short flight of steps leading to the gaoler's cellar-like quarters below.

It was a rather grim apartment, with stone floor and bare walls and several cells opening on to it. In the middle of the room was a big wooden table, laid for tea, and the gaoler, one or two policemen, two prison warders and Sangret were standing talking together. We all sat down round the table, with the exception of Sangret and the warders, who took their tea standing, buffet style; pretty obviously because Sangret didn't wish to join the tea-party. The atmosphere of the gathering was somewhat out of this world. Dr Simpson, Dr Grierson and the gaoler chatted together on the subject of juries. The policemen were discussing football. I couldn't overhear the conversation between Sangret and the warders, but it sounded amiable enough. I sat silent, eating bread-and-butter and drinking good hot thick tea from an even thicker tea-cup. Every now and again I tried to stare at Sangret without staring at him.

Sangret was a strongly-built young man of medium height, with his Red Indian blood clearly predominant. Straight features, quite impassive, cold, glittering dark eyes, straight dark hair, and a red-bronze skin. With an appetite not at all impaired by the ghastly predicament in which he found himself he enjoyed a large tea, eating and drinking noisily, holding the thick slices of bread-and-butter in both hands. Not a gracious individual with whom to share a wigwam, I mused. And not likely to make anybody a doting, devoted, baby-dandling husband, either. Did he let out a blood-curdling whoop as he crashed Joan's skull in? One could very well imagine it.

However, although he was not a very sensitive-looking man, I did not like to stare at him too much. So I sat quietly sipping tea and listening to the conversation about juries on the one hand, the conversation about who was going to be top of the League on the other, and wondering

what Sangret and the warders were talking about. It was
certainly the strangest tea-party I ever went to.

At length it was over, the two medical gentlemen and
I returned upstairs to the court, and the gaoler and the
policemen began clearing away the tea things in nice
domestic style. A few minutes later Sangret was back in
the dock, facing Mr Justice Macnaghten across the crowded
court, and Dr Simpson was in the witness-box, telling the
jury how Joan Pearl Wolfe had been murdered.

And now came an historic moment. Dr Simpson took up
a cardboard box, raised its lid and lifted out the dead girl's
skull, in order to demonstrate to the jury the fracture and
the peculiar stab-wounds. It was the first time a murdered
person's skull had ever been produced at a trial. All present
craned their necks to see, including the judge; all, that is,
save one, and that one was Sangret. I watched him, but
only the merest twinge of curiosity flickered over his face.
Indeed the impassive Redskin.

The medical and circumstantial evidence combined made
an overwhelming case against Sangret and the jury found him
guilty, but rather unexpectedly added a recommendation for
mercy. Why they felt he deserved mercy was a bit of a puzzler
to me. The girl had not been killed accidentally, during a
scuffle, for the blow to her head had been a truly savage
one, delivered with full murderous intent. Nevertheless, the
jury felt Sangret deserved mercy.

This plea was duly considered when Sangret appealed,
but it was of no avail, and he was executed at Wandsworth
a week or so later.

Dr Simpson did a p.m. on him. He lay there on the
p.m. table, muscular, well-built, almost good enough for
one of Fenimore Cooper's novels, his handsome bronze
skin marked only by the imprint of the hangman's noose
around his neck, and tattooed on his arm, ironically, the
name "Pearl".

Molly Lefebure

The Heirens Case

The Heirens case has intrigued criminologists for half a century – the famous inscription on the wall above a murder victim: "For heavens sake catch me before I kill more – I cannot control myself" seems the classic expression of the torment of a compulsive killer.

I wrote about the case for the first time in 1960 in *An Encyclopedia of Murder*, co-authored with Pat Pitman. It fascinated me because it seemed so typical of what I had called "the age of sex crime", discussed more fully in the introduction to this book. The first recorded sex crimes had been simply a matter of rape – like those decribed in the diary of the 16th century Nuremberg executioner Hans Schmidt, and this has continued to be true throughout most of the 20th century. Yet the Marquis de Sade, that patron saint of sex crime, had made it very clear that sexual violence is essentially a matter of the imagination.

Now pubescent teenagers have always been subject to intense sexual daydreams – even William Blake speaks of them in one of his poems; but these daydreams are seldom put into practice, at least with the opposite sex. So the sheer intensity of sexual desire tends to lead to "perversion" – the expansion of the sexual realm through "association of ideas" – that is, through daydreams and masturbation.

When *Psychopathia Sexualis*, the first textbook on sexual deviation, appeared in 1886, the Victorians were staggered by these medical revelations – sadism, masochism, voyeurism, vampirism and fetishism. It seemed incredible that anyone could

want a woman so badly that he could experience
orgasm while drinking her urine or licking the
dirt off her shoe. These revelations made it
clear that sex was no longer the straightforward
"two backed beast" it had been in the age of
Rabelais or Shakespeare. Frustration and social
convention had lent it a morbid intensity. On the
analogy of superheated steam, I once called this
"superheated sex".

Towards the beginning of the 20th century, a
new fetish-object made its appearance. As long
ago as 1850, ladies of the upper classes had been
wearing long undergarments called pantalettes,
usually made of some hard-wearing material like
calico and reaching down to the ankles. In 1851,
a temperance campaigner named Amelia Bloomer
argued that full-length skirts were unhealthy and
inconvenient, and that it would be better to
combine skirts that reached halfway down the
shins with, underneath these, Turkish trousers,
strapped around the ankles. This ensemble was
known as "bloomers". At first regarded as rather
indecent, they gradually caught on, until by the
1880s, most women were wearing some kind of
long "drawers" (so called because they were
drawn on). Oddly enough, these do not figure
in Krafft-Ebing's list of fetish objects, possibly
because they were so ugly – often made of red
flannel – that they deadened sexual desire rather
than exciting it. Little by little, the legs became
shorter and the material less coarse, so that by the
late Victorian age, "knickers" (the name shortened from the male knickerbockers) were usually
made of wool or cotton, and their elasticated legs
reached no further than halfway down the thighs.
In the 1880s, a smooth new material, rayon, was
invented. Now at last knickers became the object
of male fetishism – as did corsets – and in Joyce's
Ulysses, set in 1904, the hero Leopold Bloom is
a devotee of "drawers", and masturbates at the

sight of a girl leaning back and displaying her underwear.

I am inclined to suspect that knickers somehow became part and parcel of western sexuality at about this time, and – against all Darwinian theory – entered the male unconscious. I can recall, in the early 1930s, being fascinated by the sight of my mother's knickers – this was long before I went to school or knew anything about sex – and even putting them on when there was nobody in the house. And when I began to experience the onset of powerful sexual desire at puberty, I found the sight of a pair of knickers in a shop window, or pictured in an advertisement, as exciting as some casual glimpse of a naked girl.

So when I read an account of the Heirens case, describing how he had begun to steal women's panties in early adolescence, and of how he eventually began to experience orgasm as he climbed in through a window in the course of a burglary, it seemed to me that this was a logical and inevitable development in the "age of sex crime".

The account that follows, from my book *The Serial Killers*[1] (1990), is based upon the only full length book on the case that existed at the time, Lucy Freeman's *Before I Kill More* (1955).

On 10 December 1945 a maid entering the Chicago apartment of a thirty-year-old ex-Wave named Frances Brown was alarmed to see that the pillow on the bed was bloodstained; in the bathroom she found the woman's naked body draped over the side of the bath. On the wall over the bed, someone had scrawled in lipstick:

> For heavens
> sake catch me
> Before I kill more
> I cannot control myself

1 Written in collaboration with Donald Seaman.

Frances Brown was kneeling beside the bath, and she was naked. A pyjama top had been folded loosely round her neck; when this was removed, police discovered a knife driven in with such force that it protruded from the other side of her throat. She had also been shot twice. The body had been carefully washed after death, and wet bloodstained towels lay on the floor.

Four weeks later, on the morning of 7 January 1946, James E. Degnan went into the bedroom of his seven-year-old daughter Suzanne, and saw that she was not in her bed, and that the window was wide open. He called the police, and it was a policeman who found the note on the child's chair; it said she had been kidnapped and demanded $20,000 for her return. Later that afternoon, Suzanne's head was discovered beneath a nearby manhole cover. In another sewer police found the child's left leg. The right leg was found in another sewer, and the torso in a third. The arms were discovered – also in a sewer – some weeks later. The case shocked the nation, but the police seemed to be unable to develop any definite leads.

Six months later, on 26 June 1946, a young man walked into an apartment building in Chicago, and entered the apartment of Mr and Mrs Pera through the open door; Mrs Pera was in the kitchen preparing dinner. A neighbour who had seen the young man enter called to Mrs Pera to ask if she knew a man had walked into her apartment. The young man immediately left, but the neighbour called him to stop. Instead, he ran down the stairs. He pointed a gun at a man who tried to stop him, then ran out of the building. Minutes later, he knocked on the door of a nearby apartment and asked the woman who answered for a glass of water, explaining he felt ill. She sensed something wrong and rang the police. In fact, an off-duty policeman had already seen the fleeing youth, and ran after him. When cornered, the young man fired three shots at the policeman; all missed. As other police answered the call, the burglar and the police grappled on the floor. Then one of the policemen hit him on the head – three times – with a flowerpot, and knocked him unconscious.

The prisoner turned out to be a seventeen-year-old youth

named William George Heirens, and he had spent some time in a correctional institution for burglary. When his fingerprints were taken, they were found to match one found on the Degnan ransom note, and another found in the apartment of Frances Brown. In the prison hospital, Heirens was given the "truth drug" sodium pentathol, and asked: "Did you kill Suzanne Degnan?" Heirens answered: "George cut her up." At first he insisted that George was a real person, a boy five years his senior whom he met at school. Later, he claimed that George was his own invisible alter-ego. "He was just a realization of mine, but he seemed real to me." Heirens also admitted to a third murder, that of a forty-three-year-old widow, Mrs Josephine Ross, who had awakened while he was burgling her apartment on 5 June 1945; Heirens stabbed her through the throat. In addition to this, he had attacked a woman named Evelyn Peterson with an iron bar when she started to wake up during a burglary, then tied her up with lamp cord; he had also fired shots through windows at two women who had been sitting in their rooms with the curtains undrawn.

The story of William Heirens, as it emerged in his confessions, and in interviews with his parents, was almost predictably typical of a serial sex killer. Born on 15 November 1928, he had been a forceps delivery. He was an underweight baby, and cried and vomited a great deal. At the age of seven months he fell down twelve cement steps into the basement and landed on his head; after that he had nightmares about falling. He was three years old when a brother was born, and he was sent away to the home of his grandmother. He was frequently ill as a child, and broke his arm at the age of nine. The family background was far from happy; his mother had two nervous breakdowns accompanied by paralysis, and his father's business failed several times.

Heirens matured very early sexually – he had his first emission at the age of nine. Soon after this, he began stealing women's panties from clotheslines and basement washrooms, and putting them on. (After his arrest, police found forty pairs of pink and blue rayon panties in a box in his grandmother's attic.) He came to think of sex as something "dirty" and forbidden. This was confirmed when, at the age of thirteen, he walked into the school washroom and found two boys playing sexually with a mentally retarded boy; he refused to join in. Being a good-looking boy, he was attractive to girls; on eight occasions he attempted some form of sex play, touching their breasts or pressing their legs, but this had the effect of upsetting him so much that he cried. There was a deep conflict between his sexual obsession and his rigid Catholic upbringing. He found normal sexual stimulation repellent. From the age of thirteen he had been burgling apartments, entering through the window, and experiencing sexual excitement – to the point of emission – as he did so. After this, he lost interest in underwear, and began to experience his sexual fulfilment by entering strange apartments through the window. He often urinated or defecated on the floor. He also began lighting small fires.

He was arrested for the first time in the same year – 1942 – charged with eleven burglaries and suspected of fifty; in many of them he had stolen guns and women's dresses. He was sentenced to probation and sent to a semi-correctional Catholic institution. After a year there he transferred to a Catholic academy, where he proved to be a brilliant student – so much so that he was allowed to skip the freshman year at the University of Chicago. Back in Chicago, the sexual obsession remained as powerful as ever, and led to more burglaries. If he resisted for long, he began to experience violent headaches. On one occasion, he put his clothes in the washroom and threw the key inside in order to make it impossible to go out; halfway through the night, the craving became too strong, and he crawled along the house gutter to retrieve his clothes.

Once inside an apartment, he was in such a state of intense excitement that any interruption would provoke an explosion of violence. This is why he knocked Evelyn Peterson unconscious with an iron bar when she stirred in her sleep. On another occasion he was preparing to enter what he thought was an empty apartment when a woman moved inside; he immediately fired his gun at her, but missed.

None of the victims was raped – the thought of actual

sexual intercourse still scared him. Sexual fulfilment came from the "forbiddenness", the excitement of knowing he was committing a crime. After the ejaculation, he felt miserable; he believed that he was a kind of Jekyll and Hyde. He even invented a name for his Mr Hyde – George. Although he later admitted that the invention of an alter-ego was partly an attempt to fool the psychiatrists, there can be no doubt that he felt that he was periodically "possessed" by a monster. This is why he scrawled the message in lipstick on the wall after killing Frances Brown. It may also explain why he eventually courted arrest by wandering into a crowded apartment block in the late afternoon and entering a flat in which a married woman was cooking the dinner as she waited for her husband to return from work. Dr Jekyll was turning in Mr Hyde. In July 1946 Heirens was sentenced to three terms of life imprisonment in Joliet penitentiary.

In August 1991, I saw an advertisement in an American bookseller's catalogue for a new book entitled *William Heirens, His Day in Court*, by Dolores Kennedy, published by Bonus Books of Chicago, and sent off for it. To my astonishment, the author argued that Heirens was innocent. Dolores Kennedy had been legal secretary to the lawyer who represented the Degnan family – although, oddly enough, he believed that Heirens should be released. In 1983, a federal magistrate ordered the release of Heirens – after thirty-seven years in jail – because the parole board had failed to comply with his parole requirements. There was immediate uproar, and the Attorney General declared: "I am going to make sure that kill-crazed animal stays where he is." The magistrates's decision was reversed.

The father of Dolores Kennedy began to work for Heirens's release, and when her father died, she went to see Heirens in the Vienna Correctional Center in Illinois to discuss what could be done. She found Heirens likeable – as did most people who had met him – and helped to form a committee for his release. But Heirens himself presented a curious obstacle. He argued that he did not want to be released on parole – or at least, that he was not willing to pacify the parole board by taking what they regarded as the essential first step in considering him for parole: admission of guilt. He declared: "In 1946 I had to plead guilty to live. I was 17 years old and I wanted to live, and sometimes I wanted to die. I am 60 years old now and I will never admit to murders I did not commit." In other words, he had been forced to plead guilty only because the alternative to this "plea bargain" was the electric chair. As Dolores Kennedy looked into the case, she began to "uncover the magnitude of the misrepresentations connected with his conviction", and decided to write a book about it.

My immediate reaction to her book was scepticism. At least fifty per cent of criminals claim they have been "framed". Where Heirens was concerned, the case against him seemed to hang together so well that I found it virtually impossible to believe in his innocence. And as I read the book, it seemed to me that Dolores Kennedy deliberately underplayed the most powerful evidence – the box of knickers found in the house of Heirens's grandmother. I wrote to her to tell her so. She replied politely, declaring that Heirens had concocted the fetishism story because he hoped to be found insane. She said that Heirens himself would write and confirm this.

In March 1992, I received a letter from Heirens in which he did exactly that. He pointed out that although he had twice been arrested for burglary in his early teens, there had been no suggestion of stealing panties. "None of these examinations remotely indicated fetishism." He also pointed out that, when he was arrested, it was the police who fired the three shots, not he.

He went on to explain how, when he was nine, he had found a trunk of old clothes on a garbage dump near his grandmother's home, and had taken from it various items, which included women's underwear – bloomers and slips – as well as some men's swimming trunks. He put these in a cardboard box and hid them behind the chimney in his grandmother's house. "None of the underwear was of the frilly sort common with panty fetishism." In fact it was made of cotton and was of the pre-war variety. There were no semen stains, as there would have been if it had been used in masturbation. And, according to Heirens, it was only after he had agreed to the plea-bargaining, which included the fetishism story – that he told the police of the whereabouts of the box, which had been there for almost ten years.

On the whole, I was not convinced. Yet I had to admit that his refusal of parole *unless* he was given the opportunity to establish his innocence was a persuasive argument in his favour. My wife suggested that perhaps he didn't really want to be released. After all, a man in his sixties is likely to find the modern world a bewildering place after forty or so years in jail. He replied to this comment by pointing out that his prison "is not as comfortable as you seem to believe . . . it is still a prison where you are told what to do and when . . ."

I asked if there was any documentary evidence indicating that the box found in his grandmother's attic contained a mixture of male and female clothing; he replied that, as far as he knew, no inventory had been made.

When the publisher of this present volume asked me to compile an anthology of murders of the 1940s, it was obvious to me that Heirens had to be included, and that I had to make some mention of Dolores Kennedy's belief that he was innocent. That is why I decided to write to Heirens and ask him to write me a simple and brief account of his own side of the story, which I would print alongside my own account of the case. This is it.

My name is William Heirens. I have been imprisoned in Illinois for 47 years for murders I did not commit. Many of you over the age of 50 will remember the murder and dismemberment of six-year-old Suzanne Degnan in January of 1946. If you are younger, you may have read about it in crime anthologies or studied the case in classes. And, based on your reading, you may have been satisfied that the person responsible is paying for the crime.

I did not murder Suzanne Degnan. I did not murder Frances Brown and Josephine Ross – two women whose unsolved murders I was also forced to take the blame for to save my life.

Over the years many writers have canvassed my case in crime anthologies. Almost without exception they have been carelessly written with no regard for the facts and aimed at titilating the reader. A hallmark of such articles state that the lipstick message left by the killer in the Brown case was found on a mirror when it was actually found on the apartment wall. For the first time a crime anthologist has asked me for the truth of what happened in 1946.

Chicago, January 6, 1946 – midnight. On this clear, cold winter night, blond, blue-eyed Suzanne Degnan was taken from her bed in a house on the north side of Chicago and murdered. The next day her dismembered body was found in catch basins near the family residence.

Investigation disclosed that the child had been strangled. She had not been raped. Her body had been expertly dismembered into five pieces and distributed among various catch basins in the area. The dismemberment had taken place in the laundry room of an apartment building near the Degnan home. On the floor of the child's bedroom a ransome note was found.

The horror of the crime swept through the nation. The murder of a child is not uncommon, but decapitation is unusual, and dismemberment is rare and unthinkable. The effort made by those responsible for the crime suggested that the creation of horror was intentional. How much easier it would have been to dispose of the body in nearby Lake Michigan. One catch basin would have held the child's body without dismemberment. The scattering seemed to invite discovery.

The crime created dread and fear among Chicago parents. Emotions surplanted rational thinking. And, of course, the Chicago police were under enormous pressure to solve the crime. The case was ripe for a quote from Oscar Wilde: "It matters not if one is guilty as long as someone is found guilty."

The police arrested hundreds of suspects, grilled many and brutalized several in an effort to secure a confession.

The five Chicago newspapers, freed from the incumberance of wartime newspaper rationing, vied with each other for circulation by reporting every detail of the crime and the investigation that followed. I remember reading daily accounts of the Degnan murder, little suspecting that one day I would be held responsible.

Six months after the murder of the little girl, on June 26, 1946, I was arrested for burglary. Detected in the act of burglarizing a north side apartment, I fled the scene, but the police cornered me. A struggle followed during which I was severely beaten over the head, rendering me unconscious. I was taken to a police hospital where suspects were held. Almost immediately a newspaper reporter suggested to the police that I might be guilty of the Degnan murder. Before I regained consciousness, I was strapped spread-eagle to a bed in solitary confinement. For the next six days, without benefit of counsel, I was accused, questioned and threatened. I was 17 years old.

During those six days and nights of police grilling, I continually denied murdering Degnan. I was illegally questioned under the "truth serum" and denied murdering Suzanne Degnan. I was forced to undergo two lie detector tests that confirmed my denial. The police, however, claimed my prints matched a partial fingerprint found on the ransom note. The state's attorney announced to the press that the killer of Suzanne Degnan had been found.

My parents hired attorneys to represent me and I was finally released from police custody, charged with a couple dozen burglaries, not murder, and put in the county jail where I spent a week in the jail's infirmary recovering from my ordeal with the police.

On July 7th my attorneys were summoned to the prosecutor's office. They were told that the prosecution was anxious to settle the case on a plea bargain. In exchange for confessions to the murders of Suzanne Degnan, Frances Brown and Josephine Ross (two women whose murders had not been solved) and pleas of guilty to the murders and all other charges brought against me, the prosecution would guarantee one life sentence with all sentences running concurrently. If the offer was not accepted, the prosecution would seek the death penalty in the Degnan murder and, even if no conviction was obtained, sentencing for the burglaries would be so contrived that I would be imprisoned for life.

The attorneys informed me of the offer and I refused it. I had not murdered anyone and had no intention of taking the blame for it.

During this time, the Chicago newspapers, in the midst of a circulation war, printed everything they could to convince the public that I was responsible for the murders, even manufacturing "evidence" of guilt in order to "scoop" the other papers. Defense counsel kept me informed of what was appearing in the newspapers and discussed the effect of the publicity on my trial.

On July 16th, three weeks after my arrest and before I was indicted for any murder, the Chicago Tribune manufactured and printed my "confession" to the three murders. Only *after* I was sentenced did the newspaper boast:

> For the first time in newspaper history, the detailed story of how three murders were committed, naming the man who did them, was told before the murderer had confessed or was indicted . . . So great was public confidence in the Tribune that other Chicago papers reprinted the story solely because the Tribune said it was so. Never have a newspaper's contemporaries and competitors paid a higher tribute to its reputation for veracity . . . For awhile, Heirens maintained his innocence, but the world believed his guilt. The Tribune had said he was guilty.

The possibility of a fair trial was now impossible, defense counsel told me that it looked "very likely" that I would get the electric chair, and so I agreed to accept the plea bargain offer.

The problem was that all I knew about the murders resulted from what I had read in the newspapers and what I had been told by others. The Tribune's fake confession could be followed to some extent. I found myself in the position of Scheherazade, a spinner of tales to save my life. I knew I could make up a story; after all, our librarys' fiction shelves are filled with credible but untrue stories. However, I had a problem other story tellers did not face – my story was to be presented to a prosecutor who would renege on the plea bargain if he did not find it plausible.

During those long days and nights in jail, my seventeen-year-old mind constructed a substructure, an easel, to hang my story on. It had to be something that was self-effacing, certainly not self-serving. In those days sex was a taboo subject and I thought that its interjection into the confession stories would upset the interrogation so unanswerable questions would be abandoned. It would give me some control over the questioning.

On one of my burglaries I had obtained some books on sexual dysfunctions, read them and became intrigued with the practice of fetishism. I decided to use what I had learned and selected women's underwear, which was very common, as the fetish that I would claim. The police had removed everything from my living quarters and examined the contents. Not one item of women's underwear was found to support fetishism and to get around that I would claim I stole women's underwear eight years previously and the act transferred itself into the act of burglary instead. I didn't know if the psychology of transferrence worked that way but expected nobody else would know either.

Once it was decided that I would accept the prosecution's offer of a plea bargain, defense counsel began rehearsing the confession story with me. They corrected me when my account didn't check with the facts and I changed my story accordingly. Finally, defense counsel had the confession typed and presented it to me and my parents in the jail chapel to be signed. Even at that stage counsel had me change the typed version because of inconsistency. In spite of the rehearsal, I later learned that many aspects of the confession were at variance with the facts.

The murder of Frances Brown had occurred on December 10, 1945, between the hours of 4:00 and 5:00 a.m. She was 33 years old and was shot to death with a .38 caliber gun in her apartment. It was a bizarre murder during which the killer had written on the wall in lipstick: "For heaven's sake catch me before I kill more. I cannot control myself." A smudged partial fingerprint was found on a door jamb. After my arrest, the police announced that this print did not compare with my fingerprints. Ten days later they claimed there was a match.

Josephine Ross, 43, was stabbed to death in her apartment on June 5, 1945. Although there was no evidence of any kind to link me to the crime, the prosecution insisted that I confess and plead guilty to this crime.

The authorities attempted to establish a pattern between the three murders but it was difficult. The three females were in different age groups, did not look alike, were killed at different times of the day and by different methods (strangulation, knife and gun). In my confession story I tried to link them by saying the victims had surprised me in the act of burglarizing. It was a weak motive but never questioned. I had been interrupted in burglaries many times and instantly fled the scene, harming no one. Furthermore, I had my own modus operandi which included making certain no one was at home before I broke in. Burglary hours always occurred in the early evening before people went to bed. That way I could tell by the lights inside whether anyone was at home. None of the murders occurred during that time. And lastly, despite my "pack rat" habits, not one item taken from the scene of the murders was found in my possession. Few of the facts matched my confession, but no one cared.

Once defense counsel felt that I could hold my own, I was taken to the prosecutor's office which was filled with more than 30 officials. The prosecutor had newspaper reporters waiting outside in the hallway for copies of the confession stories as they unfolded. After some preliminary discussion, the prosecutor made a statement I hadn't heard before. He said he wanted the "truth" and I responded with "Do you really want the truth?" He replied "yes". Questioning about the murders began and when I was asked if I had murdered Suzanne Degnan, I responded by saying that I had no memory of killing her. Questioning ceased and my attorneys took me in another room. They were angry and asked me what happened. I explained that the prosecutor was insisting on the truth and that's what I gave him. I reminded my attorneys that they never asked me for the truth themselves. My parents were called to persuade me to go along with the agreement and I told them the same thing. I was taken back to my cell.

Several days later my attorneys again talked to me in jail and by this time I had gotten over my anger about the "truth" issue. For weeks I had lived in fear for my life with no other emotion. The "truth" demand had gotten me angry, an anger that swept away my fear. No longer scared, I reacted as I had. By the time my attorneys saw me the anger had passed and I was back to being scared and compliant. One British reporter covering the case wrote home in the London Sunday Pictorial under the headline "Condemned before his trial, America calls this justice", and discussed my conviction in the Chicago press.

I finally agreed to go through with the plea bargain and another date was set. However, by this time the prosecutor was angry because I had embarrassed him in front of his colleagues and the newsmen he had assembled in the hallway. Now the plea bargain became three consecutive life sentences if I went through with it. At this point there was no longer a choice and I gave my confession to the three murders as rehearsed.

As I had anticipated, difficulties arose about matters I didn't know the answers to and I could see that the prosecutor was getting angry about my "don't remember" and "don't know" answers. It was then I volunteered the sex angle, and, as expected, the prosecutor abandoned the line of questioning and asked for more sex input. I was then taken to the scenes of the murders for a reenactment and did exactly what I was told to do. I made many mistakes when asked questions at the scenes.

The next phase of the agreement was a psychiatric examination limited to finding out if I were sane enough to plead to the charges. This was merely a continuation of the confession phase because if there was a sanity question it would have been looked into before the plea bargain was accepted. The psychiatrists never considered my sanity at the time of the crimes.

The psychiatric examination was exhaustive. The psychiatrists didn't believe the fetishism and wanted proof. My family regularly visited my grandparents on weekends and they lived in the suburbs of Chicago. The area hadn't yet been built up and there were open fields for my brother and I to play in. There was a lot of landfilling going on and we examined the dumps for toys and other interesting things people threw away. There was a huge dump, a former clay pit, at some distance that we would visit in the evening on our bike to hunt for junk. I was alone at the big dump when I found an old trunk somebody had thrown out. I opened it hoping to find a treasure but all it contained was old clothes.

I sorted out the cotton items, which were mostly women's undergarments and put them in a small cardboard box. The items were clean but frayed. I also found a clean bedsheet that wasn't badly torn and put that in the box too. I took the box to my grandmother's house. I removed the sheet and my brother and I made a sail out of it which we mounted on our wagon so the wind would give us a ride down the empty streets (it didn't work well as we could only go with the wind and then had to walk back). The rest of the box I secreted in my grandmother's attic with the intention of making guncotton out of the material once I could get the acids needed for the process. At the time I was interested in Chemistry and read about making explosives in a chemistry book I got from the library. I was only nine years old at the time and my brother was six. Needless to say I couldn't obtain the acid – too young. So I forgot about the box in the attic. But I remembered it in 1946 when I was considering using the fetishism story. I told the psychiatrists where to find the box and they recovered it, supporting my claim of fetishism.

We also got into dual personality because the newspapers were playing up the Jekyl-Hyde angle. When the police used sodium pentothal on me to make me talk, I was unconscious most of the time but when I was coming out from under the drug I remembered talking about a George and saying that maybe George did it. At the time a common saying was "Let George do it" when passing off a job to someone else. I knew very little about dual personality, only common knowledge gotten from magazines of the time. The psychiatric report had a lot of material on the George alter ego. As to the murders, the psychiatrists recorded one statement I made to them: "I still believe yet that I didn't do it". After I was sentenced one of the doctors came to my cell and asked some more questions. The doctor reported what I said to the newspapers and that was: "As far as the murders are concerned, I don't know whether I did them or not."

About the only thing of merit that came out of the psychiatric examination was their finding that I was unusually susceptible to suggestion but then all immature people are to one degree or another.

On September 4th I was taken to court and pleaded guilty

to all charges. The police fingerprint expert testified to the fingerprint match in the Degnan and Brown cases.

We've tried to get copies of the fingerprint evidence so we could have it examined by independent experts. The state's attorney has refused to comply with this request. Modern fingerprint expertise could well tell a different story than was told in 1946. The prosecutor's handwriting expert, Herbert Walters, testified my handwriting matched that on the ransom note and lipstick message. Incidently, before my arrest, this same expert had compared the lipstick message and ransom note and declared they were not written by the same person. Recently five independent handwriting experts reexamined the same material used by Walters and determined that the messages were written by different people and neither matched my writing.

The confessions were read into the record and the psychiatrists made their report to the court.

Then the prosecutor rose and told the court how grateful he was to the newspapers and to my attorneys for helping resolve the case. He explained that without the cooperation of defense counsel in obtaining my confession, a conviction would have been impossible in the Ross case and a sincere public doubt would exist in the Degnan and Brown murders.

My attorney then rose and told the court that although at the outset he thought he had a duty to me and to me alone, he ultimately determined that his public duty was greater. At that point he cooperated with the prosecution to secure my convictions. I have since learned that my attorneys failed to investigate potential alibis (which people volunteered later) and gave confidential information to the Tribune in order to encourage my confession.

And that is why I have spent 47 years, from ages 17 to 64, in prison. Since that time, I have continually sought the fair trial denied me in 1946 through our appellate courts. One such appeal is pending now. So far our judicial system has denied me the opportunity for an advesarial trial before an unbiased jury. One attorney appointed to help me in an appeal commented: "When William Heirens stands before a court of law, justice peeks."

I was wrong to be burglarizing in my youth but I never

thought it would get me into so much trouble. If it wasn't for that, I would not have been in a no-win situation.

My sentence includes provisions for parole as part of the sentence I received under the plea bargain contract. The day after I was sentenced the prosecutor breached the plea bargain by sending a "Pen Letter" to the prison, telling the parole board not to parole me. Although the parole board has unfettered discretion, the board has admitted they do honor such pen letters. Several other breaches have occurred since then. In 1946 my attorneys told me that I would have the same chance for parole as any other prisoner that behaves himself in prison. This assurance was made to give me hope of a future in order to encourage me to accept the plea bargain. At the time it wasn't much of an inducement because parole eligibility was 20 years in the future but as time passed it became something to look forward to. 30 times parole has been denied.

Needless to say, over all these years I've learned more about the murders in a quest to establish to everyone's satisfaction that I did not murder anyone. The rational approach to solving any murder is to look for the cause; every event has a cause. The cause may be in the past, in the present, or in the future. Revenge is a cause out of the past. I knew none of the murder victims or those close to them, eliminating the revenge motive in my case. A common "present" cause is a reaction to a threat; rape-murders fall in this category because the victim's survival threatens exposure. I always fled when detected burglarizing. Neither Suzanne Degnan, Francis Brown or Josephine Ross were raped so they weren't killed under that scenario. A "future" cause is often for remuneration of some sort so that some murders occur for insurance money. Very often the one who profits from the victim's death is the murderer. In the Degnan case there was a bid for a ransom but the police, by immediately publicizing the discovery of the child's body, thwarted a follow-through in apprehending those who collect the ransom. I was a petty burglar, not a kidnapper.

I thought I had a hot clue some years ago. In the Brown murder, ballistics matched the bullet to one fired at another woman a month before. Two published accounts had the police recover the gun under the woman's window so that the Brown murder weapon was last known to be in police custody. One published account of finding the gun said the writer relied on the other published account.

The writer of the first account said she got the information from police reports or somebody told her and couldn't remember which. A search of old police reports was futile, they had been destroyed over the passage of time. In my confession story, though I complied with the demand to show where the Brown murder weapon was the police didn't find the weapon there.

William Heirens: *His Day in Court* by Dolores Kennedy, a book published by Bonus Books of Chicago in 1991, covers my case thoroughly and I commend it to the reader.

Am I convinced of the innocence of Bill Heirens?

Let me put it this way: I am now far less certain of his guilt than I was a year ago.

In the *Encyclopedia of Murder*, I also wrote an account of the Lindberg kidnapping case. There again, it seemed abundantly certain from the evidence presented in court, that Bruno Richard Hauptmann was guilty of the murder of the Lindberg baby. The chief evidence consisted of the various bills of the ransom money which were found in Hauptmann's house – which, after all, looks quite conclusive. (He was arrested when he used one of the ransom bills to pay a garage.) But the main back-up was the evidence of a piece of board which was missing from Hauptmann's attic. The prosecution alleged that one of the rungs of the ladder which was found below the window of the kidnapped baby was made from this piece of board. The ladder itself was made of yellow pine, and an eighteen month search of timberyards finally established that the pine might have been bought at a yard in the Bronx; this yard later proved to be the one used by Hauptmann. Another convincing piece of evidence of Hauptmann's guilt was a telephone number written on a closet door in his house – the telephone number of "Jafsie" Condon, the doctor who acted as contact-man between Lindberg and the unknown kidnapper.

Between the Lines

HANDWRITING AND DOCUMENT EXAMINATION
115 NORTH ARLINGTON HEIGHTS ROAD
ARLINGTON HEIGHTS, ILLINOIS 60004
(708) 255-5855

ELIZABETH M. BIESTEK

Statement of handwriting experts attending
workshop on May 9, 1992

Based upon our examination of the handwriting as
presented in the book, <u>William Heirens, His Day in
Court</u>, it is our preliminary opinion that the
handwriting on the Suzanne Degnan ransom note and
the handwriting on the Frances Brown wall do not
compare favorably with the handwriting sample
attributed to William Heirens and most probably
were written by someone other than William Heirens.

Elizabeth M. Biestek
Diane Marsh
Marie Gerage
Frederick J. Dudink

inter-graph associates, inc.

4020 West 111th Street
Suite 202
Oak Lawn, Illinois 60453
(708) 424-4443
(708) 424-4447

MR. PAUL LAURENT
Assistant Public Defender
Cook County Public Defender
2650 S. California
Chicago, IL. 60608

April 14, 1990

Re: William Heirens

Dear Mr. Laurent,

    On April 12, 1990, photocopies of script were delivered to
my office via U.S. Mail. Enclosed were exemplars of Mr. William
George Heirens. Also enclosed were documents of questioned origin.

    Please refer to the attachments. The page marked "A" are
taken from the ransom note. The letters underlined in brown
are from the questioned document. Those underlined in blue are
from exemplary material offered by Mr. Heirens. These are all
comparisons of indivdual letter structures.

    The page marked "B" show comparisons from the note written
on the wall. The letters underlined in brown are of an unknown
origin. Those underelined in blue are from exemplary material
offered by Mr. Heirens. These are all comparisons of individual
letter comparisons.

    The page marked "C" show word grouping comparisons. The
words were taken from the ransom note. The words underlined
in brown are of an unknown origin. Those underlined in blue
are from exemplary material offered by Mr. Heirens.

    The samples provided were subjected to all the measuring
prescribed by our profession. It is the finding of this examiner
none of the questioned material matches the writing of Mr. Heirens.
So different is the script that no comparisons could be found.

Sincerely,

R.W. Hellstrom

R.W. Hellstrom
Certified & Licensed
Examiner

Hauptmann protested that the ransom bills had been left in a box in his house by a business associate named Fisch, who owed him money. Fisch had died after his return to Germany, so when Hauptmann found that the box contained "gold certificates", he felt he had a right to help himself. In fact, Hauptmann's story about Fisch checked out in every detail. So is it possible that Fisch was the kidnapper? Possible, but unlikely. Bills of the ransom money were on sale in New Yorks underworld at a heavy discount long before Hauptmann was caught; Fisch, who was a dubious character, may well have purchased some of them.

As to the ladder, Hauptmann pointed out that it was such a botched job that any professional carpenter – such as he was – would have been ashamed of it.

Then what about the rung made from wood in his attic? In fact, Hauptmann's wife had made the mistake of moving out of their house soon after her husband's arrest, giving the police and reporters free access. One reporter admitted that it was he who wrote Condon's phone number in Hauptmann's closet. In *The Airman and the Carpenter*, Ludovic Kennedy has argued that it is likely that Detective Bornmann, in charge of the case, prised up the board from the attic floor and sawed out the telltale rung. After all, why should Hauptmann, who had plenty of timber at his disposal, prise up a board from his own attic?

Moreover, the footprints found below the baby's window were definitely not Hauptmann's. *If* he was involved in the kidnapping, then he was not alone . . .

In short, there is a very strong possibility that Hauptmann was not guilty, and that some of the evidence presented in court was fabricated.

What Dolores Kennedy's book makes quite clear is that William Heirens did not receive a fair trial. Just as in the Lindberg case, the police were feverishly anxious to charge someone with the crime, and a powerfully-built seventeen year old burglar seemed the ideal suspect. He was pressured until he confessed, and then told that unless he entered into plea-bargaining and pleaded guilty, he would receive the death sentence. Under such circumstances, most of us would agree to plead guilty.

There is also the fact that Heirens has pressed hard to have the fingerprint evidence – on which he was convicted – re-examined. If, in fact, such a re-examination showed that the fingerprints found at the scene of the attack on the nurse *were* his, this would obviously badly damage his case. This has been pointed out to him by his legal representatives, yet he still persists in asking for the fingerprint evidence to be re-examined.

But for me, the most powerful piece of evidence in Heirens' favour is the two documents reproduced here, in which handwriting experts testify that the writing found on the bedroom wall and the writing of the ransom note was not that of Bill Heirens. Like the "wrong footprints" in the Lindberg case, it is the piece of evidence that has the effect of throwing doubt on the whole prosecution case.

In a sense it is all irrelevant. Heirens has served a far longer term in prison than most people sentenced to "life". If he is a killer, then he has paid his debt to society. Yet for some reason, he declines to plead guilty – which would probably lead to parole – and quietly slip into obscurity; he insists that he is innocent and that his case should be re-examined. I do not know how you, the reader, feel after reading his statement – you may be totally unconvinced and pity my gullibility in even accepting the possibility that he may be innocent. But surely there can be no one who would disagree that, under the circumstances, he at least deserves what he is asking for: a re-examination of the evidence against him?

Colin Wilson

Neville Heath: The Sadist

June 21, 1946 – the day Margery Gardner's bruised and lacerated body was found in the Pembridge Court Hotel, Notting Hill – was five days before my fifteenth birthday, and I can still recall the sensation caused by the discovery. The police were already looking for the man with whom she had spent the evening, Neville Heath, for his "help in the murder enquiry". At that time, the British public knew little about sadistic murders – the trial of Gordon Cummins had been rushed through with such speed that no one had noticed it. But a woman found naked and dead in a hotel room with lash marks all over her body was the kind of material that tabloid editors dream about – particularly in the "silly season" – and the search for Heath received maximum publicity. Three weeks later, after Heath had been detained by the police, the naked body of another girl was found lying in undergrowth near a Bournemouth hotel, again horribly mutilated.

Heath's trial, which took place two months later, was probably the great British murder sensation since Jack the Ripper. I can clearly remember the general reaction to it – a kind of shivery horror, incredulity that human nature could be so depraved. There was nothing quite like it until the Christie trial in the following decade.

I recall meeting a journalist who had known Heath, and whose theory was that Heath was so good-looking that he could virtually take his pick of pretty women; this, the journalist thought, had led to a kind of Byronic boredom which in turn led to experiment in sado-masochism. I find this hard to accept. All the evidence is that sadism starts fairly early, in childhood, and develops if and when it is given the opportunity. But Heath certainly strikes me as an interesting example of the con-man killer – Ted Bundy is a modern example – whose murders spring out of a low sense of self-esteem, a desire to be a Somebody with a capital S. "Group Captain Rupert Brooke" was fundamentally a man who was unsure about his own identity, and who suddenly felt he knew "who he was" when he allowed himself to turn into a monster and abandoned himself to an orgy of beating and slashing.

This account is taken from *The Sound of Murder* (1973) by *Daily Express* crime reporter Percy Hoskins.

The Heath case presented the authorities with a terrible dilemma. Sadist and pervert Neville George Clevely Heath had already committed one murder in London, during which he flogged, bit, suffocated, beat and savagely mutilated a young woman.

He was a monster, wild with desire after gorging on one murder and clearly capable of, and likely to commit, murder again soon. It was absolutely vital to warn the public to be on their guard. The best way of doing that, in 1946, was to issue his picture to the newspapers.

The police were able to do it: Heath had a record and they had a photograph of him in the files. *But* the only positive evidence they had that Heath had accompanied the woman to the hotel where she was murdered came from a cab driver who took them as fare. And here was the dilemma: if Heath's picture appeared in the newspapers before the trial, the defence would almost certainly maintain the taxi driver had been unduly influenced by its publication. In plain English, defence counsel would infer he was claiming to recognise a face he had only seen in the newspapers. On that, a case could founder.

So a calculated gamble was taken that Heath's photograph would be circulated to the police only, in the hope and belief that someone, somewhere in uniform would pick him up before he murdered again.

The gamble failed. That decision cost another life, for Heath did murder a second time. No-one knows if that life would have been spared had the alternative course been taken – of saying, publish and be damned! – but it is possible, even likely. That was a hideous dilemma for all those CID chiefs saddled with the responsibility of decision. Their feelings when the news of the second murder broke can be imagined.

A curious-sideline to the Heath case is that Fleet Street's reporters knew Heath well, under one name or another, long before the murders. We didn't like him whatever the label he wore. Incidentally, one world famous figure who thoroughly distrusted him is Denis Compton the former international cricketer and footballer, born – like me – at Bridport. Denis, who of course is now a colleague of mine on the *Sunday Express*, rated Heath a dangerous phoney.

World War 2 had just ended. Millions were still in uniform, and it was fashionable in many quarters for temporary officers and gentlemen to cling to their wartime rank even when demobbed. The pubs were packed with returning warriors, and the hangar doors were open in every saloon bar every day. In Fleet Street we suffered "Group Captain Armstrong" almost daily. The dashing Groupie, alias Heath, was such an obvious exhibitionist, such a patent fraud to us old cynics. It has always been a source of amazement to me that women should fall so easily – and fatally – for his brittle, surface charm.

Our instinct was right, our suspicious noses had caught the right scent. Ladies' man Heath was in fact a brute, a sadist, and quite horrific killer. Now his blood was roused, and he was prowling through the hotels and pubs of London like any animal in the jungle looking for prey.

On the night of 20 June, 1946, Neville Heath was drinking and dancing with thirty-two-year-old Mrs Margery Gardner at the Panama Club in South Kensington, in London. Mrs Gardner was an experienced young woman who liked men. Heath fascinated her, with his crinkly blond hair, pale blue eyes and baby-smooth skin. Around midnight they left the Panama, with many a drink on board, and took a cab to the Pembridge Court Hotel in the Notting Hill district. Heath had booked in there some days before with another girl friend, whom he allowed to leave quite unharmed, and had signed the register "Lt. Colonel & Mrs N. G. C. Heath".

He still had a front door key to the hotel from that booking, so on the night he arrived late with Mrs Gardner no-one in the hotel ever heard them or saw them together. *The only witness to their arrival together was the taxi driver who brought them from the Panama Club.*

At two o'clock the next afternoon the chambermaid used her master key and went into the bedroom they had used after knocking two or three times without answer. One twin bed was soaked in blood. In the other lay the body of Mrs Gardner, with sheets drawn up to her neck. The "colonel" was missing.

Detective Inspector Shelley Symes and pathologist Dr Keith Simpson were called to the hotel. It was clearly a sex murder and the work of a maniac. Her ankles were still tied together, and her face and body, front and back, were covered in bloody weals. They appeared to have been made with a metal-tipped cane or riding crop. Her face was severely bruised consistent with blows from a clenched fist, and there were more bruises on her throat, as though strangulation had been attempted. (It was later proved that suffocation with a pillow was the actual cause of death.) Her face had been washed before the killer left – why was never clear.

A hunt was started for "Colonel Heath". His background was interesting. His schooldays were shared between a Roman Catholic school and grammar school, which he left at the age of seventeen. Date of birth: 1917. Place: Ilford, Essex.

In February 1936 he obtained a short-service commission in the Royal Air Force. He won his wings as pilot, but the next year he was dismissed the Service for a number of civil offences. He stole an NCO's car, went absent without leave and "bounced" a few cheques. After he was dismissed from the Air Force, he went around posing as "Lord Dudley" – rank and title always seemed to fascinate Heath – and bounced more cheques, whereupon he was placed on probation for two years. In the summer of 1938 he was sent to Borstal for housebreaking.

He was sentenced to three years there, but was released on the outbreak of war so that he could volunteer for the Armed Forces. He did so at once. He joined the Army this time, and by March 1940 he was once more an officer and a gentleman (so much for Selection Boards!) and was posted to Cairo. But Heath just could not keep out of trouble. There followed one escapade after another. Then, in July 1941, after swindling the Paymaster into paying him two salaries as Captain and disappearing without leave into the fleshpots of Egypt, Heath was courtmartialled and dismissed the Service *a second time*!

Most Armies would have flung a man in jail for this, but not ours: not an officer. On 27 October, 1941, *Mister* Heath, civilian, sailed from Egypt (second class, naturally, following his disgrace and dismissal) on the s.s. *Mooltan*, bound for Old Blighty's shores via Durban. Life on board ship clearly agreed with Heath. I have a sharply descriptive eyewitness report from Wing Commander Johnny Johnston, who sailed with Heath on the *Mooltan*. Wing Commander Johnston wrote to me about Heath in April, 1970:

"Heath was a handsome young man at that time, and it was obvious that some women on board were attracted to him. It may have been his good looks and aloof manner which attracted *them*, but he struck me at the time as being a very suave and plausible rogue.

"He left the ship at Durban, driven off in a large car by a well-dressed and attractive lady. The ship stayed there for three weeks, *and during that time we had inquiries from the South African police about Heath*.

"As far as I can recall now, their inquiries concerned a road accident where the body of a woman had been found in a burned-out car.

"Heath never joined the ship for the rest of the voyage."

*   *   *

Incredibly, Heath enlisted again. This time he volunteered for the South African Air Force, where he served for a trouble-free rest-of-the-war record. He collected a wife on the way. Neville Heath married in South Africa in 1942. Very little is known about the marriage. But Mrs Heath divorced him in October 1945, while he was away serving with S.A.A.F.

Heath was by all accounts a good pilot and aircrew officer: but he could not stay out of mischief on the ground. On 4 December, 1945, the South Africans made it number three – and cashiered him for a number of offences. I don't know if Heath's is a unique military record, to be thrown out of the service of the Crown three times in eight years, but it certainly is unique in the criminal world.

He came back to England in February 1946. Two months later he was in court. He was fined £10 by the Wimbledon magistrates for wearing uniform and ribbons he had no right to wear. Now he was officially a phoney, and it was at this time that "Group Captain Armstrong, D.S.O." was trying to strike up friendships in Fleet Street.

Now there was a naked, mutilated body lying in a bed in the Pembridge Court Hotel, and Heath had committed murder.

And now it was that the authorities had to make that fateful decision: to issue his picture to the newspapers or not. They did not. Instead they put out a statement and his description, saying the police were anxious to contact him "in case he could help their inquiries".

Heath was moving quietly around the southern seaside resorts, Brighton, Angmering, Worthing. He booked into the Ocean Hotel in Worthing. Then, cool as you like, he rang the same young woman who had spent the night with him at the Pembridge Court Hotel four days before the murder.

Naturally, she raised the subject of murder – in their hotel, *in their room*. The story was in every newspaper. She could talk of little else. "Colonel Heath" said yes, indeed, it was awful, but you see he had simply lent his door-key to a couple who wanted privacy and had slept elsewhere on the night himself.

Colonel Heath called on the girl at home. The visit was

not an unqualified success. Her parents did not care much for him. And when they too read in the newspapers that Heath was wanted – merely for questioning in case he could help inquiries – they made their daughter *insist* he contacted the authorities. Perhaps by so doing they saved her life. Perhaps the Fiend of Notting Hill intended her no harm: who knows? But either way there walks a lucky, lucky woman today.

Heath said goodbye to her. He never went to London. Instead he went to the Tollard Royal Hotel in Bournemouth and registered as "Group Captain Rupert Brooke". However, before he left Worthing, he sat down and wrote a long letter to the CID chief in London who was directing the manhunt for him. It was a curious thing to do. It was a curious letter, too, tantamount to an invitation to the police to pull him in for questioning. He even told them how to get in touch with him: via the personal column of the *Daily Telegraph*.

He may have written because the young lady had urged him so strongly to get in touch with the police. It may have been intended as another lie, another red herring. There may have been, though personally I doubt it, a noble motive behind the letter. Eminent counsel certainly thought so. After his trial Joshua Casswell, K.C., for the defence, said he believed Heath wished to be prevented from killing again.

Heath wrote to Det. Superintendent Tom Barratt:

"Sir,
    "I feel it to be my duty to inform you of certain facts in connection with the death of Mrs Gardner at Notting Hill Gate.

    "I booked in at the hotel last Sunday, but not with Mrs Gardner, whom I met for the first time during the week. I had drinks with her on Friday evening, and whilst I was with her she met an acquaintance with whom she was obliged to sleep.

    "The reasons, as I understand them, were mainly financial. It was then that Mrs Gardner asked if she could use my hotel room until two o'clock, and intimated that if I returned after that, I might spend the remainder of the night with her.

    "I gave her my keys and told her to leave the hotel door

open. It must have been almost 3 a.m. when I returned to the hotel, and found her in the condition of which you are aware.

"I realised that I was in an invidious position, and rather than notify the police, I packed my belongings and left. Since then I have been in several minds whether to come forward or not, but in view of the circumstances I have been afraid to.

"I can give you a description of the man. He was aged approx. 30, dark hair, black, with small moustache. Height about 5ft. 9in. slim build. His name was Jack, and I gathered he was a friend of Mrs Gardner of some long standing.

"The personal column of the *Daily Telegraph* will find me but at the moment I have assumed another name. I should like to come forward and help, but I cannot face the music of a fraud charge which will obviously be preferred against me if I should do so.

"I have the instrument with which Mrs Gardner was beaten and am forwarding this to you today.

"You will find my finger prints on it, but you should also find others as well.

signed,
N.G.C. Heath."

He never sent the riding crop to Superintendent Barratt or anyone else at the Yard. The letter was interesting: Heath was sounding out the police with an alibi. There is no sign of insanity, read it how you will.

The letter was received in London on 24 June. From then until 3 July, while his picture was circulated to every police station in the country but none shown to the unsuspecting public, Heath lived quite openly as Group Captain Rupert Brooke at the Tollard Royal. Down on the front he found his next victim, an ex-Wren called Doreen Marshall.

Doreen was a fine young woman, pretty, well brought up, and on holiday alone because she was recovering from a bad bout of 'flu. There was no mystery about how she met Heath: a smile from the dashing blond young man, a casual word on a sunny morning, a date for dinner that night – and murder.

He entertained her to dinner at his hotel and they had drinks in the lounge afterwards. As on the night he murdered Mrs Gardner, Heath was drinking hard all night. Miss Marshall tried to get a cab back to her own hotel, Heath insisted they walk – and he would escort her. She agreed. She was never seen alive again.

Before they left, Heath told the night porter he would be back shortly. He did not use the hotel entrance, but climbed a builder's ladder instead and got into his room unseen by the staff.

The night porter, a conscientious man, kept an eye on the clock. At 4.30 a.m. he went into Heath's room – and saw him asleep in bed. He noted that Heath's shoes were in the room, by the bed, and caked with sand, instead of being out in the corridor for cleaning. Heath admitted coming in by ladder, next morning.

Two days went by before Miss Marshall was missed at her hotel. The manager made inquiries. Someone remembered she had a dinner date at the Tollard on 3 July. When *his* hotel manager questioned him, Heath denied his guest had been Doreen Marshall.

Her body was discovered by a woman, out with her dog in the bushes and flowers of Bournemouth's Branksome Chine. She was naked. Her dress and underclothes were placed on top of her body. Her stockings were found yards away. She had been badly beaten, stabbed, and disgustingly mutilated. The worst mutilations were made after death. The police believed Heath stripped naked himself before the attack and that this explains the lack of bloodstains on his clothing. And that he washed himself clean in the sea after the murder, dressed and walked back to his hotel.

Heath had physically to walk right into a police station and confront a man in uniform before he was recognised, but by then it was too late to prevent another murder, too late to help poor Doreen Marshall.

All my life as a crime reporter I have tried to see the police point of view and I do not criticise them now: I merely question, as I have always done, the decision to withhold general publication of his picture.

Apart from the letter to Det. Superintendent Barratt,

there was no clue to Heath's whereabouts. Heath put his own head in the noose. When Doreen Marshall was still officially missing he rang the police in Bournemouth (as Group Captain Rupert Brooke) and offered to help them in their inquiries.

They accepted. When the handsome, blue-eyed Group Captain strolled round to the station, a sharp-eyed young detective thought he bore an uncanny resemblance to a wanted man called Heath. He held him pending further inquiries and called the Murder Squad. When they found the body next day, Heath was already in the bag.

Spooner of the Yard (a Detective Inspector in 1946) questioned Heath. On his arrival Spooner had been handed a statement Heath had written and again it was interesting, fascinating even – he was accused of nothing yet here he was offering another alibi.

He wrote that Miss Marshall (*on the dinner night, at the Tollard*), – "told me she was considering cutting short her holiday in Bournemouth and returning home on Friday. She mentioned an American staying in her hotel, and told me he had taken her for car rides. She also mentioned an invitation to go with him to Exeter but I gathered – although she did not actually say so – that she did not intend to go.

"Another American was mentioned, I believe his name was Pat, to whom I believe she was unofficially engaged some while ago.

"At 11 p.m. Miss Marshall suggested going away but I persuaded her to stay a little longer. About 11.30 the weather was clear and we left the hotel and sat on a seat, overlooking the sea.

"From this stage onward my times were vague because I had no wristwatch. We must have talked for at least an hour, probably longer, and then we walked down the slope to the Pavilion. Miss Marshall did not wish me to accompany her but I insisted on doing so at least part of the way.

"I left her at the pier and watched her cross the road and enter the gardens.

"Before leaving I asked her if she would come round the following day, but she said she would be busy for the next few days, but would telephone me on Sunday, if she could manage it.

"I have not seen her to speak to since then, although I thought I saw her entering Bobby's Ltd. on Thursday morning.

"After leaving Miss Marshall, I walked along the seafront in a westerly direction and up the path from Durley Chine, and to the clifftop, and so back to the hotel where I went to bed.

"It rained heavily before I reached the hotel."

Spooner took Heath back to London. After attending an identity parade he was picked out by the cab driver who had taken him and Mrs Gardner to their Notting Hill Gate hotel. Heath was then charged with Mrs Gardner's murder. He made no reply.

He was tried at the Old Bailey in September that year, before Mr Justice Morris. Heath's counsel pleaded insanity and called Dr William Hubert, psychiatrist and former psychotherapist at Broadmoor, for the defence.

Heath himself would have none of it. Halfway through the doctor's evidence Heath scribbled this note from the dock to his counsel: "It may be of interest to know that in my discussions with Hubert I have never suggested that I should be excused or that I told him I felt I should be, because of insanity."

Very few madmen, of course, believe themselves insane so Heath's protest was not inconsistent with his counsel's plea.

Joshua Casswell pleaded that Heath was "as mad as a hatter". And there are those who believed Heath actually murdered Doreen Marshall in a deliberate attempt to escape the hangman (for the Mrs Gardner murder) by being sent to Broadmoor.

The judge had this to say:

"The tests as to insanity to which I have referred are the tests which have in all criminal cases to be applied in regard to this matter. Whether medical men might wish from a medical point of view to frame other tests is not a question with which I need trouble you.

"We are here to administer the law.

"Equally you will see that insanity is not to be found merely because some conduct might be regarded as so outrageous as to be wholly unexpected from the generality of men.

"Strong sexual instinct is not insanity: a mere love of bloodshed or mere recklessness are not in themselves insanity: an inability to resist temptation, the satisfaction of some perverted impulse, is not, without more, to be excused on the ground of insanity.

"The plea of insanity cannot be permitted to become the easy or vague explanation of some conduct which is shocking merely because it is startling.

"The law of insanity is not to become the refuge of those who cannot challenge a charge which is brought against them."

I sat in the court and listened to the Judge very carefully. Already we were moving into the fringe battlefield of the capital punishment issue, though none of us realised it so clearly then, and I would have liked his words to be hung on the wall of every defence counsel and psychiatrist in the land.

Heath was sentenced to death. He was hanged at Pentonville, on 16 October, 1946.

Heath died coolly enough. When the prison Governor paid his final call and offered this fresh-faced, scrubbed-looking, so-handsome young man a last drink (of brandy), Heath rustled up a grin from somewhere and jokingly asked for a double. He got it. And went straightway to his death on the scaffold.

I shed no tears for the sadist Heath. But still, today, a quarter of a century later, I could weep at the decision that had to be made within the requirements of the law and led directly to the murder of Doreen Marshall. If the public had been warned, she need not have died: the likelihood is that Heath would have been recognised by some member of the public long before he could have killed a second time.

I had long talks with my friends in the CID over this (Spooner was one of them) and I know how they grieved over the Marshall murder. But is there a dry-as-dust official mind that could not care less as long as the letter of the law is obeyed?

After the case was over, I published the official picture of Heath as it appeared in the *Police Gazette*. I said this was the picture every policeman carried in his uniform pocket – but none of the public were allowed to see.

I was later told that the Director of Public Prosecutions had "seriously" considered summoning me for "publishing an official document". For the sake of the police and the reputation of the Yard, I am glad he did not. That would have made a bad decision contemptuous.

Percy Hoskins

The Porthole Murder

When I first came to live in Cornwall in 1957 – fleeing from the publicity that followed my first book *The Outsider* – I became acquainted with Dr Denis Hocking, the Cornwall county pathologist, and heard from him some interesting tales of murder and suicide. Ten years ago, when Denis was already in his mid-eighties, he sent me the typescript of his autobiography, and asked me if I could recommend a publisher. In fact, it was soon accepted, but after a delay of two years or so, the publisher went bankrupt. Denis persisted, and a few days before writing these words, I attended the launching party of *Bodies and Crimes* in a hotel in Carlyon Bay, St Austell. Among the guests was a scriptwriter who was beginning to script a series based on the book for Anglia Television, and Dennis Herbstein, who had written a book about Dr Hocking's favourite case – the one that follows.

As we discussed the porthole case, Dennis Herbstein made an intersting point: that James Camb might well have been telling the truth when he claimed that Gay Gibson simply died in his arms while having sex. Herbstein had interviewed many doctors, who had told him about similar deaths – in one case, a husband and wife came back from a party and were in the process of making love when the wife simply expired. The post mortem revealed no cause of death.

I am inclined to doubt this version of events, simply because it seems to me that if this had happened, Camb's first reaction would have surely been (a) to report the death to the captain – which might have involved his being disciplined, but not the risk of being charged with murder, (b) simply left the body where it was and made his way back to his own cabin. Having said which, I just admit that *Porthole* is an impressive piece of crime writing, and that the notion of an officer losing his head in sheer panic when he finds himself embracing a corpse is by no means inconceivable.

Bodies and Crimes is published by the Book Guild.

What I have always regarded as my most interesting murder concerned the disappearance of the actress Gay Gibson from the *SS Durban Castle* on the night of 10 October, 1947, on her passage from Cape Town to Southampton. It was intriguing because we had no body and so could let our imaginations run riot – a favourite pastime of mine. Dr Donald Teare of St George's Hospital, London, thought that she had been strangled. Prof. Webster and I thought that she had died from natural causes, possibly associated with sexual excitement.

This case has been recorded elsewhere as "The Porthole Murder' in *Facets of Crime*, published by Bossiney Books along with ten other stories. It is reproduced here by kind permission of the proprietor of Bossiney Books, Mr Michael Williams. Incidentally, the cover of his publication, depicting the victim as she would have appeared after having been thrown to the sharks is well worth the price of £1.50.

To whet your appetites, not all the evidence obtained by the Defence from South Africa was allowed to be given at the trial. We were limited to three witnesses from that country, but we had significant affidavits from a number of others. As their testimony, however, tended to attack the morals of the dead girl, it was thought that the Judge would probably disallow it. From his conduct of the trial, I felt certain that he would most certainly have done so. The significance of this unrecorded evidence was that the girl had been in the habit of indulging in unusual sexual exercises, and there was a possibility that she had lost her life during one of these adventures.

This is from memory; unfortunately the original documents have disappeared after being sent to Prof. Webster.

Amongst her sexual perversions, it was stated that "she sucks a cock".

Only one person knows exactly what took place in cabin No. 126 in the Union Castle liner *Durban Castle* on the night of 17th–18th October 1947.

This is James Camb, a one-time Promenade Deck Steward who was tried for the murder of the occupant of that cabin, Miss Eileen Isabella Ronnie Gibson, at Winchester Assizes between 18th March and 22nd March 1948.

The case is cited by Mr Justice Humphreys as "yet another instance of convincing proof of the guilt of an accused person being afforded by circumstantial evidence". Yet, to the minds of many lawyers, and even more medical experts, there was equally compelling proof of the Defendant's innocence. A great many of the known facts were not in dispute, and readily admitted by the Defendant. There is no doubt that the girl died in her cabin that night; it is how she met her death that is so intriguing.

Eileen Isabella Ronnie Gibson, quiet and friendly in manner, was just over twenty-one years of age when she boarded the *Durban Castle* on 10th October at Cape Town, bound for Southampton. The ship was practically empty, there being only fifty-seven first class passengers, most of them elderly, and apparently most of them rather bored. Gay Gibson's two main companions, with whom she usually dined, were an elderly Mr Hopwood and Wing-Commander Bray.

Her background suggested a desire for much more lively companionship. She did most of her war service in a touring company of Service personnel, having a taste for the theatre, although probably not brilliant. She was described as having been a beautiful girl, slim built with dark hair and large, dark, almond-shaped eyes. An outstanding feature was her white skin, likened by her theatrical producer to alabaster. She had the grace and poise of a good, professional actress.

She left the Forces on compassionate grounds, and when medically examined on her discharge, was graded AW1, but it was also noted that she had a chronic ear infection and she was marked as "non-tropical". After her release from the Forces, she toured South Africa with a repertory company, playing a leading part with considerable success. It was whilst engaged in this way that she met, amongst others of the cast, three people who were to give evidence of the greatest significance on behalf of the Defendant at his trial.

Through no fault of the repertory company, the play in which she was taking the leading lady's part, Clifford Odet's famous play *Golden Bay* came to an abrupt end in Johannesburg, but the producer made plans to take it to Pretoria. But Gay Gibson suddenly threw in her part and announced her decision to return to England by the next available boat, which in fact she did.

Life on board with only elderly companionship must have been dull for her, and it is therefore no surprise to find her, even when only two days out from the Cape, having chatty conversation with the young and good-looking Promenade Deck Steward, James Camb. He was rather thick set, with bright eyes and a good complexion. Confident in manner, he looked attractive and dashing in his white Steward's uniform. But nobody could say that Camb was an exemplary character. Aged thirty, with a wife and daughter of three, he enlivened his life as a first class Deck Steward by having sordid little affairs with unattached female passengers. He even boasted that "some of them like us better than the passengers. I have been with them several times on other trips." This was said during an early interview with the police (Detective Sergeant Quinlan) at Southampton; and then he added a most significant phrase – "Of course, if I was found out, I would get the sack."

This was confirmed by the Master of the ship, Captain Patey, who said at the trial that Camb, as a Deck Steward, had no right to visit any cabin, and that if found in one, he would have been logged, his book endorsed, and finally he would have been dismissed. He would find it very difficult to get another job.

Gay Gibson was presented as a young woman of impeccable character. Her mother, quite properly, said that she was one of the finest types of English womanhood, physically, mentally, and morally. One of the South African witnesses, Dr Schoub, the wife of the producer of the play *Golden Boy*, said that she liked her very much: "she was a nice, charming girl."

And yet a very different picture developed as a result of inquiries instituted by Camb's solicitor, Mr Geoffrey Wells of Southampton. Camb told him of many personal and intimate details of the girl's past life that he could have got only from the girl herself. Only three or four days out from Cape Town, in conversation with Miss Gibson's Stewardess, Miss Field, he said that Gay Gibson had told him that she was three months pregnant. Asked why she did not marry him, she replied that he was already married, but she was crazy about him. In any event, she suddenly decided to throw up her job and return to England. She had travelled out to South Africa in an emigrant ship. She was returning as a first class passenger, and there was no dispute that her fare was being paid by a Mr Charles Sventonski. In all, Miss Gibson received something like £500 from this man, but it was with the knowledge and approval of her mother, who said that it was a proposition by a wealthy and successful man who was ready to back Gay's career as a business proposition. Although, as far as was known, he had never been in England, he gave Miss Gibson a letter of introduction to the Abbey Theatre, Dublin.

A contraceptive was found in her cabin. One other thing that came out of these apparently intimate conversations was that Miss Gibson told Camb that she had gone to South Africa for her health as she suffered from asthma.

As a result of the information obtained from these conversations, Mr Wells went to South Africa and interviewed members of the cast of the repertory company, run by a Mr Gilbert, in which Miss Gibson had played the leading lady. Three of these were brought over by the Defence to give evidence on behalf of the Defendant. They were Mike Abel, Henry Gilbert, and his wife Dr Schoub.

Mike Abel testified that Miss Gibson had told him that

she had come out to South Africa because she had a chest complaint, and mentioned asthma. She often behaved in an hysterical manner, and on one occasion she collapsed, became blue about the lips, and in the corner of her mouth there was white saliva. There were times when she fainted, when she coughed a great deal, and when her breathing was laboured. On occasion, she complained of pains in her tummy and left arm – a sort of shooting pain coming right down into her fingers. These are all possible symptoms of lung and heart disease. Mike Abel went on to say in his evidence that Miss Gibson had told him that she was pregnant, and asked him for £200 to get to England to get a doctor to take care of her; she said she had no faith in South African doctors and wanted to get to England.

Henry Gilbert, also of Johannesburg, testified that he was an actor-manager, and had produced Gay Gibson as "Lorna" in *Golden Boy*. He often found her distraught and highly strung, tiring easily, sometimes drinking too heavily and becoming highly emotional. He also said that she had come to South Africa for health reasons, as she suffered from asthma. She also said, "I cannot love like other people" and "I am not like other girls".

Dr Ina Schoub, the wife of Henry Gilbert, in her evidence also said that Miss Gibson had told her, too, that she had come to South Africa because of her health, as she suffered from asthma. She tired easily and became short of breath on exertion, but the doctor said she had never seen her in an actual asthmatical attack. Miss Gibson discussed sex rather intimately, said that she had had sexual experience, and later became worried as she thought that she had become pregnant – a thing apparently known to the whole cast.

This was the background to the subsequent tragedy. A young actress of possibly dubious morality, not averse to the attentions of a very presentable and highly-sexed young man who risked his career in order to be with her in her cabin.

The Crown called compelling circumstantial evidence to prove that James Camb strangled Miss Gibson in her cabin on board the *Durban Castle* at about 3 a.m. on the morning of 18th October 1947; afterwards, he threw her body out into the shark-infested sea through the porthole of her cabin, in order to conceal evidence of his crime. It was alleged that he raped, attempted to rape, or attempted to sexually assault the girl; that she resisted and raised the alarm, and in order to preserve his job and prevent her giving evidence against him he killed her – by strangulation.

The Defence admitted that the girl died in her cabin at the material time, and they called equally compelling medical evidence that her death could have been due to natural causes. The Defendant was there at the time of her death, but because he had been disturbed and possibly recognised, he panicked and threw the body of the girl out of the ship hoping that her disappearance would be put down to suicide or accident.

The trial opened on Thursday, 18th March 1948 in the Assize court at Winchester. The court was a temporary one, formed of plywood partitions in the Great Hall of Winchester Castle, and presided over by King Arthur's Round Table.

Going into the witness-box was physically very similar to "walking the plank" of old, and felt very much like it. One mounted some four or five steps, walked six to eight feet along a narrow rail-guarded walk, and then found oneself perched four or more feet high up in the middle of the court, completely isolated. The Judge was on one's left, the Defendent on the right, the Jury in front, and Counsel seemingly lost around their table on a much lower level.

Counsel for the Crown was that able, and to a guilty prisoner, dangerous KC, the late Mr G.D. (Khaki) Roberts, with Mr H.H. Elam as his junior. The Defence was led by the equally able Mr J. D. Casswell, KC, with Mr T.J. (now Sir Joseph) Molony to assist.

The Judge was the late Mr Justice Hilbery, and in this choice Camb was unfortunate. The Judge's attitude throughout the whole of the trial was clearly against the Defendant, as was his summing-up. So much so, that one of the grounds of the ultimate appeal was that the Judge's summing-up was too unfavourable to the prisoner. But the Lord Chief Justice, Lord Goddard, sitting with Mr Justice Pritchard and Mr Justice Humphreys dismissed this argument, saying, "Undoubtedly the learned Judge's summing-up was not favourable to the prisoner," and he went on to quote an earlier judgment given in the Appeal Court to the effect that a Judge is bound to give some assistance to the Jury on questions of fact as well as on questions of law.

In the court, in full view of everybody there was the bed from cabin 126 of the *Durban Castle*, a porthole of the size of the one in the cabin mounted in a wooden frame, and the bell-push in the cabin; this was at the head of the bed, and in a narrow opening beside the bed was a small chest. Other exhibits included plans of the cabin and cabin deck, bedding and pillows from the bunk, and photographs.

On the night that Gay Gibson disappeared, she had dined as usual with her friends Mr Hopwood and Wing-Commander Bray. She danced a little afterwards, and then as it was a very hot night she left her companions to look for her swimsuit to go bathing in the liner's swimming pool. She returned about half an hour afterwards, saying that she could not find it. It was during this half hour that the senior night-watchman saw Miss Gibson and Camb talking together, and he overheard a very significant remark made by Camb, *viz*: "I say, I have a bone to pick with you, and a big one at that." This was the first of two remarks of supreme significance in this case. The obvious inference drawn by the Crown was that Camb had indeed a grudge to be paid off. His own explanation was a perfectly rational one. There was no question of these two people being on very friendly terms from almost the beginning of the voyage. As a Deck Steward, Camb was not allowed in the cabin area. Orders had been given by Mr Hopwood that Miss Gibson was to have her tea every afternoon in her cabin. These trays were prepared by Camb and left out for the Stewardess to take down to the cabin. On the 17th, orders were given for a special tea tray to be prepared. This was done, but the tray was never collected. He was angry: hence his remark. Could anything be more rational?

After his remonstrance, Miss Gibson said that she was sorry, and then asked him to leave out a rum for her to collect later in the evening. Pushing his friendliness a little further, probably with obvious intentions, he asked her if she would like him to prepare a supper tray or bring her some lemonade, adding that he had a good mind to bring a drink down and join her. Her reply was, "Please yourself. It's up to you," or words to that effect. At 12.45 that night, he noticed that the glass of rum had been taken, and in its place there was Miss Gibson's alarm clock, normally kept on the dressing-table top. That clock appears never to have been seen again.

At about 12.40 a.m., Mr Hopwood escorted Miss Gibson back to her cabin; but it was a very warm night, and some twenty minutes later, the boatswain's mate saw her leaning over the rail at the after end of the Promenade Deck. She must have made an attractive picture on this her last appearance in public around midnight, in her long black evening dress, her feet in silver dancing shoes. The boatswain's mate was in charge of a party cleaning the decks, and asked her to move on, otherwise she would get wet.

This was the last that was ever seen of her by anyone – excepting James Camb.

The subsequent tragedy was heralded in by the ringing of bells. At night-time, the bell-pushes in the cabins are switched through to the night-watchman's galley. At 2.58 a.m. on the 18th, Murray, the senior night-watchman and his assistant Steer, heard the bell ringing above their heads. Following a trail of lights, Steer arrived at cabin No. 126.

The light was on, coming through the fanlight; and – most surprisingly – both red and green lights were showing, indicating that both bell-pushes had been pressed at the same time, as there was only one ringing of the bell. One bell would have called the stewardess, the other the night-watchman.

Something very peculiar had happened, something probably of great urgency, as emphasised by the Crown; but, as always in this curious case, there was an alternative explanation as will be revealed later.

Steer said that it would take him under a minute to reach the cabin from his galley. There was no noise coming from the cabin when he reached it. He knocked on the door and tried it; it was not bolted and he opened it a couple of inches. It was immediately slammed in his face, but not before he had seen the face of James Camb, who said,

"All right." Returning to his senior, Murray, Steer told him that he had seen Camb in the cabin, and then they both went back. They found the cabin in darkness, with all lights, including the indicator lights, extinguished. Both men then decided to report the matter to the officer on the bridge, but not wanting to get a colleague into trouble, they merely reported the matter. Believing that it was probably another passenger in Miss Gibson's room, the officer said there was nothing he could do about it, and that it was not for him to interfere with the passengers' morals.

Four hours later, at 7.30 a.m. Miss Field, the Stewardess knocked on the door of cabin 126; there was no reply, and she found the door unlocked. This was unusual, as Gay Gibson invariably bolted her door at night. It was also of great significance, because whoever, including Camb, might have been with the girl in her cabin that night was obviously there with her consent, if not by her invitation. Miss Field entered the cabin and found it empty. Thinking that the occupant might have gone to the bathroom, Miss Field was not alarmed. She found the bed a little more disarranged than normal and there were some stains on the pillow and sheets, but she did not take particular notice of these. The bedclothes had been pulled back. The porthole was open, but this would be natural in tropical seas; Miss Gibson's evening dress was hanging in its usual place at the foot of the bunk; her dressing-gown, and black pyjamas were missing. Miss Field tidied up the cabin, and it was only a little later after she had asked the Bedroom Steward if Miss Gibson had had a bath, and was told "No" that she became alarmed, and reported her missing. Her disappearance was broadcast over the whole ship, but without response. Captain Patey reversed course for over an hour, but realising the futility of any further search in shark infested waters, he resumed his course at 11.40 a.m. Incidentally, amongst many other wild rumours in this case, there was the report of a shark caught off the West Coast of Africa shortly afterwards, having a woman's painted fingernail in its stomach.

Captain Patey immediately set inquiries afoot. Steer told him that he had seen Camb in Miss Gibson's cabin early that morning, and Camb was sent for. Camb, thinking he had not been recognised, immediately embarked on a series of lies designed to protect his job. He said he was nowhere near any passenger cabin, since retiring at 12.45 a.m. He continued on this course, until his line of defence was broken by the police after arrival of the ship at Southampton. He got himself into serious trouble by this line of conduct, and the first devastating question asked in crossexamination at his trial by Mr Roberts was, "Would you describe yourself as a truthful man?" He obviously was not, at that time, anyway.

Captain Patey, at the first interview, did not tell Camb he had been recognised in Miss Gibson's cabin. He merely suggested that Camb was suspected of being in the neighbourhood of the cabin at about 3 a.m. Camb's reply was a flat denial. The captain then sent for William Pott, a steward who shared a cabin with Camb. Pott said that contrary to normal practice, Camb turned up that morning wearing Steward's full dress, a long-sleeved jacket, to do the ordinary routine work of cleaning-up. Was there something on his arms that he wanted to conceal?

Captain Patey decided that Camb should be medically examined. By this time Camb's nerves were becoming somewhat frayed, but he agreed to be examined by the ship's doctor, Dr Griffiths.

Dr Griffith's findings were of the most importance. He gave evidence at the trial that he found three main groups of injuries on Camb. First, there were some scratches over the back of the right shoulder, quite recent, and similar to those made by a cat's claws. The inference was that they could have been done by a woman's finely-pointed fingernails. Camb explained these away by saying that he had done them himself with a rough towel – a quite reasonable explanation. Secondly, there were some rather old scratches on the left collar bone, obviously of no recent significance except that they did bear out Camb's contention that he had recently been scratching himself rather severely with rough towels. The really important group of injuries was the third, on the front of the right wrist. These injuries were of intriguing interest. There were about twelve of them, some linear, some crescentic, running more of less horizontally across the inside of the right lower arm, commencing some four to five inches above the wrist. Dr Griffiths described these injuries as having been done probably by digging with finger-nails into the flesh. This was an important feature in the evidence, but as usual in this trial, there were divergent opinions as to how they might have been caused. The Crown said by Miss Gibson, who being manually strangulated, had attempted to tear away the hand of her assailant by pulling on his arm, digging her nails into him in the process. The Defendant offered an alternative and completely acceptable explanation as will appear later. These marks, however, had obviously caused Camb to wear his long-sleeved jacket on the morning of Gay Gibson's disappearance.

Camb, now thoroughly rattled, then wrote two notes to his Captain. In the first, he denied again having been anywhere near the girl's cabin on the night, and in the second he gave rather unconvincing explanations as to how he came by his injuries – mainly by scratching himself with his nails or with rough towels.

On the morning of 25th October, the liner steamed into Southampton and at 1.25 a.m. Detective Sergeant Quinlan boarded the ship; at 5.25 a.m., after preliminary inquiries, he interviewed Camb. Camb continued to deny that he had ever been near Miss Gibson's cabin on the fatal night, but after a while, he sensed that the night-watchman Steer had given away to the authorities the fact that he had been recognised in her cabin, and he made the not unexpected remark, whether he was innocent or not: "That puts me in a tight spot."

Later the same day, Detective Sergeant Quinlan decided, quite properly, to increase the pressure, saying that he had definitely established that Camb had been in Miss Gibson's cabin at about 3 a.m. on the night of her disappearance. A very worried Camb then confessed that he *had* been down to the cabin that night, asking Miss Gibson if she wanted some lemonade with her rum; she was looking for a swim suit – confirmed by her friend, Mr Hopkins. She asked Camb to leave her rum in its usual place. He still denied having gone later to the cabin. Later Detective Sergeant (Acting Inspector) Gibbons said to him, "You are being given an opportunity to make any explanation you may care to about this. That explanation, so far, has been a categorical denial that you know anything about the death of Miss Gibson. You may find that such a complete denial will be difficult to explain if later you are called upon to explain it." Camb replied: "Does that mean I murdered her and that I shall be charged with murder?" Gibbons said that he could not say whether or not a charge would be preferred. And then there occurred a conversation which set in train all the investigations that became the basis of the evidence for the Defence.

Gibbons said: "We have to give particular care to any explanation which you may put forward. You may be able to give a reasonable explanation of the cause of her death and her disappearance." Camb replied: "You mean that Miss Gibson might have died from some other cause, other than being murdered? She might have had a heart attack, or something?"

How does one interpret such a remark?

One explanation, put forward by the Crown, was that it was a heaven-sent invitation to Camb to adduce a heart attack as the cause of Miss Gibson's death. The other is that it is equally consistent with the mental attitude of a worried man who had racked his brains to find some explanation as to why a woman should suddenly die in his arms, and, in a flash, the explanation comes to him. After only a short while, during which he boasted that he and other members of the crew were often preferred at night-time by female passengers, he elected to make the following statement:

"I have already stated to you that I went to Miss Gibson's cabin at about eleven o'clock, and during the course of conversation with her I made an appointment to meet her that night. I knocked at the door after I had finished work at about one o'clock, but there was no answer. I opened the door of her cabin and found it empty. I then went forward to the well deck, where I sat for about half an hour smoking. I then returned to Miss Gibson's cabin at about two o'clock and found her there. After a short conversation I got into bed with her consent. Intimacy took place. Whilst in the act of sexual intercourse she clutched me, foaming at the mouth. I immediately ceased the act, but she was very still. I felt for her heart beats, but could not find any. She was at that time very still, and I cannot offer any explanation as to how the bells came to be rung, as I most definitely did not touch them myself. Thinking she had fainted, I tried artificial respiration on her. Whilst doing this, the night-watchman knocked at the door and attempted to open it. I shut the door again, saying it was all right. Then I panicked, as I thought he had gone to the bridge to report to the officer of the watch, and I did not want to be found in such a compromising position. After a few minutes I could not find any sign of life. After a struggle with the limp body – by the way, she was still wearing her dressing-gown – I managed to lift her to the porthole and push her through. I am fairly certain that at the time she was dead, but I was terribly frightened. I then went forward and turned in. The time would be about 3.30 a.m."

After saying that he was glad to have got the matter off his mind, Camb then added: "What will happen about this? My wife must not know about this. If she does I will do away with myself." Camb's Counsel, Mr Caswell, believed that this was absolutely true and proved his innocence. He had lied like a trooper up to this point to save his job, but it still did not occur to him that he might face a murder charge.

Camb is then alleged to have said something to a Detective Constable, unconfirmed, which no man in his senses (anticipating that he was about to be charged with murder) would make. The Detective Constable said that when he was alone with Camb, the Steward said to him, "She struggled. I had my arms around her neck and when I was trying to pull them away she scratched me. I panicked and threw her out of the porthole. It was a hell of a splash when she hit the water. I can't understand why the officer of the watch did not hear something." This was manifestly ridiculous. The porthole was some twenty-five feet above the water line, there was backlash from the bow wave immediately below, and machinery in the dummy funnel above all would have drowned any sound of splashing, as was confirmed by Captain Patey. The Detective Constable who made the statement had "left the Force before the trial to better himself, but was still unemployed".

The Prosecution produced two more important witnesses.

The first was Dr Montgomery, a senior Scientific Officer at the Metropolitan Police Laboratory at Hendon. He had received various exhibits in the case for scientific examination. The only things of any significance that he found were:

On the top sheet, two small blood spots, each about the size of a sixpence. The blood was of Group "O". This was not the group of Camb, which was Group "A". On the bottom sheet, there were faint blood spots, too small to group. No hair from the accused was found, and nothing of significance was found in scrapings from around the porthole, or elsewhere in the room. It was obvious that no fight had taken place there.

I later examined all the exhibits with important results that will appear later.

The last, and very important witness for the Crown was Dr (now Professor) Donald Teare, then Assistant Pathologist and Lecturer in Forensic Medicine at St George's Hospital, London.

Dr Teare described the signs he would expect to find in a case of death by strangulation, the most important relevant to this case being probable slight haemorrhage from the lungs or upper air passages due to constriction of blood vessels by pressure on the neck, and hence in this case, the possible explanation of the blood on the sheets. The blood might also have come from scratch marks by the victim injuring her throat during attempts to relieve the pressure. Unconsciousness would supervene in a matter of only a few seconds, probably not more than fifteen, and death would be within a minute. Dr Teare refused to express any opinion concerning the scratch and other marks on the body of Camb. He agreed that signs of muddiness in Miss Gibson's finger-nails, noticed by her friend Mr Hopwood, would indicate that the girl was suffering from some circulatory defect, confirmed by pains down the left arm, and that she was possibly suffering from some form of heart disease associated with asthma. On balance, however, he felt that what had been found was more in keeping with death by strangulation than death from a heart attack, although in all conscience what had been found was very little.

Dr Teare concluded the evidence for the Prosecution, and then came the turn of the Defence.

This was outlined at the beginning by Mr Casswell. His main contention was that Miss Gibson was a young woman not at all averse to the attentions of a presentable young man, even to the extent of not opposing his visiting her in the early hours of the morning in her cabin, more or less naked. There was a well-authenticated history of longstanding illness, though not by any means of a serious nature; also very experienced medical evidence that the girl could have died in exactly the way described by the Defendant, and with signs exactly as were found. Camb knew nothing about the significance of Miss Gibson's past medical history. Indeed, it was remarkable that he should have told a story about what happened on the fatal night, so close to what might have been *expected* to happen in the circumstances. Confirmation was surely almost complete.

The first witness for the Defence was the accused himself.

He outlined the increasing friendliness that grew up between himself and Miss Gibson during the early days of the voyage, and confirmed his part in preparing tea and drinks for her, to be taken down to her by the night-watchman. He explained, too, his use of the phrase: "I have a bone to pick with you."

He then went on to detail the events of the fateful October night.

After the episode of ordering the rum for the night, he went to the cabin soon after 2 o'clock. The door was not fastened. As, according to Miss Field, Miss Gibson invariably bolted her door after retiring to her cabin, Camb's advent in the early hours of the morning cannot have been a surprise to her. She was wearing nothing underneath a yellow quilted dressing-gown. Camb was emphatic, and could not be moved, that she was not wearing black pyjamas. There were no black pyjamas in the room, and he did not throw them out of the porthole after the girl when he put her through. Much was made in cross-examination of the loss of these pyjamas. The Crown contended, most reasonably, that they were missing because the girl was wearing them and was therefore not inviting intercourse. They were never found. Rumour again had it that they were, in fact, in the cabin of a distinguished male fellow-passenger who is alleged to have said that he would come forward if there was any danger of Camb's being hanged – which there was not, as capital punishment was in abeyance, fortunately, at that time. There is indeed an interval of time, from about 1 a.m. to 2 a.m. completely unaccounted for, but of course the girl could have gone back at once to her cabin after being moved on by the crew swabbing decks.

However that may be, the couple talked, for some time, about the dullness of the dance. Then almost inevitably Cambs climbed on to the bed beside her. Raising no objections, she unzipped her dressing-gown, revealing her nakedness beneath. He then went on to describe exactly what he mentioned in his statement to the police. He added, however, that she had her right hand round his neck with her left hand holding his right arm. When her body stiffened as she was gasping for breath, her right arm was still round his neck, and her left hand holding his forearm, gripped tightly. Of course, a perfectly rational happening, which would account for the nail mark injuries seen in his neck and arm. Verbally he added somewhat to the content of his written statement to the police – and it was of significance. In his own words: "I immediately got off the bed. She was completely relaxed, as though she was in a dead faint. One eye was just slightly open. Her mouth was a little open too. There was a faint line of bubbles, which I assumed to be froth, just on the edges of the lips. It was a muddy colour and appeared to be slightly blood-flecked. I was rather stunned for the moment. First of all I listened and felt for her heartbeats. I could not find any and I attempted to massage the stomach towards the heart to bring back circulation." It was at this stage that in all probability Camb pressed his thigh against the bell-pushes, and set off the alarm that was his undoing. He swore that Gay Gibson herself did not ring the bells, nor did he know how they had been rung. Confronted by Steer, he panicked and thought only of destroying any evidence. His whole career was now in jeopardy. He hoped people would presume that she had fallen overboard. It was at this point that Camb had a gruelling cross-examination by Mr Roberts, who quite rightly said that he had wilfully destroyed the only positive evidence. If there were no marks on her body, and other things were found out by a postmortem examination showing that she was not a healthy girl, then his story would have been proved to be correct, and he would have been completely exonerated. This was a point hammered home by the Judge in his charge to the Jury. It was certainly a very valid point, but one can perhaps visualise the man in his dreadful predicament behaving as he did.

The whole of Camb's cross-examination was a testing experience, but he stood up to it superbly, without being shaken or departing in one detail from his account of the way in which the girl died. So composed was he that the point told rather severely against him in the eventual final speech to the jury by Mr Roberts. Mr Roberts said: "Camb says he threw her through the porthole in panic. Did he panic? Panic? Do you think he is the sort of man to panic? Did you see any sign of panic at all? Did you see any lack of poise, or composure, or full control of the thinking facilities?" The same point was also pressed home by the Judge.

The main plank in the evidence on behalf of the Defendant was the medical evidence.

Professor Webster, Professor of Forensic Medicine at Birmingham University and a Home Office Pathologist, had been asked by the Director of Public Prosecutions to review the medical evidence and give his opinion as to the possibility of Camb's statement being correct. He did so in characteristic no-nonsense terms, saying that, in his opinion, Camb's statement was perfectly possible. On this account Professor Webster was naturally offered to the Defence. What impressed him most was the detailed description of the way in which Gay Gibson died, by a man without any possible medical knowledge. Professor Webster said: "The account given by Camb of this girl's death could have occurred." He instanced three cases in his experience in which death had occurred during sexual intercourse, when there was no question of any violence. In none of them had the dead person shown any previous sign of any disease. Death could occur from the rupture of a small aneurysm in the brain, or from heart disease, the latter either primary or secondary to some other condition, including asthma. (An aneurysm is a thin-walled dilatation of a blood vessel. It is not unusual, and rupture frequently occurs. Such rupture in the brain can cause instant death in many cases, an occurrence which is by no means rare in young people, and more likely to occur under strain or excitement. With regard to heart disease this can, of course, be primary, due to some affection of the heart itself, or secondary. Secondary causes of degeneration of the heart muscle include chronic infection resulting in bacterial poisoning of the tissues, or such conditions as asthma, which throw an increasing strain on the heart to pump blood through increasing resistance in the lungs.)

He thought that in Gay Gibson's case it could have been heart disease associated either with asthma, or her chronically septic ear. Professor Webster's conclusion was that the chances of natural death were equal with those of strangulation. Dr Teare put the chances of strangulation as greater than those of natural death, but admitted to the latter possibility.

I was called in to the case on two grounds. Firstly to help assess the possibility of natural as opposed to violent death; and here I agreed entirely with Professor Webster. I assessed the chances as about equal. Secondly, I had been asked to re-examine the bedding. This revealed something of very great importance which had hitherto been overlooked.

On the top pillow, I found a light smear of blood mixed with cells from the mouth, and digestive ferments found in saliva. This was proof that the blood had come most likely from congestion in the respiratory tract, and not from any external damage that might have been done to the girl. Something of much more importance was evident: on the top sheet, not visible in ordinary light, but showing up quite clearly when examined in ultra-violet light, was a stain, roughly oval in shape, measuring fifteen inches by six inches. It was dried urine.

This finding set off a whole chain of examination and cross-examination questions. In the first place, it provided the Prosecution with a missing link in their evidence. It was almost certain proof that Gay Gibson had died in her cabin, and that she was dead when thrown out of the porthole. This apparently was a great relief to public opinion. Mr Roberts seized on this additional information at once, as confirmation of strangulation. Voiding of urine almost inevitably occurs when a person is strangled, but it occurs equally in many cases of sudden death by natural causes, so that its occurrence is no actual proof of strangulation. Mr Roberts also argued that urine on the top sheet showed that the girl was lying on her back at the time of her death, covered by the sheet. Urine voided by a female lying on her back, of course, goes upwards. This finding, according to Mr Roberts, was also proof that Camb could not have been lying on top of the girl, as he said, at the time of her death. But, unfortunately for Mr Roberts, this finding completely destroyed his previous contention that, at the time of her death, the girl was wearing her black pyjamas. He obviously could not have it both ways. Furthermore the finding of the urine on the top sheet did not mean that the girl was covered by the sheet. If she and Camb were lying on the top of the bed together, and she passed urine this would run down on to the uppermost, i.e. the top sheet, as was found – again confirming Camb's statement. It does not seem reasonable to suppose that these two, having intercourse, would have covered themselves with a sheet.

That, then, was the evidence in the case.

The trial had lasted for four days. The Judge's summing-up lasted about four hours, and the Jury brought in their verdict of Guilty after a retirement of only forty minutes. Mr Casswell complained bitterly about the Judge's summing-up, reminding him of many matters in favour of the Defendant which he had not mentioned, but Mr Justice Hilbery, brushing this aside, said: "I have not attempted to mention everything, and I am not bound to do so".

The case naturally went to Appeal. It was dismissed without even calling on the Crown to answer Mr Casswell's arguments.

At the commencement of the trial, the Clerk of Assize read out the indictment: "James Camb, you stand charged upon the indictment with murder, and the particulars state that, on the 18th of October last year, on the high seas, you did murder Eileen Isabella Ronnie Gibson; to that charge do you plead Guilty or Not Guilty?"

Camb replied: "Not Guilty."

After conviction, the Clerk of Assize asked him, as is usual, if he had anything to say before sentence of death was passed upon him. His reply was not unworthy of note: "My lord, at the opening of this case I was asked to plead Guilty or Not Guilty; I pleaded Not Guilty, and I repeat that statement now."

Guilty or Not Guilty?

Mr Casswell thoroughly believed in his innocence, as he repeats in his own account of the affair in his book *A Lance for Liberty*. Professor Webster and I thoroughly believed that Camb's account of the happenings on that tragic night was medically possible and reasonable, with at least a fifty-fifty chance of being correct. Dr Teare agreed, but put the chances considerably less in favour of the accused.

Camb's neat appearance and supreme confidence in himself never left him throughout the whole ordeal of his trial, but in many ways he was his own worst enemy. He completely lost any sympathy the Jury might have had for him by his own utter selfishness in putting his job and future before the life of a young girl. He "concluded that she was dead" but was not certain, and he made no attempt to summon any medical aid for her. He thought only of himself. He denied that he could have inadvertently rung the bells, although it was quite possible, and denied that he had received any injury from the girl which was one of the main planks of his defence.

To Mr Casswell's mind, the Jury convicted him because they could not forgive him for his brutal and callous action.

The case has often been debated by lawyers, pathologists and medico-legal experts. On balance, I would say that generally the legal minds supported the conviction, whilst the medical men supported the opinion of Professor Webster and myself. After all, why kill the goose who is laying the golden eggs?

Mr Justice Humphreys, one of the judges who sat in the Court of Appeal is alleged to have said afterwards: "That man wasn't given a chance".

Nobody knows what he meant by that remark.

A full account of the trial was published in the series of *Notable British Trials*, edited by Geoffrey Clark, William Hodge & Co.

It even attracted interest in the United States, where a transcript was published under the title *The Girl in the Stateroom* by Charles Boswell, Louis & Louis Thompson.

The most fascinating account, however, has been written by Denis Herbstein in his book *Porthole*, published in June 1991 by Hodder & Stoughton. He not only gives a complete account of the Court proceedings, but also most skilfully analyses all the aspects of the case.

I have suffered remarkably little abuse during my career, in fact really only on one occasion connected with this case of Gay Gibson.

One newspaper reported a short paragraph recording my evidence that this girl might have died from natural causes. The reader wrote "liar" across the paragraph and sent it to me.

The other incident was an anonymous letter sent to me in the following terms:

> "Dear Sir,
> "I see by the enclosed press report you said in evidence in the Camb trial that it was perfectly possible for Miss Gibson to die as you say. Well now, you being a pathologist should know that what you said was a lot of damnation rot and many thousands are of the same opinion as myself that you was a Bluddy old waster to give such evidence to try and influence the Jury on the verdict they come to a right conclusion for Camb was nothing more than a blasted rotten blighter; what about the other 3 young women who he tried to strangle the same as he did what did the Judge say about her epitaph.
> "What Camb did was to enter Miss G's cabin with

the intention of criminally assaulting her and when she objected he seized her around the throat with his hand his own words and thereby strangled her to hide his result and put her out of the porthole but what about the blood on the bottom sheet does this not prove her to have been a virgin as her mother said you ought to know but it appears you know Bugger all about it and so the sooner this dirty rotten Bugger is *hung* the better it will be for the general public and as for you you are too a rotten dirty, Bloody old waster, there was no need for you to have poked your nose on the case at all so once more to Hell with such a rotten old Bugger for you are nothing more I wonder what you would have said if it had been *your* Daughter its a pity it wasn't you rotten old scoundrel and Bugger you once more."

It was not signed.

Dennis Hocking

Marcel Petiot:
Murder for Profit

In post-war France, the Petiot trial was the most sensational since that of "Bluebeard" Landru in 1921. Petiot was another "con-man killer", like Heath and Haigh. According to Pat Pitman's article on him (in our *Encyclopedia of Murder*) he had been stealing since his schooldays, and even when he became mayor of Villeneuve in 1928, was in trouble with the police for robbing a gas meter. An attractive housekeeper became pregnant and then disappeared – but of course, she may simply have gone back to her parents. But when a patient called Madame Debauve was robbed and killed in 1930, and another patient went around accusing Petiot, this man also died suddenly. Petiot ceased to be mayor when he was sent to prison for theft.

This account of the case, from Alister Kershaw's *Murder in France* (1955) originally struck me as too long for this book, but after looking at a few more, I decided that Kershaw was far and away the best.

A mong other aspects of a lunatic world, the German-controlled Paris press for Saturday, 11th March, 1944, reported heavy and successful Nazi counter-attacks in the Ukraine and the sinking by Japanese naval forces of two U.S. destroyers off New Guinea. At Limoges, a group of "terrorists" had been variously sentenced to death or to forced labour, and British air losses over Germany were mounting daily.

All this was the press of any country at that time, differing only in accent.

More specifically local notes were struck elsewhere in the exiguous news-sheets, combining to form an impressionist glimpse of a Paris at once astonishingly transformed and essentially unchanged. Yves Montand and Edith Piaf were singing at cabarets which bore familiar names but were required to close at the uncanonical hour of midnight. On that day all but a few especially favoured restaurants and hotels were prohibited from serving wine. The inevitable news of current literary events was juxtaposed with angry accounts of Jewish perfidy.

There was no reference to the bitter ersatz coffee, the stodgy yellow bread which had replaced the traditional crisp French loaf or to streets given over almost entirely to bicycle traffic except for an occasional German staff car going about its owner's secure and weighty business. Yet these, in all likelihood, were the colourings of their world which Parisians found most irksome, and probably more relevant than the immense events taking place in Russia or the Pacific or the skies above the Reich. For "the French character" – if one dares to make another generalisation on the subject – is stubbornly and admirably concerned with the tiny important assaults on individual life. Complaints of ill-cooked meals, unsmokable cigarettes or the scarcity of wine, never seem incongruous to a Frenchman merely because there is a war in progress or because the Gestapo is questioning "doubtful elements" (that sinister abstraction!) around the corner in the rue de la Pompe. This loyal preoccupation with the minutiae of man's existence is another of France's contributions to the human heritage: a Frenchman stands for individual man and his pitiful, vital rights.

M. Jacques Marçais, living at 20 Rue Lesueur, was a Frenchman and his neighbour's chimney was smoking. The official horrors of 1944 made this no less objectionable and constituted no sort of reason for tolerating it any longer. Rue Lesueur is a sober and dignified street near the Etoile, running between the avenue Foch and the avenue de la Grande Armée; No. 21, which annoyed M. Marçais, was, until its recent demolition, a good, grey building of the

sort which the French call a *hôtel particulier*. The whole
atmosphere fairly forbids chimneys, or anything else, to
misbehave themselves. Since the first Thursday of this
particular March, however, the furnace at 21 had been
emitting singularly unpleasant and acrid fumes; by Saturday
the thing had become insupportable. In the absence of the
guilty proprietor – who seemed not to live on the premises
but only to cycle over from some other address in order to
light the troublesome fire – there was nothing for M. Marçais
to do except telephone a complaint to the local police station.
This he did and was assured that the police would attend him
immediately.

The arrival of these officials in so select a quarter caused
some excitement and the local residents were only too happy
to give what sparse information they had on the shadowy
owner of No. 21. His pyrophiliac activities, it was explained,
had not previously caused annoyance; but for the last few
days, possibly due to some unusual movement of the wind
or to an alteration in the fuel employed, the chimney had
made life intolerable. Beyond this nothing was known of
the man, but a card affixed to the front door invited
inquirers to address themselves to 66 rue Caumartin. The
Paris directories enable one to locate a telephone number
from the address, and a call was therefore made by one of
the police to Pigalle 77–11. A Mme Petiot answered, brought
her husband to the telephone, and Dr Marcel Petiot was duly
informed that a fire had been notified at his house in rue
Lesueur.

The doctor replied that he would present himself at that
address forthwith and in point of fact did so. Not, however,
quite quickly enough. The smoke continued to pour oilily
from the chimney, the police became apprehensive that
a fire had started in the building, and, before Dr Petiot
had appeared, the fire brigade was summoned to make an
entry. Firemen accordingly broke into the house without
delay, and with still less delay broke out again, crying (as
recounted dramatically in the following Monday's *Matin*):
"This is no job for us! The place is full of corpses!" It was
a pardonable exaggeration. Not altogether full, perhaps,
but certainly well-stocked. A number of human heads were

scattered about the dark congeries of cellars beneath the ponderous, respectable building – a smouldering corpse explained the loathsome smoke – and a body had been literally split from skull to groin in order (it was presumed) that it might more easily be added to the reeking contents of the furnace. These scraps, littered among various wretched bits of clothing, were the gruesome advance-guard of the twenty-seven men and women with whose deaths Dr Marcel Petiot was to be charged within a year, representatives of the sixty-three people he himself insistently asserted he had destroyed.

While the local police were contemplating this abominable handiwork the artist himself arrived. He even descended into the cellar for a last look round, although it is hard to account for such foolhardiness, and then turned casually to leave. The police thought differently, but the doctor, with his unvarying sense of expediency, muttered in a convincing undertone that he was "a patriot – risking his head – on business for *la Patrie*". Hadn't they understood? They had uncovered an execution chamber of the resistance movement.

Fortunately for Petiot, the policemen were also patriots and made no further effort to hinder him. Dr Petiot thanked them on behalf of the French underground forces and vanished into the dusk. He was not seen again by any of those most anxious to confer with him for eight months.

Organised society's task of trapping its deviationists would be immeasurably facilitated if every murderer revealed himself in his childhood by some ugly and unmistakable tic of behaviour. Such tics actually are evident, but they are shared by those children destined to become acceptable members of the tribe. In Petiot's case, as in so many others, much has been made of an early taste for deliberate cruelty to animals, and no doubt this disagreeable trait did exist in his make-up; at the same time, a close investigation of the childish diversions of a bishop or businessman would reveal identical enthusiasms. Indeed, a murderer can be roughly written down as merely one who fails to shed (or conceal) on reaching manhood the instinctive criminality of the child. Childish ruthlessness, childish egotism, a childish belief in the basic rightness of any act which begets his own pleasure or profit – these are the qualities which lead a man to the death-cell unless he applies them to such morally unexceptionable forms of personal satisfaction as social-climbing or floating bogus companies. In *Murder for Profit*, a title too suitable for the present study to be resisted, William Bolitho suggests that, stripped of the "mountainous trappings" bestowed on them by self-justifying society, murderers would "dwindle to homunculi, perhaps no bigger, no wickeder, no redder even, than new-born babies, kicking and screaming to have their will" – in a word, men who at no age reach years of discretion.

At all events, it is certainly impossible to detect in the earliest youth of Marcel-André-Henri-Félix Petiot even the tiniest quirk which might have marked him out from any potential lawyer or functionary. He was born in Auxerre (Department of the Yonne) on 17th January, 1897, the son of a minor postal official, and led the normal existence of a French provincial child. Until middle adolescence, the solitary variation from the average lot was his becoming an orphan when only thirteen years of age, his father dying in 1905 and his mother in 1910.

It has, inevitably, been suggested that this early disappearance of parental control may have been responsible for the later horrific performances of the man, and parental admonitions, it is true, do tend to inhibit some of the less attractive attributes of children; Petiot's guardian, his aunt, may well have been less worried by his young waywardness than his own parents would have been, and less solicitous to check it. But the idea of any murderer, let alone the colossal Petiot, being so merely because he was too seldom cuffed over the head as a child is comically unconvincing. True, if an exploit which he carried out when aged sixteen had been adequately punished, it might have caused his happy-go-lucky (so to speak) self-confidence to diminish, but one can hardly say more than that. It was a trivial business – a matter of robbing letter-boxes in the district – but it was leniently viewed, and this may have implanted in Petiot his lifelong conviction that he could get away with things.

The war of 1914–18 provided evidence in support of his theory. He had begun studying medicine in 1916, but he patriotically interrupted his course (French mobilisation laws are impartially severe) in order to join the army. Characteristically, his first thought, even in the midst of the surrounding horrors, was to find some profitable side-line, and in due course he was arrested and tried for having stolen drugs from the casualty clearing stations in order to retail them to those whose need was not officially recognised. (It would be interesting to know how many of the 22,000 known drug-addicts in France in 1918 had dealt with Marcel Petiot.)

Men were shot at that strange time for a variety of strange offences: an enthralling list might be compiled of the artificial crimes which have been codified by our masters since 1914. But the large-scale creation of new wickednesses has called a resistant strain into being among the human race, and Petiot was the classic representative of this immune group. While such dark army malefactions as sleeping or running were punished with death, Petiot's trafficking in narcotics was not only mildly judged but actually rewarded. He had been wounded earlier in the war, and the ludicrous logic which rules in the army decided that his grenade-shattered foot had somehow caused a condition of "mental debility". Consequently, while tired or terrified human beings were stood against the brick wall, Marcel Petiot was given a spell in the psychopathic ward to recuperate, an honourable discharge from the army, and a pension for life.

This surely was the moment when he decided that the imbecile contemporary world was worth dicing against. Intelligent and, above all, endowed with a positive genius for knowing a good thing when he saw it, he must have appreciated that he ran small risk in gambling with such simpletons. He had twice broken the law (perhaps more often than that) and in the first case had been treated with forbearance, in the second and more serious case had been rewarded. Everything, including his indifferent acceptance of his own death, indicates that at some point he adopted a deliberate philosophy of crime and was prepared for the returns and hazards equally. Unless one has been completely conditioned by this our age, one cannot help but take an immoral satisfaction in the triumph of the unrighteous, and it is essentially amusing to reflect that but for the irrational leniency of the military mind, those charred corpses might never have lain in the cellar of 21 rue Lesueur.

The war over, Marcel Petiot emerged into the helter-skelter of peace with his sturdy notions of self-interest unimpaired. By way of having something to fall back on, he resumed his medical studies, and in 1920 was working at the Sainte-Anne lunatic asylum, the *médecin-chef* of which, Professor Bessières, more than twenty years later was to discover that the provincial intern had possessed an "unstable temperament". This notwithstanding, the young man's thesis – *Contribution à l'étude de la paralysie ascendante aïgue* – was sufficiently esteemed to earn him his doctorate; and he managed to retain this honourable status despite subsequent spells in prison, in the midst of amorous scandal, and in the face of general suspicion (long before it was proved) that he was a murderer.

Dr. Petiot set up practice in 1921 in Villeneuve-sur-Yonne, not far from his birthplace of Auxerre, having first circularised the district with a remarkable document setting out his powers and attainments in the fashion of eighteenth-century apothecaries. He was handsome in a dark heavy way, and had considerable charm, as well as that genial manner which persuades the great self-doubting majority that so much self-assurance must be based on solid merit. His practice soon became extremely satisfactory.

Like many provincial doctors, he also participated in the social and political life of the neighbourhood, and here too with a good deal of success. During his twelve years in the Yonne, Marcel Petiot held office variously as Councillor, General Councillor, and Mayor of the canton. A convinced socialist, he was a frequent and appreciated speaker at the League for the Rights of Man. He was married, in 1927, to the charming and attractive Mlle Georgette Lablais of the same district. They had one son, Gérard.

Certain incidents intrude discordantly on this gentle biography. In the doctor's early years of practice, for example, he employed a servant girl whose physical charms seem to have been more noteworthy than any intellectual or spiritual qualities she may have possessed. Her presence in the bachelor household need not itself have caused any scandal – might even have been welcomed as a juicy subject of conversations; and even the fact of her becoming pregnant need not have been disastrous had the doctor elected to change her status to that of permanent and unpaid house-keeper. What did happen, however, was that the girl simply disappeared, and the manner of her disappearance – with not one farewell made – occasioned much regrettable specula-tion. She has still not returned to clear the doctor's name.

Further unpleasantness resulted from the death of Mme Debauve. This lady, coincidentally one of the doctor's patients, was the manageress of a local shop and known to have substantial sums of money very often in the place. In 1930 she was murdered and the establishment robbed, and certain enemies of socialism and the rights of man spread the astounding rumour that Dr Petiot had been guilty of this unprofessional conduct. He bore these slanders with almost Christian resignation, even going so far as to offer to treat one of his chief accusers who was suffering from rheumatism. With remarkable lack of dignity, the man accepted and within a few hours of swallowing the doctor's tablets was dead. The autopsy, conducted by Dr Marcel Petiot, revealed that this sudden death had been from natural causes.

No aspect of the man's background is more intriguing than that, in spite of all this, he nonetheless continued to hold political office, and it is reasonable to explain the fact by there having been somebody who was solicitous to protect him. Whoever this mysterious good fairy may have been, it is clear that the influence was powerful as well as benign, for in 1944, when a Paris journalist remembered the theories about Mme Debauve's murder and went to check the police dossier of the affair, he announced that it had completely disappeared.

Not long after Mme Debauve's death, Petiot was again in trouble, and this time there was no room whatever for speculation. There had been a whole series of thefts from the municipal stores and eventually the Mayor himself, Dr Petiot no less, was caught in the act. For this application of his socialist principles he was sentenced to three months' imprisonment and removed from office.

The doctor could tolerate this pharisaic hostility no longer and, in 1933, he and his wife were installed at 66 rue Caumartin, a populous street near the Madeleine and distinguished by the quantity of unusually attractive prostitutes who make it their promenade. Still in the boisterous eighteenth-century tradition, the doctor had a broadsheet distributed in which it was announced that he had opened consulting rooms "using the most modern and highly perfected equipment, with X, UV and UR rays, faradisation, ionisation, cryotherapy, diathermy, electric scalpel, ozonotherapy, aerotherapy, etc." "Dr Petiot," the pamphlet added, "ensures painless childbirth; he also gets rid of pain in cases of cancer, ulceration, neuritis, etc."

For three years after his arrival in Paris, Dr Petiot, as far as is known, applied himself exclusively to the mysteries of faradisation and aerotherapy although, remembering his past, it seems probable that he managed to fit in one or two unofficial diversions which were never recorded in his dossier.

In 1936, he was arrested for stealing from a bookshop in the Boulevard St Michel. What book? It was said to have been a "technical" work, and it would be interesting to know what technicality was then occupying him but, unfortunately, the fact is not at this date discoverable. Petiot himself always asserted that he had pocketed the volume in an unaccountable spasm of absent-mindedness (he, the least scatter-brained of men!) but one may be forgiven for believing that a natural taste for criminality was finding renewed expression. It is perhaps significant that a number of his offences were oddly motiveless, as if the enjoyment of cocking a snook at the upright world were a reward in itself. However this may have been, a liberal court, having heard the opinions of Dr Ceillier, decided that Petiot could scarcely have so manifested his contempt for the ethical system which they represented unless he had been insane, and the accused was therefore discharged along with a recommendation that he submit himself to some form of psychiatric treatment.

As a reasonable precaution against possible mishaps, medical men suspected of insanity are customarily dissuaded from practising; but still no medical board saw fit to remove this errant creature from its rolls. The *Conseil des Médecins de la Seine*, it was later explained by the President, Professor Balthazard, was never so much as informed by the responsible authorities of its wayward member's defections. Was this also attributable to the beneficent fairy's magic wand?

There is no limit to the number of sterile speculations which one can make in regard to Marcel Petiot, of all famous killers the one in whose history there are most lacunae; and, for just this reason, the guessing-game is irresistible. What, for instance, were his thoughts on 3rd September, 1939? Was he one of those haggard men who gathered in otherwise empty Paris along the boulevards, waiting for the next bulletin to be posted up outside the newspaper offices? Absurd rhetoric! He was egotistical to the uttermost extent – an individual being, never a social one – and he had learned by direct experience that international conflicts could be of very considerable use to the adroit man on the spot. There is no way of knowing and it is, of course, possible that he shared his compatriots' tragic apprehension of doom; it is possible, but the chances are rather that there and then he looked about for a method whereby he might personally take advantage of the chaotic future which was so clearly imminent. And, into the bargain, there are grounds for supposing that he may even have contemplated the world ahead with considerable satisfaction.

What is certain is that either just before or just after the war began, he utilised his professional standing (yet another example of his gift for making the most of circumstances) to set up as a drug-peddler – a means of livelihood very possibly held in mind since 1917.

It may be worth while at this point to dispose of a proposition sometimes put forward that he was an addict himself. For a number of reasons this is unlikely. To begin with, it is almost never the case that a trafficker becomes an addict; he knows too much about the consequences of such distractions. Then, again, there is no record of Petiot during his various incarcerations, when presumably narcotics were not available to him, having shown the least need of them. Lastly, it was not in his psychological structure to submit to any authority – whether that of society, or individuals, or hypodermics.

Sooner or later the inspectors of the Narcotics Squad intrude on the sub-world for which Petiot was catering at this time; and the very basis of these men's work consists of patiently linking the first transgressor whom they discover to his nearest associate, that associate to the next in the chain, and so inexorably back until they locate the chief begetter of so much pleasure, so much pain. Early in 1942 a young female drug-addict was picked up by the Paris police; under interrogation she involved her lover, Jean-Marc Van Bever; he, in turn, charged Dr Petiot with having provided the means for his mistress's melancholy diversion. The doctor rejected the slander with weary urbanity.

Released on bail, the young man made no effort to conceal his determination to sustain this allegation, and it can hardly surprise anyone who has followed Petiot's career up to this point that Van Bever, like the servant girl at Villeneuve, abruptly disappeared.

In the same year Mme Kahid died. This lady's daughter, Mlle Baudet, had been under treatment by Dr Petiot for drug-addiction, and Mme Kahid held that there were better ways of curing her offspring's unfortunate quirk than by supplying her with morphine and heroin at something over normal retail prices. Believing this, she announced her intention of interviewing the doctor and threatening him with exposure unless he employed a more conventional technique of disintoxication, and, as far as is known, she did set off on this pious jaunt. Once again, one is simply guessing as to what happened after the devoted parent left for her meeting with Dr Petiot; all that one can assert is that she was never again seen by her family. M. Kahid was later to depose that he had made inquiries of the doctor and had "read in his eyes that he had killed my wife". He may even have communicated this alarming discovery to the police, who certainly interrogated Petiot regarding the lady's disappearance, but there was no evidence which might have proved his involvement in the affair.[1] A certain consistency was beginning to emerge in respect of the fate of those acquaintances whose continued existence was likely to embarrass the doctor.

Other events occurred in 1942 to strengthen this tradition. There was, for instance, a young provincial housewife on whom Petiot performed an abortion, who, when the countryside gossips guessed all too well the reason for her trip to Paris, had the weird idea of demanding a certificate from Petiot – a certificate which would attest that she had required an altogether different medical treatment and which would thus confound the neighbours.

Under Marshal Pétain's benevolent régime, abortion had been declared a capital offence (five abortionists were guillotined during the Occupation) and the young woman's request revealed to Petiot that she was a possible, a probable threat to his security. The consequence was therefore foreseeable: she disappeared. According to a letter received by her husband, she had crossed into the Free Zone of France (M. Kahid had had a similar note from his wife) but, like Mme Kahid, like M. Van Bever, she has still to return to liberated Paris.

Petiot's solitary vexation as a result of these incidents was a (suspended) sentence of one year's imprisonment plus a fine of 10,000 francs in connection with Van Bever's mistress's drug-addiction.

Two years prior to all this, the Wehrmacht had entered Paris and had instituted just such conditions as Marcel Petiot found most suited to his undoubted talents. Under German governorship, both Jews and those sworn friends of European civilisation, the Communists, were submitted to severe control. Even though the latter were at this time disposed to view Nazi triumphs in a tolerant light – M. Molotov was actually moved to send his personal

1 It may be noted that Mlle Baudet testified at the time of Petiot's flight that her mother had previously had an interview with the doctor, and in the presence of Mme Petiot. If true, this would establish that the latter was aware of at least one aspect of her husband's activities. But, as she was later to point out in another respect: "My husband was not the sort of man of whom to ask questions."

felicitations to the Führer on the entry into Paris – yet their situation was a hazardous one. Like the Jews, they lived in unceasing expectation of more aggressive treatment. Understandably, then, they preferred to carry their concept of European culture to greener fields, while others, less politically enlightened, had in mind London and the slowly-gathering army of General De Gaulle. To meet the needs of this ill-assorted group, a low-voiced travel agency came into being, its branch offices located in scores of Paris cafés. Here, to the accompaniment of a coffee-substitute decanted from the familiar complicated mechanism which dominates all French bars, men with names like *"Roland le Roi de l'occase"* and *"Georges Bras de Fer"* whispered suggestions as to the whereabouts of people able to arrange conducted tours of South America or the United States. Among the principals so recommended was Dr Marcel Petiot, to be seen by appointment only at 21 rue Lesueur in the 16th arrondissement.

Petiot had bought this house (sufficiently grandiose to have been at one time the residence of Cécile Sorel) in September of 1941 with a definite object in mind. That it was no haphazard purchase is proved by his having in the following month engaged builders to effect some curious (but plausibly explained) alterations to the place. One room was to be windowless and as far as possible sound-proofed (it was to be used for the installation of a rather noisy transformer); a magnifying spy-glass was to be imbedded in the wall of this chamber (in order that the scientist might study the workings of his contraption without the fatigue of entering); and from this small cell a passage was to lead to his consulting-room, a passage traversed by three doors (that the racket of his transformer might not disturb the thoughtful fellow's neighbours). In contrast to this considerate move, he gave instructions for the building of a high wall which completely obscured the view of any nearby residents who might be curious as to what went on in the courtyard. Finally, a block and tackle was set up over a pit beside the garage in the courtyard (whatever explanation he gave for this arrangement has not been revealed) and, naturally, a check was made to ensure that such a feature of a respectable establishment as the furnace was in proper working order.

At 21 rue Lesueur he interviewed the clients whom he discovered for himself or who were sent along by his agents. One such, who had second thoughts about accepting help from a man he found inexplicably disquieting and who stayed alive in consequence, has recorded his meeting with the doctor, and doubtless it represented a standard form. Petiot, it seemed, confirmed that a trip to the appropriate country could be promptly arranged at a cost ingeniously calculated in relation to the applicant's known means; and he recommended (what more reasonable?) that the victim should gather together all his or her available cash or jewels and bring them along to the subsequent rendezvous. He was prodigal in his counsels and explanations; uniquely he hesitated to provide any details as to the port of departure, the port of arrival.

No one has survived to provide an account of the second – and crucial – encounter, but one may reasonably guess that the genial medico insisted then on rendering yet another service: this was the inoculation of the would-be traveller against those diseases notoriously prevalent in foreign countries. That Hippocratic civility performed, a last, never-to-be-realised meeting was fixed and the visitor shown to a door which led, the doctor observed casually, more conveniently and discreetly to the street. *A demain*.

How many wretched men and women, a burden at last removed from their anguished minds, passed through that innocent-seeming door? Impossible to know; but each and every one found him- or herself eventually in a tiny triangular apartment; the door by which they entered slammed behind them and was bolted; the door ahead was a fake, masking a brick wall. Here, while Petiot contemplated their writhings through his spy-hole, the "inoculation" took effect and they died.[1]

---

1 This is supposition: Petiot's method of killing was never definitely proved. A high police official, who had been directly concerned with the case, has told me of the possibility that a toxic gas was pumped into the "death room" and certain wall-fittings give some support to this theory.

Their bodies were carted out into the courtyard and low-ered into the pit. It was filled with quick-lime, and whatever scraps remained after this treatment were consigned to the furnace.

Petiot's first known victim was acquired by his own unaided efforts. This was one of the doctor's neighbours in the rue Caumartin, a middle-aged Polish furrier named Joachim Gusbinov under treatment by Petiot for some unspecified illness. He confided his anxiety to quit France, obtaining in return the gratifying news that this could be arranged for no more than the 25,000 francs needed to sweeten certain intermediaries.

Wonderful and efficient machinery! Joachim Gusbinov kept his appointment at rue Lesueur and was duly shep-herded to the quick-lime. In addition to the original down payment, this operation netted the doctor 2,000 U.S. dollars and 2,000,000 French francs.

Gusbinov was killed in January of 1942, but no one can imagine that Petiot waited so long before putting his ingenious business into profitable operation. Some evidence for this belief is to be found in the fact that, even before he had bought the house in rue Lesueur, a number of corpses had been located around Paris, for whose presence none of the official extermination squads could be held responsible. Moreover, these bodies had all been dismembered in a manner identical with that observed in the case of several of the corpses located at 21 rue Lesueur. It is probable that Petiot bought that property when he felt it to be increasingly risky to scatter his handiwork in the parks and vacant lots of the city.

In the tradition of modern business, Petiot even trans-formed social encounters into profitable deals. At a bridge-party given by his wife's cousin he made the acquaintance of a Jewish colleague, Dr Paul Braunberger, and within a few days the latter was making and receiving mysterious telephone calls, waiting vainly at pre-arranged meeting places, settling on code-words, being whirled faster and faster in the mad helterskelter which Petiot seemed gleefully to impose on his clients as if in deliberate mockery of the Resistance Movement's tragic complexities. When at last the game became wearisome, a final appointment was fixed from which Dr Braunberger never returned.

Simultaneously and under the name of Dr Eugène, Petiot was investigating prospects among quite a different social class. Less imaginative than himself, such men as "Jo the Boxer" and "François the Corsican" had carried on with their peacetime trade of theft, assault, armed robbery and similar banalities. They, too, had their reasons for desiring to quit France; they, too, made and kept their appointments at rue Lesueur; and, apparently, were crammed into the furnace as expeditiously as elderly doctors and ailing furriers.

It is typical of Marcel Petiot's epic opportunism that he did not initiate his business of large-scale murder until conditions seemed wholly favourable; and it is a mark of his intelligence that he judged conditions so well. Never in the twentieth century had there been a time when individuals, even those with families and friends, could vanish in a great city with so few inquiries resulting. The French police might reasonably surmise that any such disappearance was by the wish of the Gestapo; the Gestapo itself, less satanically well-informed than is popularly believed, might interpret it as another escape from occupied territory. Resistance groups and Fascist militia complicated the situation still further, and for mere individuals with some interest in the whereabouts of a friend or relation, it was only sane, not craven, to avoid asking questions.

Even if not omniscient, the Gestapo was nonetheless a notably efficient organisation. One by one, criminals, shopkeepers, merchants, Frenchmen, Dutchmen, Poles, men, women, and children, Petiot's clients vanished; and as steadily, Dr Yodkum, chief of the Gestapo's Section IV B, added to his dossier on the adroit and notorious "Dr Eugène". The link with Dr Petiot was easily established and the minor question of proof was entrusted to a wretched Jew blackmailed into the service of the Germans. This man was instructed to present himself to Petiot as one desiring, for obvious racial reasons, to get out of France; in this way he was to acquire evidence in support of their suspicions and then report back to his superiors. He obeyed orders, interviewed Petiot in the cunning guise agreed on, was accepted by the doctor as being what he claimed to be – and left by the same door as so many others, after sardonically submitting to the obligatory inoculation.

This sinister and unconscious joke had less serious consequences for Petiot than might have been anticipated. When their agent failed to report to headquarters, the Gestapo concluded that he had taken advantage of his contact with Petiot in order actually to leave the country, nobody having any reason to suspect the real destination of the doctor's visitors. It was therefore on a charge of having for payment aided the departure of "those having an interest in leaving France" (the terminology of police-states ranges from the brutally insulting to the venomously discreet) that Petiot was arrested by Dr Yodkum's men.

It was in May of 1943 that he was imprisoned by the Gestapo, and he remained in their care for eight months. At the end of that period he was released – an unusual termination to such a history – and was able to resume his career without, apparently, any apprehension. Had the Gestapo visited 21 rue Lesueur immediately on arresting him (he was picked up at his home in rue Caumartin) they would have discovered some significant bric-a-brac. As it was, they never called on that atrocious building at any time, so Petiot need not have ensured, as he did, the speedy transfer to the country of the miscellaneous garments and suitcases which had accumulated as by-products of his monstrous trade.

"This is no job for us." The firemen's concept of where their duties ended was a reasonable one, and the question of the unconventional fuel in the furnace of 21 rue Lesueur became the concern of another department of the Republic. Commissaire Georges Massu, Chief of the *Brigade Criminelle*, arrived at the unholy crematorium of the 16th arrondissement without delay. Passing from room to room on his preliminary inspection, he found the building unfurnished, dust-covered, unused except for the little cluster of rooms on the ground floor: the doctor's consulting-room, the passage, the execution chamber.

The Constitution of the French Republic holds that a private house is "inviolable", and expressly prohibits anyone from entering uninvited at night except in the case of fire or flood. This proscription is equally binding on the police as on any other citizens, and it was therefore not until the legal hour of 6 a.m. on Sunday, 12th March, 1944, that Commissaire Massu's inspectors were able to enter Dr Petiot's residence at 66 rue Caumartin. Here they discovered every evidence of a hurried departure, but no evidence whatever of anything else – unless one is disposed to regard the presence of an "erotic statue" (a homely feature of so many worthy households) as being in any way noteworthy.

On Tuesday the investigation shifted to the vicinity of Petiot's earlier life and works, to Auxerre where his younger brother, Maurice, had a radio repair shop which apparently provided him with a most satisfactory income. He had even been able to purchase (for 130,000 francs) a house in the rue des Lombards large enough for the overnight entertainment of any friends who might call. One such had clearly passed Monday night there, and the police were interested enough to ask the identity of the guest. It was, Maurice explained, a friend from the nearby town of Courson and, on the insistence of the officials, he provided the friend's name. Seemingly, there was some confusion in his mind, as the friend, when questioned in turn, had no recollection of the event, and Maurice Petiot was arrested on a charge of making a false statement. Two hours later the doctor's wife, Georgette, was likewise arrested in Auxerre. The doctor himself remained invisible.

Interrogated the following day in Paris, Mme Petiot was willing to be communicative. After the doctor's departure from the rue Caumartin in response to the telephone call made by the police on Saturday evening, she had awaited his return all night. On the Sunday she concluded that he had made a sudden trip to his brother in Auxerre, having forgotten (perhaps in a fit of absent-mindedness such as had afflicted him while browsing among the bookstalls in 1936) to let her know in advance. Equally impulsive, she decided to follow him, but the improved conditions of daily life so characteristic of wartime included an absence of trains to Auxerre that day. She attended church, strolled along the boulevards, and, being disinclined to return to rue Caumartin, passed Sunday night at yet another of her husband's properties, 52 rue de Reuilly. On Monday evening she took the train for Auxerre. She knew nothing of Marcel's present whereabouts, knew nothing of his activities at rue Lesueur. Being assured, however, that these had taken place, and being given some idea as to their nature, she volunteered an interesting observation: "It is possible that at rue Lesueur my husband got rid of people who had been reported to him as traitors." She gave no hint as to which of the many currently offered causes these persons might have betrayed.

For Maurice the *juge d'instruction* had prepared a "*coup de théâtre*" of the kind most appealing to officials with a dramatic sense. Police inquiries had established that the quick-lime which was so essential a commodity in Marcel's business had been transported from Auxerre by his brother. After listening patiently to Maurice's flatly persistent assertions that he knew absolutely nothing of the doctor's pursuits, the *juge d'instruction* suddenly revealed that the tie-up was known. Maurice clearly lacked the appropriate feeling for theatricality. In the face of this announcement he limited his response to an indifferent: "It's up to you to prove it."

The inculpation of Maurice and Georgette Petiot represented no more than the modest beginning of a lavish series of arrests. On 21st March, three of the leg-men who, in bars and at street corners, had conducted their discreet publicity campaign for Dr Petiot's dark profession, were arrested; and a fourth joined them next day. These men were a mixed lot, but all inhabitants of a twilight world in which they met with the sort of people eager – and able to pay – for a quietly-arranged trip. And all told a similar story: they confessed that for a percentage of the fares (50,000 francs for Spain, as much as 200,000 for South America) they had conducted the prospects to 21 rue Lesueur; but none of them guessed that the voyage came to an end there. They were tidied away into the cells.

The gathering-up of such riff-raff was small compensation for the continued coy seclusion of the man they served, nor were their protestations of virtuous ignorance of much service. But on 24th March a better-informed witness was added to the group, one who gave the first hint as to the scale of Petiot's operations. Réné Nézondet had known both Marcel and Maurice for some considerable time and was for this reason required to make a statement. It was rather more than anyone had bargained for.

Long before M. Marçais had been bothered by his neighbour's smoking chimney, Réné Nézondet had enjoyed a confidential chat with Maurice Petiot, in the course of which the latter had given the disturbing assurance that "My brother has killed at least fifty or sixty people". Nézondet had felt free to discuss this intelligence with the doctor's wife, but an understandable delicacy had withheld him from passing on his knowledge to the police. For this failure to report a crime as required by law, he was added to the slowly-mounting number of prisoners. It must be added that both Maurice and Georgette disclaimed any recollection of these startling conferences having taken place but, even so, Nézondet's revelation of the extent of Petiot's private war obtained far more public interest than did the "massive new raid on London" which official German sources stated to have occurred the previous day.

Nearly a week passed without there being any development, the police continuing their search for Marcel Petiot, whose ubiquity, as always in these affairs, was downright uncanny. Reports of his presence in all parts of France – sometimes simultaneously – arrived incessantly at the Quai des Orfèvres and were each checked, but the doctor had caused himself to disappear almost as completely as his various victims.

Another search was taking place concurrently for the odds and ends – mostly suitcases – known to have been removed from rue Lesueur at the time of Petiot's seizure by the Gestapo. These were located, with aid from Maurice, at the end of March: they had been confided (by Maurice) to the care of a certain M. Neuhausen of Auxerre. M. and Mme Neuhausen followed their friends to prison.

There is something almost piteous in the determination of the police, deprived of the one captive they really wanted, to imprison *faute de mieux* whoever came their way: the number eventually reached fourteen and even included such cousins-german to the case as the former servant of the doctor's late father-in-law.

As from 7th July, however, official enthusiasm seems to have been superseded by official despair. On that date two of the leg-men were released, Mme Neuhausen was set free on 12th August, and Mme Petiot on 1st October; the others followed them, and with their emergence from behind bars, they step from the midst of this ghastly history into their private ambience of assumed names and hateful recollections.

In the outside world, whose stupendous actions Petiot so deftly parodied, immense events were taking place which could yet not wholly drive the doctor's already legendary name from the front pages. In the early morning of 6th June, 1944, the Allies had effected landings on the French coast and begun their advance across Europe. On 20th July, at the Führer's headquarters, a bomb exploded within feet of Hitler, who stepped from the room unhurt to direct the liquidation of those who had sought his death. On 24th August, the first detachment of General Leclerc's armoured division entered Paris where civilians sniped the retreating Germans or, in the name of patriotism, executed men and women against whom the patriots had a private grudge. Ramshackle barricades had been thrown up in scores of streets, there were collaborators to be judged and summarily executed, women to be dragged naked through the city for having possibly slept with German soldiers, accusations to be made and refuted. There was work for all.

Somewhere amongst this mingled squalor and splendour moved Dr Marcel Petiot, appraising conditions as dexterously as ever, considering how best to take advantage of them, acting on his decisions, preparing a new rôle for himself.

Not altogether new, perhaps; merely an elaboration of one which had already proved ideal. In the circumstances, what could be better than a full-blown performance of The Resistance Leader? He did not, however, come before the public in this guise until after repeated allegations in the daily press that he had all along been a Gestapo agent. The slight was insupportable; and he addressed a letter to the newspaper *Résistance* insisting that he had throughout been – as who at that time had not? – a loyal worker for the Underground, and was currently an officer in the F.F.I. He evinced no eagerness, even so, to leave his patriotic duties and set the police right on one or two points about himself which continued to puzzle them.

But his handwritten note was the clue for which the searchers had waited. It was passed on to Colonel Roll, chief of the Parisian sector of the F.F.I., with the request that it be compared with the handwriting of all the officers under his command. The idea was sound. After a fortnight's work, the author of the letter was identified as Captain Henri Valéry, stationed at Reuilly. Captain Valéry had been a member of the F.F.I. for just six weeks.

On 31st October, 1944, as he left the métro station of Saint-Mandé-Tourelle, Dr Marcel Petiot, alias Dr Eugène, alias Captain Valéry, was arrested.

In spite of a newly-acquired beard (which gave him an unfortunate facial resemblance to his less-gifted predecessor, Landru) and in spite of his newly-acquired name and title, Marcel Petiot was essentially unchanged. At the preliminary interrogation he was relaxed, affable – a little condescending, perhaps – as he recounted his career in the Resistance Movement; and he ended his statement with a dignified observation, reminiscent of (and possibly recollected from) his electioneering days: "I have nothing with which to reproach myself. Speaking as a patriot, I am proud of everything I have done." It was presumably as a patriot that he carried membership-cards for the Communist Party, the Franco-Soviet League and a Communist-controlled militia corps. Such documents at that particular moment were almost of themselves a guarantee of respectability (the Party's recommendation of loving co-operation with the invaders had been forgotten) and it was correspondingly inevitable that Petiot, so sensitively alert to prevailing moods, should possess them.

There were other discoveries made: a ration card belonging to a Jewish child who had vanished with his parents some time previously; numerous *laissez-passers* and requisition forms: parodist of his age even there, Petiot's pockets were stuffed with almost every lunatic document which bureaucracy and political fanatics had been able to dream up.

From the day of his arrest until the day of his death, Petiot held consistently to two main claims – that since the beginning of 1941 he had served in the Resistance, and that he had only "executed" traitors or Germans. No one could deny that he had indeed participated in the Underground Movement – in fact Captain Valéry had so impressed his companions at Reuilly with tales of his own ardour and courage that many of them remained convinced of his disinterested patriotism until the end. They were ready, even eager to testify on his behalf, but not one witness could be found to bespeak the doctor's devotion to the Allied cause prior to September of 1944.

Petiot himself named various men (all of them dead) as one-time superiors of his in the Resistance; but he was oddly unable to give any details about them other than those splashed in the exultant post-liberation press. And he spoke readily of his own underground organisation, known, he revealed, as *Groupe Fly Tox* – but known to whom? None of its other members came forward to claim the distinction of having served with Petiot. Then there was a "secret weapon" invented by himself and handed over to the Americans, but Washington had never heard of it. The Argentinian diplomat who, by Petiot's account, had helped smuggle those victims of Nazism from France (for the doctor candidly admitted that he had indeed arranged such trips) was sought in vain.

He was, however, no more elusive than the clandestine travellers themselves. What had happened to them, Gusbinov, Braunberger, and the rest? Petiot could not help: his job, he made clear, had finished once the clients were outside France; if then they took it into their heads to change their itineraries, that was no concern of his.

Nonetheless, it was a teasing mystery and led inevitably to some scepticism in considering his claim to have killed none but the enemy and the enemy's friends. Were the owners of such Hebraic names as Wolff, Marx and Kneller likely to have been serving in the Wehrmacht or on terms of jovial familiarity with the Gestapo chiefs of the rue Lauriston and the rue de la Pompe? And if not, and their undeniable visits to Petiot made in the course of escaping from the occupation – then where were they? Petiot shrugged.

Considered from another viewpoint, who were the collaborators whom he had executed, who were the German soldiers? Again Petiot proved unhelpful. It was felt that if he had from time to time – in the course of business, so to speak – included a Gestapo man or collaborator among his victims, it must have been due more to a genial lack of selectivity than to nationalistic fervour. But it should count in his favour, for all that; one name, just one.

There was no answer to be had from him, but he did provide one piece of information which may or may not have caused some official embarrassment: during all the time when he was being sought in the provinces, he had been installed in Paris. The old Resistance trick had worked again, Petiot having persuaded a M. Georges Redouté that he was hiding from the German or German-dominated authorities.

Whether this revelation upset officialdom or not, the dominating mood was one of understandable satisfaction and this benevolence expressed itself on 4th January, 1945, when eleven persons implicated in the affair, including Maurice Petiot, were discharged in consequence of a finding of Not Proven. As to the doctor, the *Chambre des Mises en Accusation* three weeks later remanded him for trial before the Assizes Court of the Seine. The date was set for 18th March of the same year, and the defence was entrusted to Maître René Floriot.

Petiot appeared at his trial shorn of his beard but, by way of compensation, endowed (it was noted by the press) with a pair of strange and hypnotic eyes. These terrifying organs are obligatory on all mass murderers, but Petiot's photographs hardly help to support the legend. On the other hand, it must be admitted that it would have been in keeping with his sardonic character to have affected a glare of that sort in mere derision of commonplace concepts of the Typical Killer. This ironic streak in him had already been remarked and, after the charge had been formally read, President Leser referred to the "Accused's disquieting fits of temper". Petiot eyed him with derisive reproachfulness. "Ah, now come," he said gently, "if we start off like this there's bound to be trouble."

He was right; but most of the trouble was created by himself. Alternating with his blithe jests were outbreaks of querulousness, rage, bitterness, as he sought to maintain the familiar thesis that he had been a selfless patriot and had all along acted as such. He did not deny that he had killed a number of people (himself raising the estimate to sixty-three) but the issue was whether they had been legally despatched (for the benefit of a particular social system) or illegally (for the benefit of an individual). Petiot held to the former view. Collaborators and German soldiers had been his meat, no one else. He knew nothing of those antique mysteries – the murder of Mme Debauve, the disappearance of his maidservant, M. Van Bever's abrupt and permanent departure. He had found the human debris in the cellars of rue Lesueur when he returned from the prison of Fresnes where the German authorities had kept him; he presumed that it had been piled there by fellow-resisters; and he had no comment to make on the government pathologist's conviction that the morsels bore unmistakable signs of having been sliced up by a practised professional hand.

Most damaging of all to Petiot's cause (if he can be said to have had one) was his austere refusal to name his companion-in-arms in the Resistance cell whose sentences he claimed to have carried out. They were all, he affirmed, yearning to give evidence in his favour but he himself would not permit them to be implicated in such a sordid business. One would have thought that these daredevils who had helped Petiot capture German soldiers from crowded streets in full daylight would have come forward despite this prohibition, but none did so – a fact which did not inhibit the doctor from demanding on their behalf, as well as his own, that they be decorated with the Cross of the Liberation – presumably in absentia.

The first day's hearing ended as it had begun with a cheerful quip from the man in the dock. "Oh, you can keep going," he announced when, at 6.30 p.m., the court was adjourned, "personally, I'm not at all tired."

Most of the debates during the succeeding days were boring even to the person most concerned. Petiot slept, or affected to sleep, through much of the most damaging evidence, and diverted himself by writing little poems of which one is remarkable for its ferocity if not its technical skill. Very roughly translated:

> Ah! It is fine to see, haphazardly assembled
> In one or another of these adjoining rooms,
> The black birds of the night preparing their meal –
> Three judges and a prosecutor drawn up in a square.
>
> It is fine to see within this confined court
> The heavenly crew juggling the law at will,
> Sticky with ambitions and carrying in their faces
> All the hidden vices by which they are devoured.
> But it would be better still to see the city in arms,
> Crying "Down with the rogues!" or fearlessly
> Sacking the court; but best of all,
>
> Hacking at this one and stringing up that,
> It would be fine to see them die a slow death
> And to see ten judges' skins for sale at ten sous.[1]

Little poems and little jokes are poor substitutes for a

1 This was not his only literary achievement. While in prison he completed a curious work entitled *Le Hasard Vaincu* (Imprimerie Roger Amiard, Paris, 1946). Sub-titled *Les Lois des Martingales*, the volume is decorated with several odd and possibly significant designs by the author. The text is printed in a facsimile of Petiot's manuscript and consists largely of elaborate mathematical propositions and columns of figures. It is sardonically dedicated "*à vous – qui m'avez fait ces loisirs*" and as an additional jest it is recorded that "the researches have been executed by Dr Eugène, ex-chief of the Fly-Tox Resistance Group; the columns of figures have been drawn up under the command of Captain Valéry of the 1st Army, 1st Paris Regiment; the mistakes in the operation have been committed by Dr Marcel Petiot . . ."

The book gives additional and superfluous proof of Petiot's preoccupation with chance and the avoidance of its ill results; and it is unnecessary to point to the irony of his having seen all his carefully-planned activities ruined by the sheerest hazard – a smoking chimney and a testy neighbour.

strong defence, and even the fabulous Maître Floriot could hardly create that out of Petiot's unsubstantiated claims and provable lies. Witness after witness demonstrated how tenuous were the Accused's connections with the Resistance; while Petiot himself could manage no more than a sequence of grateful clients and childhood friends. It was evident from the beginning that the Cross of the Liberation would not be awarded this time.

Yet somehow a vague, unhappy notion grew up that Petiot *had* been in one way or another involved in patriotic endeavour – but then he had been involved in everything. And whether or not some of his murders had benefited his country, the fact remained that some had benefited Petiot and were therefore criminal. At ten minutes to midnight on 4th April, 1946, the jury, after two and a half hours' deliberation, returned a verdict of guilty and he was sentenced to death. "Let me be revenged!" he called to the public.

Marcel Petiot was awakened at dawn on 26th May, 1946, and told he was to die that morning. The bitter, intelligent face showed no sign of fear, but when, as called for by tradition, he was adjured to have courage, he snarled an exasperated vulgarism which might be translated as "Get the hell out of this." His wife had brought him some clean clothes the previous night and he dressed himself with care; then he borrowed a pencil to write a last letter to his wife and, having finished it, turned to the waiting officials with: "And now, gentlemen, I am at your disposal."

It is some distance from the condemned cell of the Santé Prison to the courtyard where the guillotine is erected when an execution is to take place, but Petiot walked unperturbedly all the way to his destination. He stopped *en route* in one of the corridors where a temporary altar had been set up. He declined to hear Mass but, after a moment's hesitation, decided to pray "to please my wife". He refused a glass of rum but smoked a final cigarette.

In the courtyard he contemplated the guillotine without apparent emotion but muttered that he wanted to urinate. The executioner was in a hurry; he begged the doctor to control his bladder for a moment, adding consolingly that it would not be for long. Petiot nodded in acquiescence.

One last effort was made to persuade him to confess and to elucidate the mysteries still surrounding those vanished travellers and their heaped suitcases. Nothing could have been more apropos than Petiot's reply: "When one sets out on a voyage," he remarked, "one takes all one's luggage with one."

Monsieur de Paris's work was done by five minutes past five in the morning.

As a character Petiot seems, at first glance, to have no more interest than is attached to him by his awe-inspiring massacres. The reports from his schools fail to single out any notable quality in him; the psychiatrists charged with the task of examining him were unable to do better than record their conviction that the murderer of sixty-three people was "morally retarded"; he evinced no precocious inventiveness as did Troppmann, nor had he that terrible and tawdry sense of theatre which was one of Landru's fascinating quirks. The solitary surviving example of his verse is not impressive, and his wit was impudent rather than epigrammatic. For the rest, he struck all except those who had a few moments for reflection before dying at his hands, as a charming and worthy fellow, extraordinary only in the degree of his amiability.

The servant at 66 rue Caumartin (even when given a perfect chance to claim premonitory sapience) asserted that she had never remarked any oddity in his behaviour or manner; and Mme Legros, a neighbour in rue Caumartin who had some acquaintance with the Petiots, deposed in the course of a newspaper interview that "so pleasant a man could not possibly have committed such crimes". His electoral triumphs in Villeneuve indicate that he was respected and liked in the district, and there were even those who maintained ever after that there must have been some mistake in the matter of the servant girl, the municipal funds and all the rest.

Yet there is a definite interest in Marcel Petiot's character, and the reason lies perhaps in the fact that he hideously caricatured the world in which he lived. Modern bureaucracy has created in people a sense of wary opportunism; Petiot perfected this sullen defence and applied it to his own better-ment with absolute logic and completeness, transforming it in the process from defence into aggression. His abominable trade was scarcely a distortion of the brutish techniques of big business, and his killings a tiny imitation of the Gestapo and the MVD. What was his drug-trafficking but an individual parallel to government hand-outs designed to keep the slaves quiet? And what were his thefts but insig-nificant personal equivalents to the organised gangsterism of mankind's masters?

The war, with its mass executions, obliteration bomb-ings, its evil underground manœuvrings and employment of decoys and spies, was a thing too vast in its horror to be understood; it enveloped everything so utterly as to seem almost normal and beyond questioning. In Petiot's actions the whole complicated foulness was seen reduced to comprehensible dimensions. He needed only to have made a private *Baedeker*-raid on the Louvre to have completed the analogy.

The great puzzle in the Petiot case is the identity of the person or persons who throughout a period of nearly twenty years would seem to have been concerned with his well-being. That he did in fact enjoy some sort of powerful protection becomes, at the very least, a reasonable supposition if certain questions are posed. Chronologically, these are as follows:

1. How was he able to retain political office despite the widespread local suspicion that he was guilty of having murdered his servant girl, Mme Debauve and the chief unofficial prosecutor in respect of that case?

2. How was it possible for Petiot to conduct the autopsy on a man who had died under his treatment?

3. Why was he never interrogated regarding the murder of Mme Debauve? And how did the dossier on this case, believed to have contained the murderer's fingerprints, come to vanish from the files?

4. Why did no report of his various court-room convictions

and sojourns in psychopathic wards ever reach the Medical Council?

5. How did he come to be released by the Gestapo in 1943 on the grounds (ludicrous for such an organisation) that there was insufficient evidence? Petiot claimed that he had purchased his release for 100,000 francs; but in every other such case the figure was considerably higher – and why did the negotiations take so long to complete?

6. Was it a mere coincidence that his eventual arrest, so long delayed, followed quickly on the liberation of Paris?

All these questions may, of course, be explicable on depressingly commonplace grounds; but it is also possible to answer them by presuming the existence of a protection more powerful and far-reaching than any individual could provide. In short, it is a fair guess that some organisation was looking after Petiot.

As already mentioned, various Resistance newspapers, shortly before his arrest, argued that the doctor was a Gestapo agent. The charge at that time was a not uncommon one and Petiot's membership of the Communist Party by no means conclusive proof to the contrary: the theory was, at any rate, more applicable to his case than to thousands of others similarly accused. There are, however, serious objections. If he was one of their employees, why was Petiot ever arrested by the Gestapo at all? And surely the Gestapo, if they employed him, would have known all his addresses, so why did they not visit 21 rue Lesueur at the same time that they were busily searching all his other properties?

Another proposition sometimes put forward is that, while politically innocent at the time of his arrest by the German police, Petiot subsequently obtained his release by agreeing to become one of their undercover men. But this would not account for whatever protection he may have enjoyed extending back to 1930.

If, then, he was in fact the protégé of some powerful group, it must have been one of the several German secret services which functioned independently of the Gestapo and long before that malignant force came into being, allowing nonetheless that initially Petiot may not have known who or what was behind his immediate benefactors. There was some measure of rivalry and a very spasmodic co-operation between the various German intelligence services,[1] and this lack of liaison would account for his arrest by the Gestapo and, assuming that his own superiors later made representations, his eventual release.

Further, it is quite possible that the German authorities learnt at some point of his murderous activities and, believing them to involve only "persons having an interest in leaving France", gave their unofficial blessing to the enterprise.

M. Marçais having brought the French police into the business, even the occupying Power would have hesitated to side publicly with Petiot; but they might (and it has been alleged that they did) attempt to abort the French efforts to locate him, hamper the inquiry in a variety of ways, and it is worth noting that the German authorities insisted on receiving a detailed daily report of the progress of the hunt. Such weighty interference (perhaps applied deviously, without the police even realising what it was that hindered them) might well have kept Petiot at liberty until such time as the Germans were no longer in Paris to obstruct the traditional skill and patience of the Police Judiciaire.

All of which is the sheerest supposition: Petiot took all his luggage with him.

Alister Kershaw

As a footnote to this case, it is worth mentioning *Petiot, Victim of Chance* by Ronald Seth. Seth was in Paris at the end of the war as a member of Military Intelligence, and argues persuasively that Petiot *was* a member of the Resistance, and that his defense may have been basically true. Seth argues that the evidence in the case was so

---

1 Cf. H.R. Trevor-Roper's *The Last Days of Hitler* (Macmillan Ltd., London): "In Nazi Germany neither war production, nor manpower, nor administration, nor intelligence was rationally centralised; and Ribbentrop's protest at Nuremberg that foreign intelligence was not supplied by the Foreign Ministry but by thirty competing agencies is substantially true. The structure of German politics and administration . . . was in fact a confusion of private empires, private armies, and private intelligence services."

complex that no jury – "even a jury of geniuses" – could have grasped it, and that even though Petiot lied and repeatedly changed his story, he was probably telling the truth when he declared that he was in the Resistance. The reason, Seth thinks, is that Petiot could never have dealt with so many bodies without some help. He often had two bodies to dispose of, and sometimes as many as six. Yet before March 1944, when the smoke from his chimney caused his downfall, no one had noticed heavy smoke – even though Petiot had been killing since January 1942. Seth suggests that Petiot was a member of a Communist group, and that he was afraid to speak out because they would have killed his wife and son.

Seth seems to believe that the Communist group killed the victims to raise money for the Resistance. If this is correct, then Petiot was not innocent; he was a kind of hired killer, and deserved to go the guillotine with his co-conspirators.

At all events, I must confess that, having read three books on the case, I find it very hard to feel much sympathy for Marcel Petiot.

C.W

The Black Dahlia

Like the case of Donald Fearn, described earlier, the Black Dahlia case has always struck me as one of the most horrific in the annals of sex crime. When I first read it – in this account from David Rowan's *Famous American Crimes* (1957), I remember feeling utterly shocked and nauseated; I recall that it was the account of suspending her upside down and burning her with cigarettes that so revolted me.

The crime writer James Ellroy has written a powerful novel called *Black Dahlia* that suggests, probably correctly, that Elizabeth Short was involved in drugs and porn movies. In Ellroy's novel, the killer is an extremely sick sadist with a badly disfigured face. It sounds appropriate, yet somehow I doubt it. Few sadistic killers look like the hunchback of Notre Dame.

It has been suggested that Elizabeth Short's murderer was the killer known as "the mad butcher of Kingsbury Run", who killed and dismembered a dozen or more victims between 1935 and 1938 in Cleveland, Ohio. (An account of the case – by my son Damon – will be found in my *Murder in the 1930s*.) It is an interesting speculation, but seems to me unlikely. The mad butcher killed both men and women – often two at a time – and dismembered their bodies. All the evidence indicates that he was a homosexual sadist – I suspect the women were killed because he hated women, but that there was no kind of sexual motive. Such a man would hardly have travelled to Hollywood nearly a decade later to kill one would-be film actress. Only the horror of the cases serves as a connection.

Down in the heart of Hollywood, well away from the much-publicised glamour of the film stars' mansions, some of the side streets tell a sad story. Here is all the cardboard tawdriness of the disused film sets stacked behind the big studios. Here, a short ride from the world's most expensive hotels, the cheapjack stores shriek a thousand vulgar boasts, in garish neon lighting. But when the lights are out, little is left but the dirt on the plaster façade – and for hundreds of the pretty girls who arrive each year in search of a Hollywood fairy-tale, this is the reality . . .

Nobody cares. The masters of the film studios may be among the richest and most powerful men in the United States, but Hollywood is only a suburb of Los Angeles. And who notices what becomes of a pretty girl in a city with more than one and a half million inhabitants?

In the normal way, nobody would have noticed what happened to Elizabeth Short. She was just another of the countless failures, the forgotten souls sacrificed on the altar of a gaudy myth. Yet she, alone, broke through the callous flow of public indifference.

Elizabeth Short was murdered. That, too, was of little moment in a city which has an average of one murder a day. But the manner of her killing has ensured that her name will be remembered when those of the lucky few – the ones for whom the Hollywood fairy tale came true – have sunk into oblivion.

A tall, unusually beautiful girl, Elizabeth Short had several of the qualities which can make for renown in the extravagant, nerve-stretched capital of make-believe. In her personal appearance, she adopted a peculiarity of dress well calculated to attract the attention of a passing film producer. To emphasise her milk-white complexion and striking head of raven hair, often set off by a white flower, she rarely wore anything but black. Tight-fitting black dresses, the sheerest black underwear, black court shoes, even a jet ring on her pale hand. The habit had quickly earned her the nickname of "The Black Dahlia" – and possession of a nickname like that is another useful means of standing out from the ordinary film crowd. In her origins, she conformed with the favourite version of the studio publicity men in that she was born as far from Hollywood as possible, and in a small town or village rather than a big city. Miss Short, in fact, had come right across the continent, more than three thousand miles, from her home in the little manufacturing town of Medford, Massachusetts.

Finally, in her private life, "The Black Dahlia" had traits which, though morally reprehensible, testified to her high spirits and guaranteed her a solid basis of experience. Despite her stern New England background, she was wild and independent. Early in the war, she had been arrested as a juvenile delinquent, for drinking with soldiers in a café. When she gravitated to Hollywood a couple of years later, she loved to be taken to night clubs frequented by the film stars. It was not long before she fell in with a certain section of the film colony, whose morals were in inverse proportion to their potential influence. Although one may condemn her, it has to be admitted that quite a few young actresses, now famous, have won their first screen part by similar means . . .

For a while, Elizabeth Short did manage to find regular work as an extra, but that was all. There were so many girls like her. And soon after the war, when the studios went through a bad period, even that work dried up. Facing the facts of life, she moved out and got a job in San Diego, the booming seaport town a hundred-odd miles to the south. It was near enough for her to return to her old haunts for a day or two, every now and then, in the faint hope that one of her old film friends would remember her.

Yes, there were so many girls like "The Black Dahlia" – until a bleak, windy morning in Los Angeles in mid-January, 1947. Somewhere behind that wretched, grubby little pattern of her life is the clue to a discovery which, when they saw it, made hardened detectives vomit where they stood.

On that morning, alerted by a passing motorist, police rushed to a vacant building site beside a local "lovers' lane". There they found two halves of a female corpse.

It was nude. It had been cut in two at the waist. It had been hideously mutilated, beyond recognition. As a last refinement, the murderer had carved the initials "B.D." deep into one thigh.

Worse was to come. Pathologists who examined the body established that most of the bestial injuries had been inflicted *before death*. From their reports, police deduced that the victim had been overpowered and suspended by her ankles. Her legs, hands and feet had then been bound with wire or rope. In this position, head downwards, she had still been alive when the killer began mutilating her with a knife.

In its unspeakable sadism, I can think of only one comparison in recent criminal history – that of Neville Heath, the British sex murderer who was hanged the previous year. It happens that I was among the first newspapermen on the scene of Heath's first murder, a Notting Hill boarding house, just after the body was discovered. One of Britain's most famous detective chiefs told me then that, throughout his twenty-five years in the police, this was the only time that the sight of a murder victim had made him physically sick. The men of the Los Angeles Homicide Squad suffered a similar revulsion with the "lovers' lane" victim. On reading the medical reports, one of them muttered: "I hope to God she died of shock first – before the bastard had finished." Unhappily, the reports showed that, when the passing motorist saw the severed body, the victim had not long been dead. From the place where the murder was committed, wherever that might have been, the killer had taken the body and dumped it on the vacant site only a short while before it was discovered.

At this stage, the initials "B.D." cut into the body conveyed nothing to the police. Because of the obliteration of any recognisable features, it seemed likely that identifying the victim would be a long business, if not impossible. Experts were able to take impressions of some of the dead woman's finger-prints, however, and these were sent out for nation-wide checking. It was purely a routine measure. Unless she had been a criminal or an alien, or perhaps had worked in a confidential government job, there was little hope that her prints had been recorded. But now the police had the first of their very few breaks in the case. From the vast finger-print files of the Federal Bureau of Investigation, one punched card dropped into place. By a chance that could be reckoned in millions, the victim had given her finger-prints – *voluntarily* – to the F.B.I. while working during the war as a clerk in the U.S. Post Exchange (roughly the equivalent of the British NAAFI). She was, of course, Elizabeth Short, "The Black Dahlia". At the time of her death she was just twenty-two years old.

It had taken only a few hours to overcome this first hurdle, and the Los Angeles police made good use of their luck. Under Captain Jack Donohue, of the Homicide Squad, detectives rapidly traced the dead girl's mother, Mrs Phoebe M. Short. Her daughter's body had been cut up so terribly that she was unable to confirm the identification, but she did give the police a new lead. After quitting Hollywood, she told them, Elizabeth had written to her from San Diego, saying that she had found work there in an Army hospital or in some connection or other with the armed forces.

A hurried call to San Diego established that Elizabeth Short had left her room there six days before her death. She had taken no luggage with her – so it seemed possible that she had been planning to stay in Los Angeles with a woman friend, who could provide her, if necessary, with extra clothes and make-up. Meanwhile, other detectives scoured the less savoury back streets of Hollywood in search of anyone who had seen "The Black Dahlia" during her last visit. At one period one hundred policemen were engaged on different aspects of the case.

They found two bartenders who said that they had served drinks to Miss Short two or three days before the murder. Each time, she had been accompanied by one or more women friends.

They built up a description of "a man with red hair", who was believed to have been the last to see the victim alive. At the same time, they sought one of her former room-mates, who had disappeared on the very day the body was found.

All the time, too, they were building up a strangely mixed picture of the dead girl's character. Neighbours told them that she was "crazy about clothes" but that otherwise "she seemed to be a nice girl". A woman with whom she had once lived in Los Angeles said that Elizabeth had described herself as a friend of Ann Todd, the British film actress. When police checked the story, however, Miss Todd denied that she knew her. Next day – only three days after the crime was discovered – they made their first arrest.

The suspect, a thirty-eight-year-old cook named Edward Glen Thorpe, of Laramie, Wyoming, was handed over to them after fellow-passengers in a long-distance bus had heard him mumbling in his sleep – apparently about the murder. He was alleged to have muttered: "I forgot to cut the scar off her leg." Thorpe denied all knowledge of the crime but was said to have been unusually nervous during interrogation. Police also stated that they found what appeared to be blood-stains on his jacket. There was all the tense expectancy which immediately precedes the solution of a major crime . . . and then, as suddenly as it had begun, the enquiry fizzled out and the "Man from Laramie" was released. His description, it was announced, did not fit that of the "man with red hair" for whom the police were looking, and he was in the clear on other counts.

Only a few hours later, detectives brought in a man who did answer the required description. He was Robert Manley, a twenty-five-year-old salesman, formerly a musician in the U.S. Army Air Force. He had red hair – and he admitted that he had had a "flirtation" with Miss Short. But Manley, who had a wife and four-month-old child, denied any connection with her death. Lie-detector tests showed that his conscience was clear, and his wife supported his statement that he had been visiting friends with her on the night of the murder. Once again, the enquiry had come to a dead end. Before his release, however, Manley gave the police one hopeful lead. At one of his meetings with "The Black Dahlia", he recalled, he saw scratches on her arms. When he asked her about them, she explained that she had a friend who was "intensely jealous."

Despite these two setbacks, the hunt for the killer was proceeding along lines which could normally be expected to produce a solution within a week or two. The "Dragnet" series of television films has given many people an excellent insight into the methods of the Los Angeles detective force – and, for that matter, of detectives throughout the world. It is all a matter of routine thoroughness, of unending questioning, the elimination of each name on a list which may run into the thousands, the constant checking and cross-checking of every statement, every rumour, every known activity of the victim throughout his or her life. And all backed by scientific experts who can deduce a man's appearance from two short lengths of hair, or his job and probable home town from a speck of dust. No detail is too small to neglect. Intuition and inspired hunches, with which the detective-thriller sleuths are so gifted, do play their part in real life, but not often. One of Scotland Yard's greatest detectives, Mr William Rawlings, Deputy Commander of the C.I.D., has estimated that 97 per cent of all successful solutions are reached solely by the method of infinite pains.

So it was with the murder of "The Black Dahlia". Unmasking the culprit seemed only a matter of time. Under Captain Donohue, detectives questioned literally thousands of people. They came to know every place where the victim had ever worked, her likes and dislikes, her personal habits. They spread out from her known friends and began to amass a list of her more casual acquaintances, one link in the chain leading to the next. It was not easy, for her circle of acquaintances was large and indiscriminate, although the job appeared to have been simplified by another stroke of luck – in the shape of an anonymous letter received by a local newspaper in the week after the murder. The letter contained Elizabeth Short's birth certificate, social security card and address book. The envelope was addressed with portions of newspaper headlines relating to the case, crudely pasted together. A terse note inside said: "Here are Dahlia's belongings. Letter to follow." Exceptionally clear finger-prints were obtained.

But there the Homicide Squad's good luck ran out on them. This time, there was no record of the finger-prints in the files of the F.B.I. or anyone else. Nor did a minute scientific examination of the headlines and paste on the envelope yield anything of immediate use. The police laboratory experts could identify the newspapers (down to the exact edition) and the make of paste, but both could have been bought almost anywhere in the city, and Los Angeles covers a bigger area than any other city in the world. Even Miss Short's address book, in which she had written the names of her many men friends, produced little but hard work and disappointment. Several detectives were assigned to the sole task of tracing each name (a few of them surprisingly prominent and one of them actually a Hollywood millionaire). Occasionally they turned up somebody who gave them reason for suspicion; always, after further enquiry, they had to give him a clean sheet – so far as the killing was concerned, anyway. When the long, tedious job ended, it was as if they had never begun it . . .

Apart from their misfortune in being unable to uncover a vital lead, the men of the Homicide Squad were hampered by two factors beyond their control. The first was that, in addition to their usual one-a-day murder rate, they now had to contend with a whole series of brutal killings closely resembling that of "The Black Dahlia". Murderers are notoriously imitative, and detectives always know that if, say, a woman has been asphyxiated with a pillow and considerable publicity is given to the case, somebody else is sure to try the same method within the next few weeks. The death of the young film extra, and the enormous amount of space devoted to it in American newspapers, sparked off at least half a dozen sex killings of a similar type in the Los Angeles area. One came only three days after the Dahlia murder; the victim, Mary Tate, was savaged and then strangled with a silk stocking. Next month, the body of Mrs Jeanne French was found, atrociously mutilated; obscenities had been written on the corpse with lipstick. On March 11th, Mrs Evelyn Winters was slashed to death; she, too, had been slowly mutilated beforehand. Throughout the summer, as the Dahlia investigation dragged on, three more women suffered exceptionally gruesome deaths. Rosenda Mondragon was clawed and strangled with a silk stocking; Mrs Dorothy Montgomery was stripped bare and mutilated; Mrs Laura Trelstad was ferociously beaten and then strangled. In each of these six murders, there were other features, best left unmentioned, which suggested that they had been inspired by the manner of Elizabeth Short's death. Not only did these crimes have to be solved, but detectives had to make sure that there were no direct links between them. It was always possible that one or more of the six had been committed by the original Dahlia killer.

The second big obstacle to police progress turned out to be even more serious. From the start, Homicide Squad detectives were bedevilled by fantastic interference from ordinary members of the public. Day after day, an unending stream of misleading information and dubious "tipoffs", mostly motivated by a desire for publicity or personal revenge, poured into police headquarters. Yet, inside the framework of essential thoroughness, each one had to be examined closely before it could be rejected.

Above all, there were the false confessions. In the early days of most sensational murder cases, one or two cranks can be sure to give themselves up, wildly confessing their guilt of the crime; it is a common phenomenon. The Dahlia murder attracted at least *twenty-eight* of these claimants – far more than for any previous killing in U.S. criminal history.

Despite its gruesome nature, Elizabeth Short's death might long have been forgotten by now; but the phoney confessions have ensured it a place among the classics of American crime. For their character, the reasons behind them and behind the other forms of public interference in the case, lifted the stone and exposed an ugly growth: the hysterical unbalance affecting a wide section of the community.

A fortnight after the murder, Captain Donohue revealed that a thirty-three-year-old man had telephoned the Homicide Department to come and pick him up, saying: "I can't stand it any longer – I want to confess to the murder of Black Dahlia." In the patrol car which brought him in, he mumbled continually: "I killed her . . . I killed her." At police headquarters, the man, Daniel S. Voorhees, a former restaurant employee, signed a statement which was displayed to the waiting newspapermen afterwards by one of the detectives who questioned him. On the sheet of paper, above his signature, was written simply: "I did kill

Elizabeth Short." Voorhees, the detective said, had refused to give any details but denied having written any of the many anonymous letters and postcards received by the police – notably one which had stated that the murderer would surrender that very day. In passing, he had revealed that he had a wife and nine-year-old daughter at Phoenix, Arizona. Another detective said that Voorhees would not be given a lie-detector test "until he recovers from his bewildered and befuddled state". Unhappily, his recovery was immaterial. As detectives grew more insistent, pressing him to elaborate on his story, he became increasingly sullen. Eventually he growled: "Ah, I'm not going to talk to you any more. I've talked too much already. I want to see my attorney." Voorhees remained in custody – as a mental case.

Ten days later, Captain William Florence, of the U.S. Army Criminal Investigation Department, announced the arrest of twenty-nine-year-old Corporal Joseph Dumais, a combat veteran of Fort Dix, New Jersey. He was convinced, the captain said, that Dumais was involved in the crime. The curly headed, moustachioed young corporal, who had just returned from forty-two days' leave, was reported to military police by another soldier with whom he had quarrelled over money. He volunteered the information that he had known Miss Short and had been out with her on January 9th – only six days before her body was found. Investigators found bloodstains on his clothing and, among his possessions, a batch of newspaper cuttings about the murder. In an alleged statement running to 50 pages, Dumais was reported to have said that his first wife, by whom he had one child, died in 1937 in mysterious circumstances (which he did not elucidate). He was then 19. His second wife bore him three children, two of whom died. While serving overseas, he married a Czech girl in 1945 and adopted two children; he did not know her present whereabouts. The alleged statement then described his supposed association with Elizabeth Short. The presence of certain marks on her body which he mentioned was said to have been corroborated. Dumais himself admitted: "It is possible that I could have committed the murder. When I get drunk, I get rough with women . . ." Yet again, however, the whole edifice collapsed when the Los Angeles police came to give it a close inspection. They merely checked his story against facts known only to themselves – then sent Dumais, too, to a psychiatrist.

Experienced detectives can usually spot a false confession in a matter of minutes, if not seconds, by asking trick questions. In the Dahlia case, their task was made easier by the fact that many details of the murder were unprintable. Even the most uninhibited American newspaper draws the line at telling its readers the exact nature of the sadistic wounds inflicted by a sex killer. Accordingly, detectives seldom had any trouble in establishing that the would-be suspects knew nothing more about the murder than had actually appeared in the Press.

Some of the confessions arose from the misinterpretation of individual boasting. In a Long Beach bar, a U.S. naval man, Chief Pharmacist's Mate John N. Andry, talked long and loud about his skill at cutting up bodies. The police were informed and Andry, aged 30, was taken into custody. There he sat back and calmly insisted that it was he who had killed "The Black Dahlia". Tripped up during interrogation, he said sulkily: "Well, I'm *capable* of doing it." Finally he admitted that he had just been "kidding". The police said that there was some suspicion that he had shortly been due for an unwanted draft overseas . . .

Men were not alone on this exhibitionistic roundabout. Back in San Diego, a tall young woman, formerly in the Women's Army Corps, walked into a police station and announced: "Elizabeth Short stole my man, so I killed her and cut her up." When she, too, stumbled over essential questions about the location and method of the murder, she agreed reluctantly that she had "made the whole story up". In Barstow, California, a bartender reported that a beefy woman customer had told him: "I know who killed Beth Short and if the reward is big enough, I'll talk." Two plainclothes men rushed out from Los Angeles to question the woman, a twelve stone brunette. She alleged that two of her men friends had been involved in the murder. They had since walked out on her; so, to get her own back, she had decided to "shoot off her mouth". Although her story was patently phoney, the detectives' journey was not wasted. They took her two friends back to Los Angeles with them and "booked" them as suspects – not for murder, but in connection with a car theft!

Such attempts to lay information for reasons of personal revenge – an unpleasant trick known to the police as a "roust" – were always treated with severity. At least three Los Angeles landlords will think carefully in future before worrying the Homicide Squad with their troubles. Each of them, soon after the murder, reported the actions of certain tenants as suspicious. And each landlord, it transpired, had been trying unsuccessfully to evict those particular tenants . . . A blonde dancer telephoned police headquarters one evening and, with an air of great secrecy, whispered: "I'm meeting a man at First and Temple Streets at nine o'clock and I've reason to believe he is the 'Black Dahlia' killer." Captain Donohue sent detectives to the rendezvous to arrest both the girl and her suspect. They found that the man was a harmless business executive, innocent of all knowledge of Elizabeth Short or her murder. He had met his accuser during the war, quite fortuitously: they had been placed in the same "share-the-ride" group – a patriotic wartime scheme to save petrol, under which car owners gave regular lifts to people along their route. She had "dogged, threatened and slightly blackmailed" him ever since. His temporary arrest was a blessing in disguise; the blonde dancer is most unlikely to pester him again.

The task of sorting out the false confessions, "rousts" and other misinformation fell mainly on two veteran Homicide detectives, Harry Hansen and Finis Brown. "Most of them were exhibitionists and publicity seekers," Lieutenant Hansen said. "One man who confessed eventually admitted that he had done so because he and his wife had separated and he could not find her. He thought that, if he confessed, he would get his picture in the papers." It must have been hard to raise a laugh, yet the flood of strange tip-offs and offers of outside assistance, made for whatever reasons, sometimes had its amusing side – tragi-comic, anyway. The Homicide Squad men themselves figured in a typical incident. A few days after the murder, two of them were in a restaurant near police headquarters, discussing the case over coffee. They returned to their office at the very moment a frantic telephone call came through from somebody who thought he had just seen the killers. The caller proved to be a waiter in the restaurant. His "suspects"? The two detectives!

Another caller, telephoning with great anxiety from a public call-box, urged the police to pick up a man who had been sitting on the stool next to him in a nearby coffee shop. The informant explained: "I'm certain he's the murderer. He had an apprehensive look and ordered only a half-cup of coffee." One old lady walked five miles to tell the police that, if Elizabeth Short's body were buried with an egg in one hand – the way they did back in Alabama, the old lady's home State – the killer would be found within a week. An astrologer from the little town of Altadena, near Los Angeles, asked for the date and exact hour of Miss Short's birth, also promising (through the resultant astrological chart) to produce the murderer's name within a week. An amateur photographer, scorning both superstition and stars, requested the loan of the dead girl's right eyeball; he would photograph the last image reflected in it, he explained, and return with a picture of the killer.

Local drunks and petty criminals soon learned to turn the case to their own advantage. The former found that, by spinning a plausible yarn to suggest that they knew something about the murder, they could avoid, for a day or two, the discomfort of their regular cure in the city's "drunk tank". One habitual inebriate thought up an uproarious game; his system was to telephone the police from one bar, saying that he wanted to confess to the crime, then move on quickly to another bar from which he could see the fun – and then repeat the process all over again. He did it six times altogether before the overworked patrol car caught up with him. Public fear, meanwhile, made easy pickings for small-time footpads and hold-up men; where before some people might have resisted them, now all they had to do was to warn their women victims to keep quiet "or you'll get what the 'Black Dahlia' got."

Since it was always possible that one of these threats or

drunken jokes might provide a genuine lead, the police could never treat them at their face value. In December 1947, for instance, the Homicide men were informed – though it would not normally have concerned them – when a pretty, nineteen-year old wife, Mrs Helen Miller, complained that a man had scarred her with a knife. The man, Donald Graeff, aged twenty-eight, had offered her shelter when she was penniless, she said, but afterwards he had held her prisoner in his hotel room for a week. Two days before she escaped, she alleged, he had decided to brand her. He had thrown her on a bed and cut his initials in her hip with a sharp knife. Mrs Miller's story appeared to be true; police found three-inch letters carved deep into her flesh. Remembering the "B.D." cut in Elizabeth Short's thigh, they subjected Graeff to an intense grilling about the coincidence. On his treatment of Mrs Miller he admitted readily: "When I get drunk, I don't know what I'm doing." But on all questions concerning "The Black Dahlia", his denials were firm. He had been strangely imitative, hadn't he? Perhaps, but he hadn't consciously been so – and he still didn't know anything about the murder. For hours the questions kept coming; for hours he shook his head stubbornly. When at last the interrogation ground to a halt, it had failed to uncover a single direct link between Graeff and Elizabeth Short.

Slowly, as the months passed, the stream of "rousts" and busybodies began to dry up – but not the false confessions, although there were now long periods of quiescence. In September, 1950, police at Oakland, California, were suddenly reminded of the case by thirty-four-year-old Mrs Christine Reynolds. She committed the murder, Mrs Reynolds told them, when Elizabeth Short left her for the company of another woman. Because of this unpleasant new twist, her story took a few hours longer to disprove than most of the others.

The police were equally careful, though equally sceptical, when a man named Max Handler, also known as Mack Chandler, gave himself up to them only eleven days later. For among Miss Short's papers, they remembered, was the card of a company for which Handler had once worked. Moreover, Handler named two places to which he claimed to have accompanied the dead girl – and she was known to have been at both places. Once again, however, there was nothing to it.

Just how deeply the Dahlia killing has exerted its unholy grip is indicated by the fact that the 28th "confession" (and the last at the time of writing) came no fewer than nine years afterwards. The claimant, Ralph von Hiltz, a forty-four-year-old dishwasher, emerged in New York on January 5th, 1956. For a change, he did not announce himself as the culprit, but merely asserted that he had been a witness to the murder. Hiltz told detectives that he saw his friend kill Elizabeth Short and that afterwards he helped him to cut up her body. Unfortunately, most of the details he provided were at variance with those in the police dossier, and his friend's identity remains a mystery.

The cranks who tried to implicate themselves in the crime faced two big traps. The first, of course, was their ignorance of several basic facts. The second, known to few people outside the police, is that detectives have long had a good idea of the type of person actually responsible. And that, I can disclose, is not a man but a *woman*.

This theory was formed by Captain Donohue within two weeks of the murder. Although he could not be absolutely sure, and the male suspects were interrogated as thoroughly as ever, he was led to the belief that the killer was more likely to be a woman for a number of reasons. Primarily, the nature of the injuries – the peculiarly vicious spite with which they had been inflicted – pointed to the "deadlier of the species". Many of the wounds, Captain Donohue noted, were similar to those found in other mutilation murders in which jealous women had hacked their rivals to death.

Various points of circumstantial evidence supported his belief. Looking back over the case, it may be remembered that when Elizabeth Short left San Diego, she took no extra clothes or make-up with her – meaning, most probably, that she intended to stay with a woman friend who could lend her some. Who was the woman? The police never found out. Again, the two bartenders who reported serving drinks to her, a day or so before her death, both said that she was in the company of one or more women at the time.

Finally, might not the "intensely jealous" friend mentioned by former suspect Robert Manley – the one who, she had told him, had caused the scratches on her arms – have been a woman, too?

Whatever the murderer's sex, there can be little doubt that the principal motive for the crime was jealousy. The stories thought up by the few women who made false confessions – to the effect that "The Black Dahlia" was killed by a woman she had deserted or whose man she had stolen – may have been nearer the mark than their perpetrators imagined. But the police have not discounted another possibility. In certain details, there is a marked similarity between the Dahlia murder, and the unsolved sex killings which followed it, and the notorious "Jack the Ripper" killings in London towards the end of the last century. Among the innumerable legends about the Ripper, the only certain facts are that he had expert surgical knowledge and that his victim – six in three months – were all poor street walkers. As a result, the most widely accepted story is that he was a doctor, who launched his terrible campaign against that class of women because one of them had caused him (or, in the more fanciful version of the story, his son) some serious harm. In other words, he sought revenge against prostitutes as a whole and not merely against the specific individuals he happened to catch. Were Elizabeth Short and some of her fellow-victims caught in a similar vendetta? One or two of them were known prostitutes; others appear to have been enthusiastic amateurs. It is at least feasible that some person whose son had been ruined by such a woman might have wreaked indiscriminate vengeance on others of the same type. And that person, to return to Captain Donohue's theory, might well have been a woman herself . . .

The murder of "The Black Dahlia" remains unsolved. But even after this length of time, there are still grounds for believing that the killer may yet be found. The grounds are psychological – developing, strangely enough, from the string of false confessions. They were first expounded by Dr J. Paul de River, black-bearded staff psychiatrist of the Los Angeles police. In March, 1947, he told detectives that the confessions did not arise just from a lust for publicity, as they thought, but could spring from masochism, exhibitionism or a guilt complex engendered by some forgotten incident of childhood. He predicted, therefore: "The confessors will keep coming." As we know now, he was right. By the same token, Dr de River concluded, the type of mind which conceived the Dahlia murder "will one day have to boast about it". We can only hope that eventually he will prove to have been right about that, as well.

David Rowan

John Haigh:
The "Vampire Murderer"

The sensation caused by the Heath murders was eclipsed three years later by the case of the "vampire murderer" John George Haigh. On Sunday 20 February 1949, a man and a woman arrived at the Chelsea police station and explained that they wanted to report the disappearance of an elderly lady, Mrs Durand-Deacon, who was a fellow guest at the Onslow Court Hotel in South Kensington. The man – dapper and well-dressed, with a neat moustache – explained that he had arranged to meet Mrs Olivier Durand-Deacon two days earlier, to take her to his place of business in Sussex, but she failed to keep the appointment; now, with her friend Mrs Constance Lane, he had come to alert the police. When the police checked on him at the Criminal Records Office, they discovered that John Haigh had been in prison for swindling.

Crime reporters flocked to the Onslow Court Hotel, and Haigh gave a kind of impromptu press conference, emphasizing his own concern for the missing woman. But the West Sussex Constabulary was already looking at Haigh's "place of business", Hurstlea Products, at Crawley. He rented a two-storey brick-built storehouse from the firm, using it for "experimental work". The police broke in, and found a revolver, and a receipt for a Persian lamb coat from a firm of cleaners. The coat proved to belong to Mrs Durand-Deacon, and further enquiries revealed that her jewellery had been sold by Haigh to a jewellers in Horsham. Haigh was arrested and taken to the police station. At first he told obviously concocted lies about his relationship with Mrs Durand-Deacon, hinting at blackmail. Then he suddenly asked the police inspector what the chances were of anyone being released from Broadmoor, the criminal lunatic asylum.

Inspector Webb was non-committal. "Well", said Haigh, "if I told you the truth you wouldn't believe me . . . Mrs Durand-Deacon no longer exists . . . I have destroyed her with acid!" He gazed at the incredulous policeman with a bland smile. "How can you prove murder if there is no body?" Like many murderers, Haigh made the mistake of believing that the phrase *corpus delicti* means the corpse, without which murder cannot be proved; in fact, it means the body of the offence or crime. Fellow convicts who knew Haigh in his earlier days in Dartmoor had nicknamed him "old *corpus delicti*" because he liked to expound his view that a killer could not be convicted so long as there was no body.

Haigh added: "You'll find the sludge that remains at Leopold Road [Crawley]. I did the same with the Hendersons and the McSwanns."

Haigh had decided that his best means of escaping justice was a defence of insanity; he continued to pursue this objective by telling the police that the motive for the killings had been a desire to drink the blood of his victims; he had an insatiable lust for blood, and after each murder, filled a glass with his victim's blood and drained it. (In fact, blood is an emetic, and a glassful would undoubtedly have made him vomit.)

Haigh had embarked on his career of mass murder with the deliberation of a businessman. After a number of spells in jail for petty fraud, he decided that the best way to avoid being caught was to kill his victims and dispose of their bodies. In 1936 he had been employed by an amusement arcade owner named McSwann; after coming out of prison in 1943, he had met their son Donald again, and proposed a business partnership. Donald was lured to Haigh's basement "workshop" at Gloucester Road in September 1944 and bludgeoned to death; then Haigh dissolved his body in a vat of concentrated sulphuric acid – he had already experimented on mice in the prison workshop and decided that this was the perfect method of destroying corpses. He emptied the "sludge" down the drain. McSwann's parents were told he had gone off to Scotland on business. Ten months later, the elder McSwanns were lured separately to the basement and disposed of in the same way. Haigh then disposed of their considerable property, forging the necessary documents, for about £4,000.

By September 1947, Haigh had spent the £4,000, and looked around for more victims. He saw an advertisement for a house, and introduced himself to its owners, Archie and Rose Henderson, and offered them £10,500 for it. The deal "fell through", but Haigh continued to see the Hendersons, posing as a rich businessman. On 12 February 1948, Archie Henderson accompanied Haigh to his "workshop" at Leopold Road, Crawley, and was shot in the back of the head. Haigh then went and collected Rose Henderson, telling her that her husband was ill, and killed her in the same way. Various letters were despatched to relatives of the dead couple, explaining that they had been close to a "bust-up", and were travelling while their relationship was repaired. Haigh forged these letters so expertly that all suspicion was finally allayed. Then he disposed of their property, collecting some £7,700.

Other possible victims – including the widow of a Wakefield business-man – slipped through the net. By February 1949, Haigh was again in debt, and realized that he had to find a victim within the next week or so. To Mrs Durand-Deacon, who always dined at the next table at the Onslow Court Hotel, Haigh suggested a business deal involving the manufacture of plastic fingernails. And on 18 February 1949, Mrs Durand-Deacon made her fatal visit to the Crawley workshop. Twelve days later, on 2 March, Haigh was charged with her murder.

When Professor Keith Simpson travelled down to the Crawley workshop on 1 March, he had little hope of finding evidence of murder; Haigh had already told the police that he had poured the "sludge" over the ground several days earlier. The sludge was lying on an area of ground about six feet by four, and was about three inches deep. Simpson was staring intently at this sludge when he exclaimed: "Aha, gall-stones." He had seen an object about the size of a cherry, lying among some pebbles that were, to the inexpert eye, indistinguishable from it. After this find, the police carefully shovelled the sludge into boxes, to be removed to the Scotland Yard laboratory. There it was searched by spreading it thinly in steel trays; because the acid was so strong, the searchers had to wear rubber gloves. But the effort was worthwhile: the sludge proved to contain a partially dissolved left foot, and intact upper plastic denture, a lower denture, three gall-stones (easy to distinguish at close quarters by their facets), 28 lb of greasy substance, 18 fragments of human bone, the handle of a red plastic handbag and a lipstick container. Haigh had left more than enough of Mrs Durand-Deacon to hang him.

Simpson took the bones to his laboratory at Guy's. He discovered the presence of osteo-arthritis in some of the joints – Mrs Durand-Deacon suffered from osteo-arthritis – and was able to identify most of the bone fragments as human. Meanwhile, the police had made a plaster cast of the left foot, and checked it against Mrs Durand-Deacon's left shoe; the fit was perfect. The plastic dentures were identified by Mrs Durand-Deacon's dental surgeon as having been supplied to her two years earlier. Haigh had no way of knowing that the false teeth were of plastic, and therefore would not dissolve in acid, nor of knowing the gall-stones cannot be dissolved in acid.

Bloodstains found on the whitewash of the storeroom were tested and found to be human. Bloodstains were also found on the Persian lamb coat, and on the cuff of one of Haigh's shirts. The handbag strap was identified as belonging to the handbag Mrs Durand-Deacon had carried when she drove with Haigh down to Crawley.

Haigh's major mistake had been in confessing to the murders, and trusting to a defence of insanity. If he had said nothing about the "acid bath", the sludge might not have been examined for many weeks, and Simpson later admitted that by that time, the acid might have consumed everything but the gall-stones and the human fat. And in themselves, these would not have constituted sufficient evidence of identity.

In prison, Haigh continued to build up the notion that he was insane, claiming that there had been three more victims – all penniless – whom he had killed for their blood alone. He explained that the urge to drink blood developed after an accident with a lorry in 1944, when his car overturned. After this, he said, he began to have a recurrent dream of a forest of crucifixes which turned into trees that dripped blood . . . He also claimed that the murders were divinely inspired. When aware of being observed, he drank his own urine.

All this was useless. A number of doctors and psychiatrists examined Haigh, and all but one concluded that he was perfectly sane. A woman friend who visited him in prison observed that he was playing the role of mass murderer with tremendous gusto, delighting in his belated "fame". The newspapers were full of accounts of the "vampire murderer" – probably no case of the century has received so much publicity – and one of them, the *Daily Mirror*, went too far and was fined £10,000, while its editor was sentenced to three months in prison. But at the trial, which began on 18 July 1949 at Lewes Assizes, all the evidence revealed Haigh as a calculating killer who had murdered for gain, and who was shamming insanity. Dr Henry Yellowlees, for the defence, argued that Haigh was genuinely paranoid, but the jury was so unimpressed that they took only 15 minutes to bring in a guilty verdict. Haigh was executed at Wandsworth on 6 August 1949.

Simpson, who was responsible for the medical evidence that convicted Haigh, later commented on the absurdly small profits that Haigh had made from five years of murder – a mere £12,000. The last murder, of Mrs Durand-Deacon, would have brought him only about £150 for the coat and the jewellery. He could have made more money in almost any honest occupation.

Keith Simpson died in 1985, at the age of 78. Like Spilsbury, he was inclined to overwork, and his publisher J. H. H. Gaute remarked in an obituary that this was the cause of his death. But his enthusiasm for his gruesome occupation was so great that he was unable to stay away from the morgue and the "path lab". Gaute recalls how, after lunching with Simpson at Guy's, Simpson asked him if he would like to come down to the mortuary, and seemed surprised when the publisher declined. "Not the keen type, eh?" he remarked drily.

The present writer did not decline a similar invitation,

and was taken into the mortuary to view the body of a male child of about 7, who had – according to a teenage baby-sitter – died after a fall downstairs. Simpson expertly opened the body in a few minutes, then, as if he knew exactly what he was looking for, plunged in his hand and drew out the liver, which was broken in half. "That wasn't caused by a fall downstairs. It's an impossibility. He must have been kicked in the stomach." Since the baby-sitter had been alone with the child at the time of the "accident", the evidence suggested that he was the culprit. I never found out the sequel to the story. But I retained the impression that Simpson had known intuitively that he was looking at a case of murder.

Colin Wilson

AFTERWORD

The crime writer Nigel Morland once told me that he had received a phone call from someone who gave his name as "Hay", and who enquired about how long it would take to dissolve a body in acid; Morland told me that Haigh pronounced his name "Hay."

For me, perhaps the most interesting story about Haigh is told by Blanche Patch, who was Bernard Shaw's secretary. Shaw and Miss Patch were eating a meal in the Onslow Court Hotel, and a child in the dining room was being a nuisance. The man at the next table – whom Blanche Patch later recognised as Haigh – suddenly snarled: "If that child doesn't shut up I'll murder him." At this, Shaw told Miss Patch: "That man is going to be hanged one day." I would like to think that this indicated some profound psychological intuition on Shaw's part, but the truth is probably that Shaw was simply reacting to Haigh's sudden loss of control, and his remark indicated distaste rather than precognition.

The Lonely Hearts Murders

The Lonely Hearts murder case caused an understandable sensation at the time; Ray Fernandez and Martha Beck were regarded as inhuman monsters. I was always fascinated by the case because it involved the syndrome psychologists call "folie a deux" – and because this so often reveals an interesting pattern of dominance of one character by the other. It was the psychologist Abraham Maslow who discovered that all human beings fall into one of three "dominance groups" – high, medium and low. He preferred to study women – because he thought they were more truthful than men – and concluded that the female high dominance group is always 5% of the total – one in twenty. High dominance women tended to be highly promiscuous, often had experience of lesbianism (without necessarily being lesbians), and were only interested in high dominance males who liked fairly rough sex. (Interestingly enough, even for high dominance females, the male had to be slightly more dominant than she was.) Medium dominance women, the largest group, were basically "one man women", who liked the kind of lover who wooed them with soft lights and flowers. Low dominance women disliked sex and thought the male organ downright ugly (high dominance women thought it beautiful; medium dominance women didn't take either view.)

What I found interesting was that both men and women usually preferred long term sexual relations with someone in their own dominance group. But sometimes, a high dominance character and a medium dominance character became involved by chance, and then there was potential for a violent explosion.

In such circumstances, the dominant partner often seems to be carried away by a recklessness that is based upon the joy of ego-assertion, and is prepared to commit acts of which he would be incapable alone. Leopold and Loeb, the homosexual killers of the 1920s, were such a mixture, Leopold referring to himself as Loeb's "slave". Ian Brady and Myra Hindley, the "moors murderers", were another example in which the male exercised almost hypnotic dominance. When I first wrote about them, Fernandez and Beck struck me as another example, except that, oddly enough, Martha Beck seemed to me the dominant partner.

When asked to write up the case for a partwork called *Murder Casebook* (on which the following account is based), I changed my mind; closer study of the case made it clear that Fernandez was the dominant partner, and that he was changed from a medium-dominance and basically honest person into a high-dominance crook by a head injury. Blows on the head often seem to play an important part in criminality; others who developed criminal tendencies after a head wound were Earle Nelson, the "gorilla murderer", Albert Fish, the American child killer, Alfred Rouse, the burning car murderer, Henry Lee Lucas, the serial killer, and a Chinese man called Lock Ah Tam, who can be found in the *Encyclopedia of Murder*. It is worth commenting, in parenthesis, that the painter Augustus John was a second rate artist until he dived into the sea and smashed his skull on a rock; from then on he became a painter of genius.

But there are, I think, few cases in which a violent blow on the head produced such bizarre and unexpected results as in that which follows.

* * *

It was a head injury that turned Raymond Fernandez into a monster. The accident happened at sea in December 1945; a falling hatch struck him on the forehead with such force that it made a dent in his skull. He spent four months in hospital, and it was later revealed that his brain tissue had been scarred. Before that, Raymond Fernandez had been a mild, unaggressive character, a hard worker and a faithful husband. The accident turned him into a criminal and a sex maniac.

Not that Fernandez was a sex criminal in the usual sense – even after the accident he would have been incapable of trying to take a woman by force. But he suddenly became possessed of such an overwhelming sexual urge that his only aim in life was to seduce women. It made no difference if they were young and attractive or middle aged and overweight. Anything female aroused his lust. He later estimated that in the next two years he seduced over a hundred women.

But first he spent time in jail for a minor offense whose irrationality baffled the court. In Mobile, Alabama, he tried to walk through customs with a huge packet of soiled linen, all marked with government stamps. It was worthless anyway – with luck he might have received a dollar for the lot. Pleading guilty to attempted theft, he was sentenced to a year in the prison in Tallahassee, Florida. And here occurred another event that was to exercise a baleful influence on his life. There were large numbers of West Indians in the jail, and much talk of voodoo and black magic. Fernandez was fascinated – particularly by tales about hypnotism. He became convinced that he possessed magical powers, and in order to test them out, wrote a letter to the judge who had sentenced him, complaining that his punishment had been too severe. Then he spent days concentrating on the judge, and trying to influence him by a kind of distant hypnosis. Incredibly, it worked. When the judge asked for guidance on the case, court officials agreed that there *was* room for leniency; they had advised Fernandez not to secure himself a council, thus depriving him of skilled advice. The judge decided to cut the sentence to six months. To Raymond Fernandez, this was a revelation. If he could infuence people from a distance, nothing was impossible. He could become rich and famous. Or, more important, have all the women he wanted . . .

Raymond Fernandez was born of Spanish parents in Hawaii in December 1914; his father was a labourer, and he treated his children harshly. Raymond, who was small and weak, was never a favourite. When his father began running a farm in Connecticut, the boy was always given the most unpleasant tasks. Raymond was highly intelligent – a later test showed that his I.Q.was 135, near genius-level; but his father refused to allow him to go to college. At sixteen, anxious to provide the family with a bird for Thanksgiving, he and two friends stole some chickens. They were caught red handed. The fathers of the other two boys offered sureties for their future good conduct; Raymond's father refused, and he went to prison for two months.

During the American depression of the '30s the family moved back to Spain; Fernandez senior became a successful businessman and mayor of the town. At the age of twenty, Raymond married, and went on to father four children. During the Second World War, he went to Gibraltar, where he worked as an ice cream vendor, picking up information for British intelligence. Many writers on the case have assumed that Fernandez's stories of being a spy were pure invention; in fact, they were confirmed by his biographer Wenzell Brown.

At the end of the war, Fernandez decided to return to America to seek his fortune. But on the voyage, he was struck on the head by the falling hatch, and his whole life changed . . .

Back in New York Fernandez went to stay with relatives. They found the change incomprehensible. The Raymond Fernandez they had known had been a shy, reserved young man with impeccable manners. This hollow-cheeked, balding man boasted and ranted like a madman, always dwelling on his favourite subjects – magic and hypnotism.

And now it was time, he felt, to put his newly-discovered powers into operation. According to the doctrines of voodoo, all he needed was some small item belonging to any woman

– a lock of hair, a fragment of clothing, even a letter – to entangle her in a web of magical desire. New York was full of potential conquests – lonely middle aged women hoping to find romance. Many of them belonged to the "Lonely Hearts Clubs" that advertised in cheap magazines, and from one of these, Mother Dinene's Friendly Club, Fernandez obtained a list of addresses.

Most of the replies that poured in were gushingly sentimental – these women were crying out to be seduced. And Fernandez was well equipped to do it. The child of Spanish parents, he had an old world courtesy combined with charm and self-confidence. At the age of thirty-one, he was far from unattractive, being tall and thin, with a gaunt face and dark eyes – some pictures make him look rather like Henry Fonda. With a toupee covering the scar on his forehead, he was a highly presentable male. And even if he had lacked these advantages, the man-shortage in post-war America would have made up for it (there were one and a quarter million more women than males.) Soon he was writing to several women at the same time. Most of them fell in love with him at the first sight, and many of them – even respectable matrons – allowed him to make love to them at their first meeting. Fernandez, of course, attributed all this to his hypnotic gaze (and he may not have been entirely wrong). His sexual appetite was omnivorous: old women, young women, thin women, fat women, rich women, poor women – he even seduced a woman who was badly deformed. In cases where the lady proved more difficult, he performed various occult rituals, such as scattering his letters with a magic powder (bought at a Jamaican shop in Harlem) and putting spells on dolls. Few women resisted for long. He was soon having affairs with a dozen at the same time – his average turnover was one a week. The sheer complexity of such an existence would have deterred most Romeos. Fernandez seemed to be driven by some obsessive compulsion, a desire to prove something.

He soon discovered that there were concealed benefits in the life of a sex maniac. Many of the women were well off, and they were anxious to press money on him. It seems fairly clear that obtaining cash was not a part of his original intention. But since it was freely offered, it seemed absurd to refuse it. And since his life was so complicated it was obviously impossible for him to bestow himself completely on any one of his mistresses. If the lady had no money, he stayed a few days. If she was rich and generous, he might stay a week or so. But his compulsion forced him to keep moving on.

In the late spring of 1947, he embarked on one of his longer affairs. The lady was a middle-aged cook named Jane Lucilla Thompson, and she lived with her mother in a large apartment on West 139th Street. She also had a few boarders, and Fernandez soon left his sister's home in Brooklyn to move in with her. By August they had decided to take a holiday in Spain. They sailed in October, travelling as man and wife, then visited Madrid, Granada, and Malaga, with Fernandez acting as guide to his own country – for although he had been born in Hawaii, he had spent most of his adult life in Spain. In fact, he had acquired himself a wife there, a girl named Encarnacion, and she had presented him with four children. Driven by the strange irrationality that had made him steal the soiled linen, he now visited La Linea, where his family – and his wife's family – were living, and actually introduced his wife to his latest mistress. It is not known how he succeeded in persuading the two women to be polite to one another – as they were for several days. But a point came where Lucilla Thompson felt that she was sharing her "husband". Or possibly Encarnacion revealed that Fernandez was *her* husband. For whatever reason, on the evening of November 7, 1947, Lucilla Thompson exploded – servants later described her screaming at Fernandez – and undoubtedly threatened to return to America alone. Since she had been footing all the bills, this would have caused her gigolo severe inconvenience. But the crisis was averted, for the next morning, Lucilla Thompson was found dead in her room. The local doctor diagnosed a heart attack brought on by gastro-enteritis. Since there were no suspicious circumstances attached to her death, Fernandez was allowed to leave town the next day.

A few months later the police of La Linea received a disturbing communication via the American Consulate. An

English lady named White had reported her suspicion that Mrs Thompson had been murdered. She had met her on board ship, and noted that her "husband" was many years her junior, and that he seemed to want to prevent her from talking with other passengers. She suspected that his interest in Lucilla was purely financial. Mrs White and Mrs Thompson had subsequently kept in touch by letter, and when Mrs White heard of her friend's death, she was shocked and suspicious. The police of La Linea soon discovered that Fernandez had purchased a bottle of digitalis from the hotel pharmacy two days before Mrs Thompson's death, and it was found, half empty, in her medicine cupboard. This would certainly have caused symptoms like those from which she died. Unfortuntely, it was now too late for an autopsy; the body proved to be too badly decomposed.

Meanwhile, Fernandez had hurried to Lucilla Thompson's New York apartment, and presented her mother, Mrs Pearl Wilson, with a document that made made him sole heir to Mrs Thompson's property. The feeble old lady was too shattered by her daughter's death to object; besides, Fernandez told her she was welcome to stay on. A closer examination would have revealed that the "will" was a forgery; it later became clear that Fernandez had simply obtained Lucilla's signature on two sheets of blank paper, then filled them in to make himself her legatee.

Now once again Raymond Fernandez took up his career of seducing lonely widows and divorcees whose addresses had been provided by Mother Dinene. His attention was immediately drawn to one woman who was far younger than the rest – a mere twenty-six. Moreover, she held a responsible position as the superintendent of the Pensacola Crippled Children's Home in Florida, and apparently had her own apartment. She sounded ideal. Her name was Martha Seabrook Beck. Fernandez lost no time in sending her a telegram announcing his imminent arrival.

Martha Beck's childhood had been even more difficult than Raymond's. She was the first child of a highly dominant mother, with whom she spent much of her life quarelling. Her mother went on to marry a man named Holland Seabrook, and Martha adopted his surname. She was born in Florida in

1920, and from the beginning had a deep attachment to her strong-willed mother; her feelings veered between love and hatred. She was a sullen child, overweight and either ignored or disliked. Other children tormented her. At the age of nine her breasts began to develop, and older men began making passes at her. Her glandular disorder filled her with violent sexual cravings, but her mother's watchful eye made any gratification impossible. At the age of twenty-two she passed her nursing exams, but failed to find a job – her physical appearance was against her. Eventually, she went to work for a local mortician, washing and laying out bodies. She spent all her spare time devouring cheap romantic magazines. Sheer frustration brought her to the edge of nervous breakdown, and she decided to get away to California. There she found employment in a large hospital. She also found sexual gratification – of a sort – picking up men around bus stations. One of these, a bus driver, made her pregnant. She pressed for marriage, and he reluctantly agreed. When he tried to drown himself, Martha was shattered, and had a nervous breakdown with amnesia. She decided to go back to Florida, where her mother was living in Pensacola; there she told everyone that she had married a naval officer named Joe. When she announced that he had been killed in action, all her acquaintances were deeply sympathetic; after the birth of her baby she obtained a job in the local hospital. (Later investigation revealed that the marriage was a figment of her imagination.) She met a local bus driver named Alfred Beck, and soon persuaded him into marriage. By May 1945, after less than six months, she was filing a suit for divorce. Now pregnant for a second time, she obtained a job in the Crippled Children's Home in Pensacola. Six months later, she was appointed superintendent.

Her major problem was her immense sexual appetite. Moreover, normal sexual intercourse gave her little pleasure; she needed a man who was rough and demanding. She began going to parties and drinking heavily. At this early stage, the home had no suspicion that its superintendent was a nymphomaniac who was fast becoming an alcoholic.

Then, in November 1947, an acquaintance from her schooldays played a cruel practical joke: he replied to a

Lonely Hearts Club in her name. Her first response was to burst into tears. Then she decided to forget caution and write an application . . .

Fernandez's first sight of Martha Beck was something of a shock. To describe her as fat would have been an understatement. She was positively gross. But Raymond Fernandez had never yet failed to provide satisfaction. Besides, she might be rich. Showing no sign of his lack of enthusiasm, he accompanied her back to her apartment, and sat down to an elaborate meal. Neither was he alarmed to discover that she had two children, and had been married twice. And when they retired to bed he was in for another surprise. The gross-looking nurse responded with immense passion. What was more important, she displayed no aversion to some of the minor sexual abnormalities that Fernandez had developed of recent years – and which many of his more demure conquests had found unutterably indecent. Full details of their sex life – which emerged during their trial – have never been published, since they were regarded as too vile. In our less inhibited age, it is probably safe to say that they amounted to bondage, sodomy, oral sex, and simple variations on these three. What we *do* know is that Martha Beck not only consented to these experiments, but suggested a few of her own. Fernandez, accustomed to prudish American ladies, and to even more prudish Spanish ones, found it an incredible experience. Each of them ended that night in a state of total sexual exhaustion.

Yet for the seducer of more than a hundred women, alarm bells were ringing. It was obvious that Martha Beck was madly in love; she felt that her good fairy had at last provided her with something she had craved all her life: a truly romantic lover. As she assured him of her undying devotion, he inwardly cringed. This one was going to be difficult to get rid of. Moreover, she was obviously as poor as he was. So after two days, he made flowery and regretful farewell speeches, and fled back to New York. The lovelorn Martha bombarded him with adoring letters, but recieved no reply. Then, one day, she received a letter with his writing on the envelope; she tore it open ecstatically. But she found what he had to say was shattering and unbelievable. She had, he assured her, mistaken his feelings for her, which were of deep respect rather than passion. They must never see one another again.

Martha escorted her children to a neighbour's house, then put her head in the gas oven. But the neighbour had noticed her distraught state, and went to investigate; when she smelled gas, she called the police. A farewell note to Ray Fernandez was lying beside her. A few days later, Fernandez received it in the post, together with a letter describing the suicide attempt. And either from motives of remorse or of prudence – at the prospect of being involved in a scandal which might alert other prospective victims – he lost no time in writing her an affectionate letter, inviting her to New York. Martha paused only to obtain a two week's leave of absence from the children's home, then caught the next train.

For Martha the next two weeks were a dream of bliss. Fernandez seemed cool, but she realised that she had to win him all over again; she cooked him huge meals, ironed his shirts and cleaned the flat. She slept in Lucilla's old bedroom; but since Fernandez experienced powerful and abnormal sexual urges several times a day, their love life was soon as passionate as ever. Yet even the insatiable Spaniard was beginning to realise that sex was not everything. He simply did not want to be tied down. So when he finally waved goodbye to the train, he heaved a sigh of relief.

Back in Pensacola, Martha had a shock awaiting her. She was told that she was fired from the crippled children's home. No reasons were given, but it was obvious that in a place as small as Pensacola, news of her torrid liaison was causing scandal. She had been fired from a previous job in a maternity hospital for promiscuity. Martha railed at the injustice, then set out to cause a scandal by taking her case to the local newspapers. The attempt backfired; it only guaranteed that she would find no other work as a nurse in Florida. Now there was only one thing to do: move in on Raymond, complete with children.

Fernandez was stunned to find her on his doorstep. He needed freedom for his complicated love life – a love life that was now his sole means of livelihood. He began by telling her sternly that he could not accept the children. Martha found this shattering, but knew she had to give in. With the aid of the Welfare Department, her mother was persuaded to take charge of the children. Martha never saw them again, nor showed any inclination to do so.

As on the previous occasion, she strove to make herself useful. It was Martha who sternly told the bewildered old lady that she would have to move, since Fernandez intended to sell the apartment. She was sent off to live with one of her sons. And now they were alone in the place, Fernandez decided to play for all or nothing. He told Martha frankly that he could not marry her, because he made his living by seducing middle aged women, and she would cramp his style.

It would be untrue to say that Martha did not turn a hair – she was deeply shocked. But her passion was so deep that it finally made no difference. He was her man, her hero, her god – a man who could seduce women from a distance by hypnosis. What did it matter if he was a petty crook? She could never leave him. The feelings of the trapped gigolo are not recorded. But since he was basically a far weaker character than Martha, he conceded defeat.

The next victim on the list was a retired teacher named Mrs Esther Henne of Pennnsylvania. Fernandez had already met her when she was on holiday in New York. Now he arrived at her home with a proposal of marriage. Yet even on a mission as delicate as this, Martha was too jealous to allow him to go alone. She was introduced to Mrs Henne as Fernandez's sister in law, and she drove down with them – in Mrs Henne's car – to Fairfax, Virginia, where they were married, then back to the New York apartment. Now Raymond applied himself to the main part of the enterprise, parting her from her cash and property. But Mrs Henne proved to be cautious and hard-headed. When she declined to sign over her insurance policies and pension fund, Fernandez ceased to be an attentive husband, and became rude and irritable. He succeeded in obtaining possession of her car and extracting five hundred dollars. By then, Mrs Henne had heard rumours from other tenants in the block about the sudden death of his previous "wife" in Spain; she lost no time in hurrying back to

Pennsylvania. She even instituted legal proceedings against him, and succeeded in recovering her car and three hundred dollars.

Fernandez was already finding life difficult. One of his mistresses was pregnant and wanted him to marry her. He decided to sell the apartment and go in search of fresh dupes. One of these – supplied by the Lonely Hearts Club – was a lady named Myrtle Young, of Greene Forest, Arkansas. When Fernandez arrived with his "sister in law" in Arkansas, Mrs Young was swept off her feet, and lost no time in accepting his proposal of marriage. But during their honeymoon – in a cheap Chicago rooming house – she became increasingly impatient as Raymond failed to consummate their marriage. The jealous Martha was doing everything to prevent it from happening. On the third day, the new Mrs Fernandez announced that either Martha should go or she would. The result was a screaming row that ended with Martha persuading Myrtle Young to swallow a sleeping draught of barbiturates. And since they now had four thousand dollars of her money, and no further use for her, they put her on a bus for Little Rock, Arkansas. On the journey, the groggy Mrs Young collapsed, and had to be taken into hospital, where she died. Her death was ascribed to a cerebral haemorrhage.

It was becoming plain to Fernandez that Martha was something of a jinx. Their next enterprise confirmed this view. The "mark" was a young and relatively rich woman in New England, and she succumbed readily to the Fernandez brand of Spanish courtesy. Unfortunately, she found his sister in law intolerable. Martha had quickly recognised that Fernandez found his new conquest attractive and suspected that he was wondering whether it might be time to settle down. Martha displayed such jealousy that Fernandez lost his temper and gave her a beating. Finally, cowed and contrite, Martha agreed to go away and visit relatives. But by now the wealthy lady had seen through Fernandez and told him to go away. Back in a newly rented apartment in Queens, Raymond could no longer stand the loneliness, and sent for Martha. She was there as soon as he beckoned.

* * *

It was a gloomy Christmas. The money they had obtained from Myrtle Young was almost finished. But at least there was a new quarry in sight. She was a sixty-six-year-old widow from Albany, New York, named Janet Fay. She belonged to many Lonely Hearts Clubs and kept up a wide correspondence. She was a Catholic, and her letters were full of religious sentiments. When a correspondent who called himself Charles Martin told her that he was also a Catholic, she entered enthusiastically into religious discussions. And when he proposed to come and visit her, she lost no time in extending a warm invitation.

On New Year's day, 1948, "Charles Martin" arrived at Mrs Fay's small apartment in Albany, together with a large woman whom he introduced as his sister. He began by explaining that he had lost his wallet in the course of the New Year's Eve celebrations, and would be grateful if they could stay there until he could send for more. In fact, Fernandez and Beck were penniless. They *had* to make this con-trick successful.

Mrs Fay was delighted with her religious pen-pal. Three days later, she was so much under the spell of the thoughtful and charming Spaniard that she agreed to marry him. The following morning, they visited various banks and Mrs Fay drew out six thousand dollars. Then they all drove back to New York, in the car that had belonged to Myrtle Young, and to a new apartment on Long Island.

The marriage was to take place almost immediately; meanwhile, Raymond suggested a delightful way of informing her relatives. They would receive sheets of paper containing the word "Surprise!", with Mrs Fay's signature. Mrs Fay not only signed the papers, but also two blank cheques. Her trust in Charles was total.

That night, apparently, she began to suspect it was misplaced. This was not due to any oversight on the part of Raymond Fernandez, but to Martha's jealousy. Mrs Fay and Martha slept in the same bed, and Mrs Fay plied her future sister in law with probing questions about her fiancé's childhood. Martha grew taciturn, then angry. And when Mrs Fay lost her temper and told her that after the marriage she and Charles were going to live alone, Martha realised that she was jinxing their latest swindle. Mrs Fay stormed out of the bedroom – in a pink chenille bath robe – and woke Charles, to explain her grievances. She was obviously hoping to persuade him that his sister had to leave in the morning. Before the discussion could reach that stage, Mrs Fay was knocked unconscious by a hammer wielded by Martha Beck.

Typically, Fernandez was thrown into a state of panic – so much so that he suggested calling the police. At which point, Martha knelt beside Mrs Fay and announced: "She's dead."

Mrs Fay was bleeding all over the carpet. Numbed with shock, Fernandez helped Martha to clean up the blood and bind a towel round the dead woman's head to stop further bleeding. When there was time for calm discussion, Martha admitted that she had struck Mrs Fay out of sheer jealousy. But that was now an academic point. How could they dispose of the body?

They devised an answer that has suggested itself to many murderers. The next day they purchased a large trunk, and Raymond's sister was persuaded to allow them to store it for a few days in her basement in Astoria. Then came a frantic search for a more permanent disposal site. Eight days later they found a house in Queens. The trunk was transported there in a jeep, and lowered into a hole in the cellar. When it was cemented over, and dust rubbed into the surface, the grave was indistinguishable from the rest of the floor. They then told the agent that the house would not be suitable after all, and left without demanding a return of their advance rent.

With such a traumatic experience behind them, it might be supposed that the homicidal lovers would think twice before embarking on another scheme of a similar nature. In fact, Fernandez's conviction of his magical powers probably sustained him. On the day of Mrs Fay's murder, he had received a letter from another likely prospect, a forty-one-year-old widow named Delphine Downing, who lived in Grand Rapids, Michigan. And although Martha was in favour of relaxing for a while on their ill-gotten gains – they had even gone back to Mrs Fay's home and stripped it bare – he was now ready for fresh adventures. Or perhaps he simply liked the idea of moving as far away as Michigan.

Delphine Downing was a young widow with an infant daughter; her husband, a war hero, had been killed in a railway accident two years earlier, just before the birth of Rainelle. When "Charles" arrived on her doorstep with his sister, she made him welcome. He was grave, thoughtful and good-looking – as well as being nearly a decade younger than she was. She even liked his sister Martha, who struck her as "loads of fun". When Charles and Martha moved in, Delphine Downing told her neighbours that Martha was the nurse who had delivered her baby.

Raymond was getting tired of not being allowed to have sex with his conquests, and he was determined that this rather attractive woman would be the exception. He told Martha so sternly, and she sullenly agreed – after all, her last fit of jealousy had cost them a great deal of inconvenience. Within days, Raymond was sleeping with Delphine, and Martha was doing her best to hide her misery and rage.

Martha's later story of what led to the murder seems somehow inadequate. She claims that Delphine walked into Raymond's room and discovered him without his wig. This led to accusations of deceit and quarrels. The story seems unlikely – a woman in love does not quarrel with a new lover because he has thinning hair. The truth is probably that Fernandez and Beck decided to kill Delphine Downing for her house and her bank account. It is also possible that it was Martha who killed her, as she killed Mrs Fay, out of an uncontrollable jealousy which erupted when Delphine Downing confessed that she thought she was pregnant. The stories they told later were understandably designed to make the crime seem less horrific.

All that seems fairly certain is that on the morning of Sunday February 27, 1949, Martha offered her rival some pills to bring about an abortion; they were actually sleeping tablets. Then, when she was in a deep stupor, Raymond Fernandez wrapped a blanket round her head, and shot her with a service pistol that had belonged to her husband.

As soon as he had done so, his nerve went. The truth was that, in spite of the things he had done, Ray Fernandez was not a bad man. Now he was sickened and demoralised by what he had done. It was Martha, the efficient nurse, who had so often laid out corpses, who thrust him aside and took over the operation. She began by tying the blanket round Delphine's head to prevent further bloodstaining, then ordered Fernandez to take the shoulders while she took the feet, and help her carry the body down to the cellar. The rest of the day was spent burying the body and cementing it over. The fact that the cement was already in the basement suggests that the murder had been planned well in advance. Then, in the evening, they went to call on neighbours with whom they had become acquainted, and explained that Mrs Downing had been called away to see a sick relative, and that they were staying in the house and looking after the child.

They spent the following day preparing to leave, and having minor repairs made on their car. It was their intention to take Rainelle back to New York – although what they then intended to do with her is not clear. But Rainelle cried incessantly. It was Fernandez who announced that she would have to be killed. At first Martha objected; but she had become accustomed to obeying her lover, and finally agreed. She carried Rainelle over to a large washtub of water – which had been bailed out of Delphine Downing's grave – and immersed the child's head. After that they dug another grave, buried Rainelle, and cemented her over.

Back upstairs, more neighbours dropped in, and were told about the planned departure – which was fairly obvious, since a car with a large trailer was standing outside the door. They left an hour later, apparently convinced by the story they had been told. In fact, they were deeply suspicious. It seemed unlikely that a woman would leave her home – and child – in the hands of strangers. And they found Fernandez's story about being a wealthy businessman highly improbable – he simply didn't look the part. That evening, Ray and Martha went to the cinema. They had only just returned home when the doorbell rang. It was the police, asking questions about Delphine Downing and her daughter. When the couple repeated the story of a sick relative, they politely insisted on searching the house. Deputy Sheriff Clarence Randle had a hunch that the bodies would be buried in the basement, and when he saw the damp cement, he knew he was correct. Within hours, Delphine and Rainelle Downing had been exhumed.

At the police station, Fernandez seemed relieved to confess. The next morning, headlines all over the country announced the arrest of the "Lonely Hearts Killers". Mrs Fay's step-daughter saw them, and suddenly knew with horrible certainty what had happened to Janet Fay. Police soon traced the house in Queens, and found the cemented grave in the basement. When news of the arrest reached La Linea, in Spain, the police re-opened the question of the death of Lucilla Thompson.

The story of how Rainelle had been drowned like a kitten shocked America; Fernandez and Beck were labelled "America's most hated killers". This repugnance was so strong that it even affected the Michigan judiciary. Michigan had no capital punishment; New York had. So when Michigan decided to hand the killers over to New York, it was with the proviso that if they were not sentenced to death, they should be handed back.

There was little chance of that happening. If the lovers had been sentenced to life imprisonment, lynch mobs would probably have broken into the jail. It was leaked to the press that the police were investigating the possibility of twenty murders, but all the law had to do was to prove one of them: that of Janet Fay.

The defense – conducted by attorney Herbert Rosenberg – was hardly convincing: that Martha was insane, and that Fernandez had no foreknowledge that Martha would kill Mrs Fay. It would have been far more plausible to argue that Fernandez had been insane ever since his head injury. Much sensational evidence about their extraordinary sex lives was offered as further proof of insanity. It was all to no effect. On July 17, 1949, after a forty-four day trial, they were both found guilty. Appeals were exhausted two years later, and on March 8, 1951, the Lonely Hearts Killers went to the electric chair in Sing Sing. Martha, taken into the death cell twelve minutes after Raymond, had to squeeze her huge bulk into the chair. It had taken only one shock to kill Raymond; it took four before Martha's body sagged against the straps.

Colin Wilson

The Cleft Chin Murder

As Edgar Lustgarten remarks in the following account, the Cleft Chin murder is not of special interest to criminologists. But it is a typical case of "folie a deux", and in that sense affords an interesting parallel with the Lonely Hearts case, and the Moors case of the 'sixties. Told in detail, the story would make a good novel – the American Walter Mitty, Karl Hulten, and the wide-eyed little Welsh nightclub stripper whose admiration led him to play out his dangerous fantasy of robbery and murder. In that sense it is the perfect example of the high-and-medium-dominance syndrome discussed in connection with Fernandez and Beck.

Perhaps because the case holds relatively little interest for criminologists, it has been difficult to find an account of it that would be suitable for inclusion in this volume. Lustgarten's is perhaps too short and too lacking in detail, but it catches something of the essence of London in the last days of the war.

This account is from Lustgarten's book *The Murder and the Trial* (1960.)

During 1944 I was working at the B.B.C. and my duties often took me to the Service ministries. To avoid the crowds in Regent Street, I made a habit of using the narrow lanes lying parallel as a quick walking route from my office to Whitehall.

About three o'clock one bright spring afternoon, I had got within a long stone's throw of Golden Square when I heard the sounds of an approaching rumpus. Presently an American soldier came round the nearest corner at a lurching trot. It was obvious from a glance that he had been drinking heavily. His head was bandaged and there were fresh bloodstains on his tunic: traces of some brawl or scuffle earlier that day. In his arms he carried several unopened liquor bottles. Behind him, at a distance, followed a shouting crowd of Soho Italians, Cypriots, and Greeks, presumably led by the owner of the shop that had been robbed. They made no attempt, however, to overtake the thief, for a good reason that was soon apparent. Every few yards, he turned unsteadily and hurled one of the bottles back at his pursuers. They jumped and dodged in terror as the glass cracked and the wicked fragments flew.

I stepped into a doorway and waited for this perilous operation to pass by. When the soldier was level with me, though, he threw into the air his last remaining bottle, and the exultant crowd now rushed swiftly forward. But still more swiftly did they halt and dive for cover. Because, deprived of simpler weapons, the soldier drew a gun and aimed it at them sightlessly as he went lumbering on.

Whether it was loaded or not, I never knew. In due course the soldier disappeared from view, the hue and cry was cautiously resumed, and I continued on my way towards Whitehall as if nothing in the least out of the ordinary had occurred. In a sense, nothing had. For this was London's West End during those hectic months when the American military invasion reached its peak, and the atmosphere prevailing in some respects resembled that of a Yukon boom-town in the gold rush of the 'nineties. This atmosphere affected, in varying degree, elements of both invaders and invaded. It generated a racing pulse of unhealthy excitement. It imparted a contempt for civilized conventions. It prompted countless minor sins of recklessness or licence. And it gave rise to at least one major act of evil – that which was popularly called The Cleft Chin Murder, but which legal records less dramatically designate the case of The King versus Jones and Hulten.

Karl Gustav Hulten was twenty-two years old. Swedish by birth but American by upbringing, he was trained as a paratrooper in the United States and ultimately dispatched with his regiment to Britain in order to assist in liberating

Europe. Instead he preferred the path of a deserter. Wearing an officer's uniform (to which his rank did not entitle him), using the bogus name of "Lieutenant Ricky Allen", driving about in an army truck he had contrived to make his own, Hulten on the run possessed in goodly measure what he afterwards described as "a build-up" for himself.

The precise form of his "build-up" – *anglice*, shooting a line – depended on his estimate of persons that he met. But as he carried a fully primed revolver at the ready – that is, with both the safety catch and the hammer back, so that it could be fired at once at any time – it was easiest for him to sustain the role of desperado, whenever that might seem advantageous or attractive. Thus his "build-up" was predetermined when he fell in with the girl whose name is now forever linked in infamy with his.

Elizabeth Marina Jones (the Marina had been Maud) was still younger than Hulten – a few months past eighteen. Most of her life had been spent in the Neath district of South Wales, against a drab background of industrial depression. Eventually she escaped to London where she worked in turn as barmaid, waitress, cinema usherette, and what is euphemistically termed a strip-tease artist (in which capacity she performed at several third-rate nightclubs for an average reward of four pounds ten a week). She lived in one small room in King Street, Hammersmith, and took most of her meals at a local eating-house. London hardly gave her the flamboyant life she craved – neither the colour not the throb nor the sensation – but at least it was not Neath, and at least she could assume a smart name like Georgina Grayson, and at least there was the shoddy glamour of the dancing floor. Above all, there were the Yanks. To the little striptease artist, as to countless other girls, America was identical with glittering Hollywood, and every farmer's boy from Tennessee or South Dakota appeared potentially a Gable or a Crosby. Better still, perhaps, a Cagney or a Bogart; the romance of brutality was very much in vogue, and Georgina Grayson responded to it ardently. Thus her course was predetermined when she fell in with the man whose name is now forever linked in infamy with hers.

Their first encounter, so powerfully charged with ruin and

not only for themselves, took place on October 3rd, 1944. They were introduced to one another in a café. This is Georgina Grayson; Georgie, this is Ricky. Pleased to meet you, Ricky. Hiya doin', babe? All right, how's yourself? Okay, okay; like to take a ride tonight? What you got to ride in? I got it, don't you worry; pick you up eleven-thirty, by the cinema. Where'll we go, Ricky? Most anywhere you like . . . Each kept the appointment, and shortly before midnight they were speeding in the stolen truck along the Great West Road.

As they drove they talked, finding out about each other. Hulten, as always, was eager to show off, and he very quickly sized up his new acquaintance. He remarked in casual fashion that he was a gunman, and that back home in Chicago he ran round with a mob; then noted complacently how his callow lie immediately won the girl's naïve admiration. You a real gangster? Sure I'm a real gangster – why, if you wanna know, I'm boss of a gang that's operating over here right now. What, over here in London? Yeah – but take it easy, Georgie; don't you go round telling no one about this . . . He took a hand from the wheel and groped inside his belt; the striptease artist gasped and thrilled – she saw the gun.

Interactions became fast. The man's conceit was flattered by the girl's enraptured awe, the girl's imagination stirred by the man's parade of toughness. To feed his conceit and her imagination further, by separate process each conjured up the same unreal world; a world that they undoubtedly derived from the same sources, a world where they were partners – a gunman and his moll. It was a platitudinous fancy, and had it ended there – he concocting tales and boasting, she receptive and enthralled – the phenomenon need not have been malignant; it would not even have been especially unusual. Make-believe is a more common adult pastime than is supposed, and play-acting the part of villain may be harmlessly cathartic. What made this pair remarkable and dangerous, forcing society to strike out in self-defence, was the way they translated their conception of themselves from the plane of air-drawn fancy to the plane of solid fact. For although neither had previously committed an offence involving any kind of physical assault, within a few hours of their meeting in the café they embarked on a positive debauch of violent crime.

Later, when each of them came to tell the story of the ensuing orgiastic days, their two accounts did not wholly correspond. The girl maintained that she was terrified of Hulten, and had only done the things she did from fear: Hulten maintained that it was she who made the pace, she who urged him on. Their respective defences were shaped accordingly and, as a result, at their subsequent joint trial at the Old Bailey, the two prisoners set about attacking one another with far more ferocity and far more virulence than a rightly temperate Crown exhibited in attacking either. Their mutual hostility was indeed so marked, and the effort of each to destroy the former ally so relentless, that they almost invited comparison with the classical "cut-throat" cases; Millsom and Fowler, for instance, or Browne and Kennedy. Such behaviour on the woman's part was at any rate comprehensible in perpetration – as distinct from inception and idea – she, it was not gainsaid, acted merely as auxiliary; making things as black as possible for Hulten offered her, albeit faintly, a prospect of escape. Hulten, however, had not even this practical excuse. On his own admission, his was the active hand; if – which he denied – criminal intention lay behind it, he was doomed; by implicating the woman, he stood to gain precisely nothing – except the doubtful luxury of malice satisfied. Nonetheless, his inculpations surpassed hers. Between the two conflicting and irreconcilable versions, that of the timid girl bullied by the brutal male, and that of the simple boy made the designing female's puppet, the jury of mankind is left to choose one – or neither.

The trial, therefore, is a dubious and indeterminate guide to the development of their personal relationship during the period in which they ran amok. But concerning broad essentials there can be no real dispute. They turned into a pair of vicious, predatory beasts. They made expeditions almost nightly in the truck, with highway robbery as their express object. They offered lifts to unsuspecting walkers; they molested cyclists on lonely country roads; they tried to hold up cars. They were absolutely ruthless and cold-blooded.

One girl, whom Hulten had struck with an iron bar and afterwards half-strangled, they threw like a discarded dummy into the Thames to drown. That in fact she survived they neither knew nor cared. There could be no looking back as their wild campaign of banditry tore towards the inevitable climax.

It came on the fourth night of their association. At half-past eleven, Hulten whistled outside the girl's lodging. She came downstairs, and joined him in the street. Where's the truck, Ricky? Ain't brought out the truck. What we going to do, Ricky? Let's go get a cab . . . She had no doubt about the underlying innuendo. "I knew the meaning of his words," she admitted to the police. "He wanted me to go with him to rob a taxi-driver."

They walked along Hammersmith Road and stood together in a doorway. A grey Ford car leisurely approached. Hi, taxi, taxi. The grey Ford pulled up opposite. You a taxi? Private hire; where d'you want to go? What d'you say, top of King Street? That'll be ten bob.

Strictly, a private hire car should not pick up casual fares. But the driver of the grey Ford was not punctilious. He had had a slack night – and didn't everybody dodge the regulation anyway? So when the American officer agreed to his somewhat exorbitant demand, he grinned affably, emphasizing the hollow in his chin – a feature that was shortly to fascinate the head-line writers, after his corpse had been discovered in a ditch near Staines.

Hulten and the girl got in, and sat in the back seat. The car moved off. Nobody spoke a word. Bored by the silence, the driver whistled softly through his teeth. He didn't specially like the look of his two passengers, and wasn't sorry when they reached their destination. Here's the top of King Street. Yeah, that's right, bud, but I wanna go further on. You said top of King Street; further on'll cost you more. Take it easy, bud; I don't mind what I pay.

On they went again, past the darkened houses, over the round-about, into the open road. The driver grew irritable, even a shade uneasy. This near where you want, guv'nor? Yea, it's near; go slow. We come a tidy way, guv'nor. Okay, we'll get out here . . . As the car came to a standstill, Hulten was holding in his hand the fatal gun.

The driver leaned across to open the nearside door. Then the final madness supervened. Without warning, without prelude, Hulten fired into his back. The driver moaned, and slumped over to the left. Hulten jumped into the front, and drove rapidly away. The driver ceased to moan and his breath came chokingly. As he died, the girl was going through his pockets.

The Cleft Chin murder – for which Hulten was hanged and the girl, reprieved at the eleventh hour, condemned to a life sentence – is not of special interest to criminologists; the minds of both criminals were crudely commonplace. It is, however, of surpassing interest to social chroniclers, for no murder has ever been more firmly rooted in its age. At any time Frederick Seddon might have poisoned his lodger. At any time Jack the Ripper might have slashed his prostitutes. At any time Alfred Rouse might have kidnapped his unknown. But for the Cleft Chin crime there could be only one occasion; the occasion when it happened; the occasion when the characters responsible had been transported by events and transformed by one another.

The brash American, physically strapping but of stunted mental growth, consigned by army order to an unfamiliar land, sought to impress the natives with his own superiority by aping the habits of a gunman or a thug. The poverty-stricken adolescent refugee from Neath, frail alike in body and in mind, vaguely aspiring but completely talentless, sought a pitiable escape in fantasies inspired by the spurious appeal of gangster films. A world convulsion brought this pair together, at a moment when life was cheap and violence sanctified; under such conditions the union was deadly. It was like holding a lighted match to dynamite, having first ensured that the latter was exposed.

And so the hapless car driver, whose facial marking gives the case its name, may be written down no less a casualty of war than those who met a death more orthodox from shell or bomb.

The Blackburn Child Murder

The Blackburn case is one of the true classics
of crime detection, an example of what happens
when both the police and the public become
obsessed with catching the perpetrator of a crime
that has caused a sense of outrage. This account of
it is by a man who was deeply involved in the manhunt, Detective Chief Inspector Tony Fletcher, of
the Fingerprint Bureau of the Manchester Police.
His book *Memories of Murder* (1986) is, in my
opinion, among the best of all autobiographies
by a policeman – I can especially recommend the
chapter in which he describes trying to take the
fingerprints of a ghost at a seance.

The Second World War was a time of hardship, death,
disaster and yet of enormous public spirit and great
self-discipline amongst most people. As always after a war,
a new world had to be built. The men in the forces,
coming home after demobilization, voted in the general
election for the first time for many years, and they put a
Labour Government in power. The Government chose to
retain rationing, believing it to be the fairest system until
a free market with ample supplies could be established.
Some resentment about this was certainly felt by many,
because in what had been Occupied Europe free markets
began almost immediately, their belief apparently being that
supplies would rapidly reach demand, if demand were not
restricted. They may have been right.

It was against this background that in May 1948 there
occurred in Blackburn a most brutal murder. It resulted
in what is arguably one of the finest enquiries involving
finger-prints in the history of criminal investigation.

Policing goes back over 600 years in this country, but it developed in a somewhat piecemeal fashion. Indeed, in the mid-nineteenth century many local police forces had as few as fifty men. One thing about them is certain; the force would know its own villains. Thieves have always travelled, but mobility has been relative to the times. If a man with stolen property hitched a lift on a slow-moving wagon he could be caught by a rider on a faster horse. A thief on a fast horse, knowing his own moors and by-ways, could get away.

It is also startling to remember that the first juries were composed specifically of men who knew the offender, because they alone were in a position to judge whether he was guilty and whether anything could properly be said in his defence. Nowadays, of course, every endeavour is made to collect a jury which does not know any of the contenders in a case and can therefore be impartial. Even magistrates are supposed to declare any private interest that might cloud their judgment. Things change but slowly, and it is only in looking back that change can be properly assessed.

In 1969 a Royal Commission on Local Government reported that "England needs a pattern of local authorities with clear responsibilities big enough in area, population and resources to provide first-class services." Thus came the death knell for several (in most cases efficient) small police forces. They were soon replaced by fewer but larger, if not more efficient, police forces. As technology has developed, so police forces, fire brigades and local government have increased their equipment; there has not been any alternative. But such expertise has to be shared and its use cover a wide area. Where expenditure is heavy, the huge police forces we have today do in fact share facilities. This is a responsible and sensible approach.

Prior to this reorganization, if a murder occurred in a small borough and the Chief Constable decided that he did not have the necessary resources to deal with the situation he would seek assistance from New Scotland Yard or from a larger neighbouring force. How the newspapers loved it when the "Yard" were called in! The placard writers worked overtime, and outside all the newsagents' shops would be the enticing words "Murder – Yard Called In". How many thriller writers have made a decent living out of the intrepid "Yard" man, whizzing up (or down) from London to take charge. What calling in the "Yard" usually meant was the arrival of two experienced officers, one of whom would be senior and expected to control the investigation, and the other his reliable right-hand man. They would need to be pretty diplomatic, too, because the local Chief Constable, having called them in, had probably offended his own head of CID. If a neighbouring force gave help, it was usually by way of extra manpower or some equipment.

Whilst not denigrating this kind of help in any way, it must be emphasized that it is the local policeman with knowledge of the area, the nature of the community and its criminals, the reaper of casual information, known and it is hoped respected by the local populace, on whom the success of the enquiry depends. In the case of the Blackburn murder, such a man was Inspector William Barton.

Blackburn has always been important to Lancashire, being a mill town with a skilled labour force, turning out high quality goods for export all over the world. Manchester is surrounded by a network of such towns and, when their goods were technically finished, they would come into the big Manchester warehouses to be run through the measuring machines, checked for faults, labelled and packed according to each customer's requirements, and shipped overseas. Blackburn, Bolton, Oldham, Burnley and the rest had been busy during the war years, and whilst some man-made fabrics had been invented and more were yet to come, cotton was still important. But like so many other places, these towns had suffered bombing and house repairs had had to go by the board because the men and materials necessary were not available. By 1948, however, a start had been made on bringing about the improvements we all hoped for, but it was not always easy.

Blackburn lies in a hollow, though it is higher above sea level than one might think, not far from windy moorlands. There were still cobbled streets here and there, and some gas lighting. Clogs were still being worn because they were practical for many trades. Blackburn was noted for good weavers and in 1948 there were about 110,000 inhabitants in the town. Most of the 35,000 houses were of the working-class type, set in compact terraces. A large proportion were two-up-and-two-down, with a backyard and an outside lavatory, though in some cases a small row would have their lavatories set next to each other in a common courtyard. On high ground, South-East of the town, stands Queen's Park Hospital overlooking Blackburn itself. It was in this hospital, on 15 May 1948, that the events which caused so much public interest, concern and co-operation took place.

Like most of the public hospitals built in Victorian times, Queen's Park consists of several buildings in grounds covering some seventy acres. A high stone wall surrounded most of it except for a small portion in the North-West corner, where there was a disused quarry. Part of the wall had collapsed at this point, but to serve as a protection a six-foot high chestnut paling fence, with interwoven wire, had been erected. The main entrance had a porters' lodge where legitimate callers entered, stating their name, address and business.

In accordance with the custom of the times, the local public assistance committee controlled the hospital's affairs, catering for mental patients, aged and infirm persons, maternity cases, general illness cases – and children. Naturally, separate wards were maintained for dealing with these specialities. Emphasizing the role of the public assistance committee was the continuing presence of a casual ward, where vagrants or tramps were accommodated for the night – mostly around ten on any one night. In all the hospital housed about 1,200 people.

The events of the day in question revolve around ward CH3, which was a children's ward at the furthest point of the hospital from the lodge entrance. There were twelve cots in it, though only six were occupied, and June Anne Devaney, almost four, was in fact the oldest patient.

She had been admitted to the ward ten days earlier, suffering from pneumonia. The only child in the room who could talk, she was a big girl for her age, and when seen in bed she could have been taken for six or seven years old. June had recovered well in the hospital, and her parents were expecting to take her home during this particular Saturday.

About twenty minutes after midnight the night nurse in charge, Gwendoline Humphreys, went round all the cots, saw their occupants were safely asleep, and then went to the kitchen near the ward to start preparations for their breakfasts. She had been in the kitchen about twenty minutes when she heard a child's voice. She went quickly back to the ward, but found nothing amiss, so she returned to the kitchen – little children quite often call out in their sleep. At twenty minutes past one she noticed a draught. She went to the porch doors and found them open, but did not worry about it because the outer door had a faulty catch and a strong gust of wind could have opened it. Then she went into CH3 ward to see to one of the babies. She saw that June was not in her cot. The drop side of the cot was still in its raised position and, as it was about four feet above the ground, it was not likely she would or could have climbed out. She appeared to have been lifted out, very neatly.

On the floor, by the side of June's cot, was a Winchester bottle. This kind of bottle comes in several sizes and this particular one was quite large. When the nurse had last seen it, an hour earlier, it had been in its usual place on a trolley at the end of the ward some six yards away. A quick glance round showed some footprints on the polished floor, one near June's cot – and they seemed to Gwen Humphreys to have been made by someone in bare feet. This was a frightening situation for her.

A quick alarm and a rapid search by hospital staff of adjoining wards and the hospital grounds did not reveal anything useful. At five minutes to two the police were told. A squad of officers carried out a systematic search of the grounds and one hour and twenty-two minutes later, at 3.17 am, June's body was found lying near the boundary wall some 283 feet away from the ward. The Chief Constable, the police surgeon and Detective Superintendent Woodmansey of Lancashire Constabulary arrived at 4 am. They saw little June lying, face down, in the grass. Her nightie was lifted a little and was dirty as though she had been rolled about on the ground. It was obvious she had been brutally raped, her left buttock had been severely bitten and she had been battered to death by being swung against the stone wall by her ankles.

The hospital area was sealed off. The immediate help of New Scotland Yard was sought and the Chief Constable of Lancashire placed the whole of his large force and its equipment at the disposal of the Chief Constable of Blackburn. The Assistant Chief Constable of Lancashire and officers manning radio cars arrived quickly. Even hardened officers can be deeply moved by the killing of a young child, and this abduction of a three-year-old girl from her bed, and her violent and nasty death, were worse than most.

A bloodhound was brought to the hospital. It was given the scent from the child's bed and the footmarks on the ward floor. It sniffed around a bit and then led its handler to the child's body; no further. Police officers followed the trail directly to where the boundary wall joined the paling fence, where there was a small gap. It was possible to climb through this gap and to reach a small ledge skirting the edge of the quarry. It needed careful manoeuvring not to fall sixty feet into the quarry before reaching Queen's Road, but somebody had done it, and got away.

A forensic scientist joined the team; he came from the Home Office Laboratory at Preston, which now operates from Euxton, near Chorley. Colin Campbell, Officer in Charge of Lancashire Constabulary's Finger-print Department, also arrived. The usual photographs were taken of the child's body and its immediate surroundings, and she was then taken to the police mortuary. At that time Colin Campbell was one of this country's foremost finger-print experts, a man of vast and useful experience.

An ordinary chap cannot imagine himself taking a little girl from a hospital cot, carrying her outside the building and killing her. Nevertheless, any investigating officer has to imagine himself doing just that; to cast round for the slightest disturbance, scratch, scuffmark, fibre, that will throw any light on the actions of the intruder.

Together with Mr Looms, the Chief Constable of Blackburn, Colin Campbell stood outside the children's ward. Both men peered through a window near the cot which had been occupied by June Anne Devaney. As they did so,

Mr Looms briefed the Chief Inspector as to all known human circumstances in the case, particularly drawing his attention to the Winchester bottle standing on the floor near June's cot.

The ward, about forty feet long and eighteen feet wide, had in it twelve empty cots. Once the murder was discovered the remaining children had been moved to another ward. A quick tour of the outside of the building showed there was a verandah on the West side of the ward; on the East, a concrete path. In each of the West and East walls of the ward were three glass doors that were never locked. At the ward's northern end was a small office containing three windows, and two of these were left open for ventilation. At the southerly end was a corridor which gave access to bathroom and kitchen, and another short corridor, at right-angles, led to the ward where toddlers were accommodated.

Obviously, there had been many open doors and windows available to the intruder, so it wasn't surprising that Colin Campbell didn't find any signs of forcible entry on which attention could be concentrated.

After this quick tour Campbell and Looms stood in the corridor at the southerly end of the ward. They stared in to the ward, looking particularly at what seemed to be a trail of bare footprints which had been made on the wax-polished floor. On more detailed examination it was seen that the foot had not been bare, as the nurse had thought, but had been stockinged, the pressure of the foot making shallow impressions in the thin layer of wax polish.

This trail appeared to begin at the door leading from the office at the North end of the ward. It travelled to the first cot on the West side, then to an instrument trolley standing against the North wall, recrossed to the West side of the ward and to the second cot from the door. At this cot the footprints were implanted side by side on the floor, as if made by a person standing alongside the cot, looking at its occupant. Similar footprints were found alongside the third and fourth cots, this latter being the one from which June had been taken. The toes of these footprints were at right-angles to the cot side and actually under its edge, showing their maker was standing very close to the cot. From there the footprints went down the ward and stopped about two feet from the South door. There, they seemed to turn round and traverse the entire length of the ward in a straight line right up to the North door. There were no footprints on the East side of the ward. It was pretty clear what this evil human being had done.

Colin Campbell selected the most distinct right and left footprints and asked for them to be photographed.

Now it was time to concentrate on the Winchester bottle found near June's cot. It was labelled "Sterile Water". It also bore twenty finger and palm impressions.

Some of these impressions appeared to have been made recently, whilst others seemed fairly old. And if you ask me now, after so many years of experience of my own, how a finger-print officer can tell the age of a print, I have to confess it is almost impossible to put into words. A print can have a "new" look; the sweat which has made it somehow looks fresh. It has not been changed by atmospheric dust molecules. One can be wrong in this judgment of a "fresh" print, but it's rare. Most important in the case of this Winchester bottle was that the recent impressions were much larger than the other, older ones. Colin Campbell took the Winchester bottle back to his own force headquarters and in the Finger-print Department the impressions were quickly photographed. After the smaller, older impressions had been eliminated as those of nursing staff (their prints having of course been obtained for comparison) a large-scale search began in the department's files.

Whilst the Detective Chief Inspector had been examining the Winchester bottle in the ward, the Home Office forensic scientist, Mr Jones, had also been busy. He scraped the wax from the floor where the footprints were implanted. Certain fibres, invisible to the naked eye, were later found embedded in these scrapings. He also measured the footprints. They were ten and a quarter inches long: not a small foot. The next examination he made was of one of the three windows which formed the bay in the small office at the North end of the ward. It had been left open, and it overlooked a concrete area at the rear of the ward. There were marks on the window which were consistent with a person having climbed through it. Adhering to the wooden window frame the scientist found fibres. He collected them, and with the other specimens took them back to the laboratory.

A special squad of officers had been established in the hospital, under the control of Detective Chief Inspector Bob McCartney. They screened the movements of all inmates, staff and patients alike. All persons who had legitimate access to the ward were finger-printed and the finger-print forms were given to Colin Campbell for elimination purposes. And providing an extra bit of news for the papers, Detective Chief Inspector John Capstick of New Scotland Yard, a name well recognized now, came with Detective Inspector Daws. Mr Capstick took control of the enquiries.

There had to be a post-mortem examination. Although it can be very distressing to relatives, it is an essential part of the enquiry. The pathologist found that June's death was due to shock caused by a fractured skull and extensive injuries. The bite on her buttock had been made before death, as had a bruise in each groin. Internal injuries were consistent with rape. Specimens were taken not only from the body but also from various places at the scene of the enquiry. Those which proved vital were:

Fibres from the window of the room adjoining the ward.
Blood and hairs from the boundary wall of the hospital.
Fibres found on the child's body.
A single pubic hair found on the child's body.
The child's nightdress.
Various swabs.
Fibres taken from the footmarks in the ward.

Add to these the finger-prints on the Winchester bottle and the footprints found in the ward, and you have an idea of the material on which the police had to work.

The hospital staff and local people were much concerned. They began to think, and think hard. Quickly came the news that at about a quarter past eleven on the night of Friday, 14 May, some nurses in the nurses' home about a hundred yards from ward CH3 saw what tradition describes as a Peeping Tom peering into a window on the ground floor. When a nurse told him to go away, he put a finger to his mouth and said, "Hush, don't tell anyone." Naturally, this looked helpful, but on the 19th of May he was traced and interviewed, showing that though he might have been up to no good he was not the man who had left the finger-prints on the Winchester bottle.

On the 18th of May a taxi driver came forward to say that just before midnight on the 14th he had picked up a man in the town centre on a road which leads to the hospital, and had set him down in Queen's Road near the quarry. When he got out of the taxi, the man had run across the quarry and was last seen going in the direction of the hospital. The taxi driver could not describe the man in any detail, but thought he had a local accent.

After giving a great deal of thought to the evidence in the ward itself, Detective Chief Inspector Campbell deduced that the murderer had entered the ward by the North door and had peeped into the first cot; he had then crossed to the instrument trolley, where he had picked up the Winchester bottle, before crossing to the second and third cots, where he had gazed at the sleeping children. He had then walked to the fourth cot, put the Winchester bottle on the floor, lifted June from her cot and had carried her to the South door. He had there presumably heard a noise and had turned and retraced his steps, walked the length of the ward and carried the child out through the North door.

A conference was called on 18 May at the Central Police Office. All officers concerned in the investigations were present.

Chief Inspector Campbell gave his assessment of the situation. He said that after the most exhaustive comparisons with both finger and palm prints of all persons who had access to the hospital, all the finger and palm impressions found at the scene had been eliminated with the exception of ten prints found on the Winchester bottle. These ten were the fresh marks which had been made by a person with a large hand.

He believed these impressions consisted of a left thumb print, a sequence of left fore, middle and ring finger-prints and a left palm print. There were two impressions which appeared to have been made by right middle and ring fingers. The remaining three were partial finger-prints which could not be allocated to any particular finger. Whilst he would not make a guess as to the murderer's age or as to whether he was right- or left-handed, Campbell did say that having regard to the span of the sequence of finger-prints left on the bottle, the clarity of the ridge detail and the absence of coarseness or temporary injuries, he believed they were made by a biggish man who was not old and did little or no manual work.

For some hours all the available evidence was discussed by those present at the conference and eventually the following four conclusions were arrived at. Firstly, the finger-prints on the bottle were undoubtedly those of the murderer, as all males in the hospital and all persons with legitimate access to CH3 ward had been eliminated. Secondly, the wanted man was someone living locally, who knew the hospital and its surroundings, particularly in view of the taxi driver's evidence. Few people could take off into the darkness and successfully negotiate the edge of this quarry; and it seemed a return trip had been made the same way. Thirdly, the man had to be reasonably tall. A small person could not have lifted June cleanly out of the cot without dropping the cot sides, and there was no evidence that this had been done. Furthermore, a small man would not be likely to have feet ten and a quarter inches long. Fourthly, the person's clothing would be bloodstained.

The big question now was how the finger-prints could best be used to trace the murderer. All prints filed in the bureaux were being examined, but this would take several weeks and, in any case, the wanted man might not have been recorded in general criminal files; and whilst this search was proceeding the trail would be going cold.

The problem was huge. A bold and courageous decision was taken to deal with it. All male persons of sixteen years or over known to have been in Blackburn on 14 and 15 May 1948 would be finger-printed. The manpower, the time and the paperwork could be provided; a matter of logistics. What was disturbing was the knowledge that at least one person in Blackburn had a good reason for not having his finger-prints taken and might be expected to do whatever he could to avoid putting himself on record. Of course many men could have left Blackburn for perfectly legitimate reasons: to work elsewhere, join the army, or even to die and be buried in the cemetery or be cremated. All these things can be checked, but it takes time.

Inspector William Barton of Blackburn Borough Police was allocated the most demanding task of all, that of ensuring that no man in the town of Blackburn slipped through the net of the finger-printing officers. It was an enormous responsibility, though he was comforted by the fact that the finger-prints on the Winchester bottle were clear and could be matched without difficulty if their maker were traced. If and when the time came there would not be a grain of doubt. Inspector Barton picked his small staff and gave them a simple instruction: "No adult male must be missed."

On occasions such as this the newspapers can be particularly helpful and through them the Mayor of Blackburn appealed for men over the age of sixteen to volunteer their finger-prints. Alongside this the Chief Constable assured everybody that such prints would not be used for any other reason and that when they had served their purpose they would be publicly destroyed. Public feeling was running very high indeed. The nation had just come through a long and bloody war which had been impossible to avoid; the hospital incident was an unnecessary and evil thing, and people were quick to help. When the special squad of finger-print officers made their first visits to houses in the vicinity of the hospital on Sunday 23 May, eight days after the killing, they found everybody on their side. This is a heartening feeling for any officer of the law.

Plans were made to obviate overlapping of visits. Thoroughness was essential. The electoral registers were used to ensure that every house in Blackburn, some 35,000 dwellings, was visited. Not every house is on the roll, but as one goes round a street armed with such a list any omissions are obvious. The registers at that time recorded all those over the age of twenty-one and thus entitled to vote. When visiting a house an officer could ask about other, younger members of the family. You might think to yourself that a member of a household could easily suspect a brother or son and omit him deliberately. True enough, but a check with neighbours either side will reveal discrepancies.

Armed with the Blackburn registers, divided into fourteen

voting divisions, subdivided into sections and then alphabetical street and road order, the finger-print squad went
into action. Carrying finger-print cards and inked pads they
worked to a predetermined pattern until every house in every
street was covered. Whilst doing this, enquiries were made
to obtain information about persons not normally resident
in the town but who were there on the night in question.
Public co-operation was truly magnificent. Each night all
the gathered information was handed in to Inspector Barton
along with completed finger-print cards.

This mass of detail meant enquiries had to be made in
all parts of the United Kingdom via local police, and to
forces in Australia, Singapore, India, Egypt, South Africa,
Canada, the USA and almost every country in Europe.
People were located in all these places, and finger-printed
for elimination.

The finger-print cards were cancelled against the appropriate entry in the electoral roll and then sent to Chief
Inspector Campbell for comparison. It didn't take long to
check an individual card, but it took a long time to examine
all the thousands. After checking, each card was stamped
"Cancelled" and filed in strict alphabetical order at police
head-quarters in Blackburn.

At the same time Detective Chief Inspector Capstick of
New Scotland Yard was seeing that other lines of enquiry
were being pursued regarding the peculiar nature of the
crime and its implications. You will realize how extensive
these enquiries can be when you study the following types
of people who were seen and finger-printed. Much of this
line of enquiry is not pleasant, but it has to be done. The
human psyche is a complex and often secretive thing.

1 About 3,600 persons discharged from mental institutions
in the northern half of the country, the nature of the crime
suggesting a person of low mentality. Many of these persons
had been convicted of offences involving indecency.

2 About 3,000 male persons of uncertain nationality; prisoners of war and Polish Army men living in camps within
twenty miles of Blackburn. This line of enquiry arose from
the biting of the child, not normal in Great Britain, but fairly
often committed on the continent in crimes of indecency.

Lancashire Constabulary officers conducted this part of the investigation.

3 Epileptics and sufferers from schizophrenia who might have committed such a crime during a temporary black-out.

4 Persons suffering from venereal disease, so far as the confidential treatment of such persons would permit. Some sufferers from this kind of disease believe, wrongly of course, that sexual intercourse with a virgin or young child will effect a cure.

5 Persons known to commit or suspected of committing sexual offences contrary to nature, that is homosexuals and the like (though the phrase "contrary to nature" would now be hotly disputed, I don't doubt). Many people in this category were the subject of anonymous letters to the police.

6 All persons having recently committed suicide and remaining in mortuaries, and those who had recently attempted suicide.

7 Casuals and other people forming the moving population of the district, who might have stayed at the casual ward on some previous occasion and thus be familiar with the hospital.

8 All persons missing from home at the relevant period.

Working on these eight groups was quite an undertaking, and indeed it is likely that some people came into more than one category. Assaults on young children are, regrettably, not uncommon and it is carefully amassed local knowledge about the kind of people who commit such crimes which can be helpful not merely to trace a wrongdoer but also to eliminate the rest.

After about eight weeks of intensive finger-printing work most of the houses in Blackburn had been visited, but no clear lead had as yet been established.

There was another source of information in 1948 which would not, so far as I know, be available to us now, and Inspector Barton did not hesitate to take advantage of it. To do whatever was possible to ensure that every person in the borough would be finger-printed, the records already obtained were compared with the records kept by the local registration officer for the issuing of food ration books. In 1948 these would be reasonably up to date, because between 30 June and 18 July 1948, new ration books had been issued to everybody in response to the completion by each person of a reference leaf from the previous year's books. If this was not done, a new ration book was not issued. The reference leaves gave the name, address, date of birth and national registration number of the holder, all filed in strict alphabetical order of surname at the registration office.

On 18 July finger-printing was suspended. The next three weeks were spent by Inspector Barton and his squad in the registration office. They compared each finger-print card with its counterpart in the registration files. When this had been done, the remaining ration book reference leaves showed the balance of the population which still required to be printed. A good deal of clerical work followed, producing new lists, separated into the sub-divisions of the borough wards.

House-to-house finger-printing restarted on Monday 9 August, but now the officers had lists giving particulars of specific persons whose prints were needed to complete the check.

On the night of Wednesday 11 August one of the squad obtained the finger-prints of Peter Griffiths, aged twenty-two, at his home, 31 Birley Street, Blackburn. His card, with others obtained that day, was sent in the normal way to Chief Inspector Campbell at the Lancashire Constabulary Finger-print Bureau, arriving at about 3 pm on Thursday 12 August 1948.

One of the experts, making the comparisons, spotted on Griffiths's card the finger-prints exactly as they appeared on the bottle. It was quite a moment. He could hardly believe his own eyes. He double checked and then exclaimed, "I've got him! It's here!"

In addition to his name and address, there was national registration number NBA 6917–188, indicating he was an ex-serviceman. News of the identification quickly went to the Chief Constable of Blackburn. His name would not have been found in the electoral register, as he had not qualified for inclusion when the last list was prepared on 30 June 1947.

Friday 13 August 1948 was not Peter Griffiths's lucky day, but it was a good one for the police. He was arrested near his home and brought to police head-quarters. He admitted his guilt in the following statement:

I want to say that on the night the little girl was killed at the Queen's Park Hospital, it was on a Friday night, the Friday before Whitsun. I left home that night on my own about six o'clock. I went out to spend a quiet night on my own. I went to the Dun Horse pub or hotel and bought myself about five pints of bitter beer. Then I went to Yates' Wine Lodge and had a glass of Guinness and two double rums. I then had another glass of Guinness and then went back to the Dun Horse again. I then had about six more pints of bitter. I was on my own and came out of there at closing time. I walked down to Jubilee Street off Darwen Street and I saw a man smoking a cigarette sitting in a small closed car with the hood on, with wire wheels, they were painted silver. I did not know him. I had never seen him before. I asked the man for a light as I had no matches to light my cigarette. I stayed gabbing to him for about fifteen minutes. He said to me, "Are you going home?" I said, "No, I'm going to walk round a bit and sober up first." He asked me where I lived and I told him. He said, "Well get in, open the window and I'll give you a spin." He took me to the front of the Queen's Park Hospital and I got out opposite to the iron railings. I don't know what happened to him, I never saw him again. I must have got over the railings, for the next thing I remember was being outside the ward, there were some children. I left my shoes outside the door, which had a brass knob. I tried the door and it opened to my touch and I went just in and heard a nurse humming and banging as if she was washing something so I came out again and waited a few minutes. Then I went back in again and went straight to the ward like, I think I went in one or two small rooms like, like a kitchen, and then I went back into the ward again. I then picked up a biggish bottle off a shelf. I went half way down the ward with it and then put it down on the floor. I then thought I heard the nurse coming, I turned round sharply, overbalanced and fell against a bed. I remember the child woke up and started to cry, and I hushed her. She then opened her eyes, saw me and the child in the next bed started whimpering. I picked the girl up out of the cot and took her outside by the same door. I carried her in my right arm and she put her arms round my neck and I walked with her down the hospital field. I put her down on the grass. She started crying again and I tried to stop her from crying, but she wouldn't do, like, she wouldn't stop crying. I just lost my temper then and you know what happened then. I banged her head against the wall. I then went back to the verandah outside the ward, sat down and put my shoes on. I then went back to where the child was. I like just glanced at her but did not go right up to her, but went straight on down the field to the delph. I crossed over the path alongside the delph leading into Queen's Park. I walked through the park and came out on Audley Street. I went down Cherry Street into Furthergate, then I went down Eanam to Birley Street and got home somewhere around two o'clock on Saturday morning. It would be somewhere about that time. I went into my house, took me collar and tie off and slept in me suit on the couch downstairs. Mother and father were in bed and did not know what time I came in. I woke up about nine o'clock, got up, washed and shaved, then pressed me suit because I was going out again after I had had my breakfast. I went out then down the town, had a walk round, then went to the Royal Cinema in the afternoon, came out of the pictures at five o'clock, went home and had my tea. I looked at the papers and read about the murder. It didn't shake me, so that I just carried on normally after that. My mother and father asked me where I had been that night and what time I came home and told them I had been out boozing and had got home at twelve o'clock. This is all I can say and I'm sorry for both parents' sake and I hope I get what I deserve.

Shortly before midnight on Friday 13 August 1948, he was charged with the murder of June Anne Devaney. His finger-prints were again taken, and also palm prints and impressions of his stockinged feet. A comparison resulted in ten of the twenty finger-prints found on the bottle being identified as his.

There was more to come. All possible samples were taken and examined by forensic scientists. Certain clothing was removed from his home. His suit, which he had worn on the night of the murder, was recovered from a pawnbroker's pledge office, where he had pawned it on 30 May. Tests showed that fibres from the window were identical with those of the suit. Fibres taken from the child's body were found to be made of wool ranging in colour between blue and violet, and agreeing exactly with the threads from which the suit cloth had been woven. Other wool fibres agreeing with those of the suit were found on her nightdress. And fibres taken from the footprints in the wax on the floor of the ward were found to match a sock taken from Griffiths's home.

Human bloodstains, sufficient for grouping purposes, were found on the lining inside the trousers at the bottom of the fly. This blood was of group A, the same as that of the child. There were more blood-stains on the linings of both trouser side pockets, on the lining at the bottom of each jacket sleeve, on each lapel, on the right front above the top button and inside the right edge, on the top button and near to the right shoulder, and inside the right bottom front.

It was interesting that the speculative conclusions arrived at during the conference had proved substantially correct, because Griffiths was not only local, and five feet ten and a half inches, but also had a good knowledge of the hospital grounds as between the ages of ten and twelve he had been a patient in the very block of buildings from which he had taken the little girl. And he was later identified by the taxi driver as the man set down near the quarry on the fatal night.

The due processes of law followed: first the magistrates' court and then on Friday 15 October 1948, he entered a plea of "not guilty" before Mr Justice Oliver at Lancaster Assizes. Many people not versed in law may wonder why anybody, having admitted guilt, pleads not guilty. In fact, this plea ensures the hearing of all evidence during the trial and a jury verdict, followed by sentence if found guilty. If a guilty plea is entered, even though a jury may be present, the judge conducts proceedings rather differently: an outline of the evidence is given, the judge makes sure that the prisoner has full knowledge of the circumstances in which he is placed, and then sentences him.

On the first day of Griffiths's trial the prosecution evidence was presented in total. It was pretty damning and the defence appeared to accept it almost without question, because there was little or no examination of the Crown witnesses. The case was then adjourned until the following Monday.

From the defence point of view the case was desperate, but Griffiths's counsel was honour bound to try and find a way out for him. An attempt was made, using medical witnesses, to prove that he was schizophrenic and therefore insane when he committed the crime. It was also given in evidence that Griffiths's father had been an inmate of a mental hospital for six months after the end of the First World War and that young Peter's condition could have been inherited. However, a medical officer from Liverpool Prison said he had had Griffiths under almost continual observation since his admission there on 14 August and his conclusion was that Griffiths was sane when he committed the crime.

On the second day of the trial, after only twenty-three minutes, the jury returned a verdict of guilty. It had been a short trial, but it was not surprising in view of the forensic evidence.

When pronouncing sentence, Mr Justice Oliver addressed Griffiths thus:

> Peter Griffiths, this jury has found you guilty of a crime of the most brutal ferocity. I entirely agree with this verdict. The sentence of the court upon you is that you be taken from this place to a lawful prison and thence to a place of execution and that you there suffer death by hanging and that your body be afterwards buried within the precincts of the prison in which you shall have been confined before your execution. And may the Lord have mercy on your soul.

The sentence of the court was carried out at Liverpool Prison at nine o'clock on the morning of Friday 19 November 1948.

The people of Blackburn had co-operated magnificently in this enquiry and the promise of destruction of finger-prints was kept: on 3 November about 46,500 finger-print cards, several hundred finger-print forms and numerous other documents were pulped at a local paper mill. The destruction was an event of great local interest, attended by the Mayor of Blackburn, journalists, press photographers and a newsreel cameraman. There had been a press announcement that if persons applied for their finger-print cards to be returned to them this would be done. Some five hundred people did so. No doubt many of these are still preserved in sideboard drawers and the popular old wooden document boxes as a memento of an event in which thousands of innocent people were caught up.

Most murders are of a domestic nature and quickly detected, and do not arouse much discussion amongst the general public. This case was different. Griffiths, of course, knew what he had done, and many people unversed in the ways of criminals thought he had been stupid to remain in Blackburn and risk detection by being finger-printed. It may be of interest to readers to outline what police reaction would have been to some of the things he could have done.

Firstly, he could have refused to have his prints taken. It will be appreciated that there are people who, being innocent and uninvolved in an event, will refuse to have their finger-prints taken on the grounds of it being their legal right. I do not think Peter Griffiths had this sort of intelligence. If he had refused, his movements on the night in question would have been very carefully looked at. If, in the likely event of his saying he was at some place other than the hospital during the relevant time, he would certainly have qualified as a major suspect when this proved false.

Secondly, he could have left the district. This again would have meant he would come under strong suspicion.

Thirdly, he could have committed suicide, but you will remember that bodies were examined and finger-printed.

Fourthly, he could have engineered an accident to his fingers. Local hospital staff were aware of this possibility and, if he had gone for help having injured the inner surfaces of his hands, subsequent enquiries would have raised suspicion. In any case his normal finger-prints could most likely have been obtained from surfaces in his home. Peter Griffiths took a chance when he volunteered his prints, and lost. He may indeed not have been bright enough to know exactly what he was risking.

A few more thoughts may occur to the reader when considering what Griffiths actually said in his statement and what came out in the course of the enquiry. He may or may not have been confused about the identity of the vehicle in which he was taken to the quarry. He says he had eleven pints of beer, two glasses of Guinness and two double rums between 6 pm and the closing time of local pubs; quite an intake, if it were true. If it were so, could he have negotiated the quarry edge so easily? When interviewed after his arrest he would have been closely questioned in great detail. In his statement he glides over the actual attack on the child, probably preferring to push it all to the back of his mind. This is not uncommon in sordid crime.

The vast majority of murder enquiries are solved by team-work. This Blackburn investigation is a perfect example. Each officer, from the highest rank down to the beat Constable and the Detective Constable, was but a small cog in a powerful machine. Each officer played his or her part to the full and in so doing gained tremendous support from the entire population of a town.

Tony Fletcher

Howard Unruh: The First of the "Crazy Gunmen"

The Unruh case deserves inclusion here, towards the end of this volume of murders of the 1940s, because it can be regarded as the predecessor of a new type of murder. In the introduction to *An Encyclopedia of Murder* (1961) I pointed to the appearance of a new type of crime: the apparently motiveless murder, which might be labelled "the crime of boredom." In March 1959, after a man named Norman Smith had been watching television in his caravan in Sarasota County, Florida – a programme called "The Sniper" – he took his revolver and went out with the intention of shooting someone – anyone. His victim, Mrs Hazel Woodard, was chosen at random, and shot through the window as she watched her TV set.

Since then, "crazy gunmen" have become a feature of crime in the late 20th century: in 1966, Charles Whitman shot nineteen people from the tower in the University of Texas; in 1974, Mark Essex killed nine people on a shooting spree in New Orleans; in 1975, James Ruppert killed eleven relatives in Hamilton, Ohio; in the same year pro-Nazi Frederick Cowan went on a shooting rampage and killed five strangers; in Ottawa in October 1975, teenager Robert Poulin raped and murdered a local girl in his basement room, then went on a shooting rampage at his school, killing one and wounding seven; in 1983, another pro-Nazi, James Huberty, killed twenty-one in a shooting rampage in San Diego, California; in 1989, Patrick

Purdy walked into a schoolyard in Stockton, California, and opened fire on Asian children, killing five and wounding thirty; in August 1987, nineteen-year-old Julian Knight opened fire on a busy highway in Melbourne, Australia, hitting twenty-six people, of whom seven died; also in 1987, in Hungerford, England, gun enthusiast Michael Ryan killed sixteen in a shooting spree; in December 1989, Mark Lepine took a repeating rifle to the University of Montreal and killed fourteen, wounding another thirteen; in April 1989, twenty-two-year-old Robert Sartin opened fire at Monkseaton, near Newcastle on Tyne, killing one and injuring fourteen. This list is by no means complete.

And so Unruh may be seen as the first of a long line of "crazy gunmen", and an ominous portent of things to come.

This account is from Brad Steiger's *Mass Murder*.

P erhaps because it was hard to believe that with each shot someone was dying, the Camden, New Jersey, residents, who lived near the intersection of 32 Street and River Road, were at first slow to take cover. Some of them heard the gun ring out five times before they believed anything extraordinary was happening.

At the sound of the shots customers in a grocery store across the street and the people in a neighboring bar-restaurant crowded to the windows to see what was going on. The setting in front of them appeared exactly normal. The relatively busy intersection carried the usual amount of mid-morning traffic, and a few cars were on 32 Street waiting for the traffic light to change. It looked like the beginning of a beautiful late summer day. The sky was clear and the morning sun was warming the air. Even the tall man who emerged from the barber shop across the street seemed to move casually, walking at an easy pace in spite of the sound of the shots.

Eyes followed the man as he walked out of the barber shop that had just been vacated by a woman carrying a little boy and girl. When the tall man reached the corner, and the entrance of the drugstore, they could see that he carried an automatic pistol. Then, as if it had been pre-arranged, out of the drugstore walked another man who practically bumped into him. There was a short pause during which the two men seemed to be exchanging words. Then two more shots rang out, and the man from the drugstore crumpled and rolled toward the street.

The observers had seen enough. The proprietors of the two establishments locked their doors, and the customers fled to the back. As the stunned and frightened people waited, they heard more shots and wondered who the gunman had killed. Although they could not have known it at the time, the killer, who moved calmly through the business establishments across the street, was in the process of setting an all-time high in rapid-fire killings. The quick action of the managers of both the grocery store and the bar-restaurant probably saved the lives of their customers. When the toll was finally taken, the methodical killer had taken twelve lives in twelve minutes, fatally wounding number thirteen, who would die before the day ended, and wounding three others who would survive.

Howard Unruh had been considered a gentleman throughout his adult life. People who came in contact with him believed him to be one of the most mild-mannered young men they had ever met. Unruh seemed to be the kind of man who would go out of his way to avoid trouble. His fellow employees, his former Army buddies, the members of his church congregation, all confirmed Unruh's quiet and responsible nature. Yet, on September 6, 1949, the twenty-eight-year-old ex-GI descended the steps of his mother's apartment, walked out on the streets of Camden and started to kill in what seemed an indiscriminate pattern of murder.

Nobody could understand what had made the quiet young man go off the deep end. But later the investigation revealed that the black day had been festering in the young man's mind for a long time.

Although it is impossible to say when Howard Unruh first began heading for that day of violence, certain factors of his personality had remained constant throughout his entire life. Even as a schoolboy he was described as quiet, although he could hardly have been classified as abnormally passive. A better-than-average student at school, Unruh went in for activities on a scholarly level. He seems to have been well received in spite of the fact that he did not participate in athletics. As a boy, he had been just another kid. Quieter than some, but still just an average boy.

His parents were middle-class working people, and even though they had begun living separately during Howard Unruh's adolescence, their separation did not change Howard's life significantly. Although still on friendly terms with his father, Howard lived with his mother. The boy's only brother was married and lived in the suburbs.

While in high school, Unruh decided to become a pharmacist and was preparing to study for that career when his plans – like those of many others – were interrupted by World War II. There was probably some speculation among Unruh's acquaintances about the kind of soldier the quiet lad would make, but to their surprise, Unruh became a very efficient fighting man.

Howard Unruh's superiors rated him a top-notch soldier. When the ground got tough to gain, the lanky boy from New Jersey performed surprisingly well from his position as a tank gunner. As part of a tank command, he took part in the Battle of the Bulge and earlier had participated in the trek up the length of the Italian peninsula.

Unruh was also accepted by his fellow GIs, even though they gave him a hard time about his refusal to drink or to go out with girls. Unruh preferred to remain by himself and read his Bible. As often as his buddies tried to set him up with an Italian or French girl, he always turned them down.

The man who was Unruh's sergeant for most of the European tour of duty said that in tense situations Unruh's demeanor never changed. He coolly did his duty at all times. The only time that the sergeant ever recalled the soldier laughing was when another GI mounted a Naples balcony and did an imitation of Il Duce. Unruh was not unfriendly, and even though he abstained from all the customary pleasures of the soldier, he never preached at his barrack mates, nor held himself above them. He was given an honorable discharge at the end of the war, and returned to his New Jersey home, eager to get back into civilian life.

But military life and World War II did have an effect on the quiet man. One of Unruh's buddies was surprised to glance at a page of Unruh's diary and find that Unruh had written with delight of the Germans that he had killed. This ex-GI – who later became a New York police officer – said that after the mass murder, it had been his suspicion that Unruh had had the soul of the murderer all along and that the Army had merely channeled his killer instinct for the duration of the war. The Army had also introduced Unruh to firearms, and he had used them well. During training, Unruh had been ranked as a sharpshooter, and his accuracy did not diminish under combat pressure.

In civilian life, Unruh continued to be fascinated with firearms. He had picked up a couple of souvenirs during the war, and he purchased other pistols to add to his collection. Unruh set up a firing range in the basement of his Camden apartment, and he spent hours there, improving his already excellent marksmanship.

Like many other GIs, Unruh had become a little rusty on his high school subjects, so he took several refresher courses in preparation for entering the university. Once again he wanted to study to become a pharmacist. Unruh was consistently at the top of the class in the preparatory courses, but when he finally enrolled at Temple University in Philadelphia, he had lost much of his ambition. He found the adjustment to civilian life less easy than he had expected. He complained to his mother that he could not concentrate sufficiently to get anything from the courses he was taking. His mother tried to reassure him by telling him that it would require patience to attain his goal.

Though things began to lose meaning for him, Unruh and his mother continued to attend a nearby church regularly, and Howard also participated in a Bible class. The only girlfriend that he was ever known to have had was a member of the church.

But Unruh's benign appearance masked an inner turmoil that was eventually to climax in twelve minutes of death for his neighbors. Howard Unruh had become what psychiatrists term a paranoid schizophrenic. He had begun to view the world around him as an alien place, its inhabitants as his enemies. This mental trauma was not something that had happened suddenly. The new Howard Unruh was the result of many years of mounting suspicion, which his twisted personality had turned into a violent hatred of his fellow men.

There were signs of the impending disaster, but the young man was so unobtrusive that it barely jogged anyone's memory when his name was mentioned. Early in the summer of 1949, Unruh ceased to attend the church he had gone to faithfully since his return from Europe. Although several members of the congregation were aware of this, no one thought it worthy of extensive consideration. About the same time, Unruh stopped dating the girl he had been seeing.

Authorities were later to discover that it was at this time that Unruh was going through some radical adjustments in his sex life and had begun to seek sexual gratification from other men. It was a crucial time in his paranoia, and Unruh felt as though the entire world was peering at him.

Unruh always left his mother's apartment by the rear door and cut through the backyard of his next-door neighbors, the Cohens. Mr Cohen was the owner of a drug store which adjoined the flat where he, his wife, son, and mother lived. On one occasion Cohen's mother had yelled out a window at the passing young man.

"Hey, you," the elderly lady said from behind her screened window. "Do you have to go through the yard?" Irritation rang in her voice.

It was not the complaint that hurt Howard Unruh so much as the fact that she had not called him by name. Back in his room he added the incident to a list of grievances that he had already recorded against the Cohens. His expression never changed as he wrote, in a very legible hand, concise statements of complaint. He listed the violation just as impassively as he had listed the bugle that the Cohens had given their 12-year-old son the Christmas before. Higher up on the list was a phrase that told of a screen door that banged late at night. A number of other seemingly insignificant incidents were also marked on the list, and behind each one was the concise abbreviation, "retal."

But the Cohens were not the only people against whom Unruh intended retaliation. He had complaints written against nearly all of his neighbors. Each of these "violations" would have been considered insignificant by a normal person, but to Unruh, they had acquired tremendous significance – for each notation marked or confirmed an individual for killing.

Unruh had begun his planning two years earlier. With each added irritation, he would revamp his plans. His weapon collection grew. He paid $40 for a 9mm German Luger, which seemed to be his favorite. His suspicions that the neighbors were talking about him behind his back mounted to the point that any time Unruh saw them in conversation, he felt certain they were speaking of him. Actually, Howard Unruh seldom entered the conversation of his neighbors. He simply was not that interesting to them.

Unruh continued to plan. He finally arrived at the conclusion that he would have to kill his mother in order to spare her the agony of the killings he would later perform. The chief target of his reprisals would be the Cohens, and his special plans for them were the most hideous of all. A machete had been added to Unruh's collection of weapons. After the crime, Unruh told investigating psychologists that he had planned to use the machete to behead Mr and Mrs Cohen.

In back of the Unruhs' apartment was an extremely small yard that was completely enclosed by a fence. On September 5, 1949, Howard Unruh sublimated his anger for one more day by installing a gate in that fence. This would allow him to get in and out of the yard without crossing anyone else's property. It was one way to prevent the prying eyes of the neighbors from falling on him. He worked industriously through the day. In the afternoon his father stopped by to give Howard a hand in fashioning the crude gate that was to hang in the middle of the back fence and open to the alley. It was not a work of craftsmanship by any standard but, to Howard Unruh, it represented a personal victory over the neighbors.

What Howard Unruh did on the night of September 5, is not known. At about 3:00 a.m., however, traveling a path that would take him through the newly constructed gate, Unruh came home. He was surprised and angered to find that the gate had disappeared, leaving only a gaping hole in the fence where it had been. As always, his calm demeanor remained, but the incident became the proverbial back-breaking straw. Though pranksters had taken the gate away, Unruh was positive his neighbors were to blame.

He walked into the apartment and began to review the plans he had made, revising and bringing them up to date. Later, the only complaint Howard Unruh had about the night was that he had had trouble falling asleep. Although he had no proof of who actually had taken the gate, there was one way in which he could be certain of punishing the true culprit – he could kill everybody.

The following morning, his mother made eggs and cereal for Howard's breakfast. Mrs Unruh was disturbed by the wild look in her son's eye, but nothing prepared her for what was to come. Howard Unruh made a quick trip to the basement and returned carrying a chromeplated wrench. His expression, and the way he handled the wrench, so terrified his mother that she ran from the house. Nearly hysterical, Mrs Unruh finally stopped at the house of a friend. When she began to tell of the hatred she had glimpsed in her son's eyes, she fainted.

Howard Unruh was a little upset by his mother's reaction. It threw his schedule off and forced him to start earlier than he had planned. He went to his room, loaded the Luger and another pistol, and put a knife in his coat pocket. All the extra clips for the Luger were loaded also, and he shoved them into the other pocket of his coat. Deciding to leave the unwieldy machete behind, Unruh picked up a tear-gas cartridge before he left the room, then walked outside and vaulted the fence instead of walking through the gateless hole in it. He made his way over a neighboring yard and then through an alley that brought him to the sidewalk on River Road, between a cleaning establishment and a shoe repair shop. Unruh's first stop on one of the deadliest walks in history was at the shoe repair shop. The time was 9:20 a.m.

Cobbler John Pilarchik had opened his shop as usual that sunny September day. He was particularly busy working on children's shoes that the youngsters would need for the beginning of school the next week. He had just purchased the shoe repair shop and business was expanding. He looked up from his work as Howard Unruh entered the store, and was met by the barrel of Unruh's Luger. Unruh's expression never changed as he squeezed off two quick shots. The blasts echoed through the little shop, and Pilarchik pitched headlong to the floor.

Taking his time, Unruh walked out of the cobbler's shop and turned to his left, heading for the corner of the block and the Cohen drugstore. But before he got there, he turned into the first door past Pilarchik's, a barber shop owned and operated by Clark Hoover.

When Unruh entered, the barber was busy giving six-year-old Orris Smith a pre-school haircut. Mrs Edward Smith, Orris' mother, was standing next to the boy, who had mounted the plastic horse on which the barber trimmed young would-be-cowboys. Mrs Smith's eleven-year-old daughter and two boys from the neighborhood were also in the barber shop. The most that could be said for Unruh's expression was that it was impatient. Unruh had come after Hoover, the barber, and the Smith boy was in his way. He shot the boy in the head, then leveled the gun at the barber himself, shooting him once in the body and once in the head. Unruh paid no attention to the other people in the barber shop. Mrs Smith snatched up her son's body and, together with her daughter and the neighborhood boys, scrambled out of the place.

The buildings leading to the corner of 32 Street and River Road are sandwiched together with hardly any space between them. Therefore it was only a short stroll for Howard Unruh to reach the corner and the entrance to the drugstore. He moved unhurriedly and was about to go in when a man stood in his way. He was the Unruhs' insurance agent, James Hutton, a man with whom Howard Unruh had no quarrel at all.

"Excuse me," Howard Unruh said.

But James Hutton stood stock still, astonished at the sight of the gun in the other man's hand.

Because the man was in his way, Unruh fired the gun twice again, one slug in Hutton's body, the other in his head. The insurance man fell to the sidewalk.

Having disposed of this temporary obstacle in his path, Unruh entered the drugstore to search for the chief targets he wanted to place in front of his Luger. But Cohen had observed what had happened at the entrance of the store and had run upstairs to warn his family. When the gunman could not find anyone in the store, he, too, walked slowly up the stairs.

Mrs Cohen had hidden her son in one bedroom closet, while she, herself, had hidden in the other. Unruh entered the bedroom and shot through the closet door before he opened it and watched the woman's body fall to the floor. He shot her again, this time in the head, apparently unaware of the footsteps of the escaping boy.

Leaving Mrs Cohen's body on the bedroom floor, Unruh walked out of this room and into the next, where he found the druggist's mother on the phone, trying to call the police. The Luger banged twice again, and the woman dropped the phone as she crumpled to the floor.

While the killer was occupied with shooting the women, the druggist and his son climbed out a window, onto the sloping roof of the building. Unruh moved to the window and picked off the man with a shot in the back. The druggist's body fell to the sidewalk. Cohen was one man Unruh did not want to miss. Taking careful aim, Unruh shot through the window again. The bullet entered the man's skull and ended his life. Of the four people who had been in the building when Unruh entered, only one remained alive.

But the gunman was far from finished. The Cohens had been his prime targets, to be sure, but there were other neighbors who had to be repaid for the stabs in the back that Howard Unruh had imagined they inflicted on him. As if he were some grim avenger measuring out justice, Unruh retraced his path, his footsteps slow and deliberate as he traversed the stairs and then the length of the drugstore. Outside, the body of James Hutton still sprawled on the sidewalk. A car had stopped on River Road, apparently to aid the luckless Hutton. Without hesitation – and again with deadly accuracy – Unruh leveled the Luger and fired. In his attempt to aid a man beyond help, Alvin Day had forfeited his life.

With practiced smoothness Unruh reloaded, then walked across the street to where a car waited for the lights to change. A woman sat behind the wheel. Before she could pull away, Unruh shot her in the head through the open window. In the car with her were the woman's ten-year-old son and aged mother. Unruh poked the barrel of the gun through the car window and blasted until the boy and the older woman were also dead.

The tall, taciturn murderer walked on as if nothing extraordinary had occurred, then attempted to enter the supermarket and the bar-restaurant. Unruh fired two shots into the locked door of the bar-restaurant before recrossing the street on a diagonal that brought him back to the shoe repair shop where the carnage had begun. Down River Road, a truck driver was climbing from his cab. It was a long shot, but Unruh proved his marksmanship once again when he hit the driver in the leg.

On the other side of the cobbler's shop, was a tailor's establishment. Tom Fegrino, the owner, was out, but Unruh entered the shop and proceeded to the back room where he found Fegrino's terrified wife.

"Oh, my God, don't," the woman sobbed. Mrs Fegrino's pleas had absolutely no effect on the killer as he impassively triggered the two shots that ended the woman's life.

Outside again, Unruh chanced to see a movement in a nearby window. Most of the residents had sought cover, but three-year-old Tommy Hamilton had wandered to a window and was looking curiously through it when the glass shattered in front of him and the boy fell to the floor, dead.

Unruh left River Road by way of an alley running between the tailor's shop and the cobbler's shop. Knowing that he was low on ammunition, Unruh walked to a house that opened to 32 Street and entered it.

Mrs Madeline Harrie was at home with her two sons, Leroy, fourteen, and Armond, sixteen. Though Mrs Harrie's first thought was to retreat, she decided that she was not going to be driven out of her own home. She turned and held her ground in the kitchen. Her older son went further, however, and rushed the gunman. Perhaps because of the body flying at him, Unruh's aim was, for the first time, inaccurate. He shot twice and only wounded both Mrs Harrie and her son. He would have shot again, but, mercifully, he had run out of bullets.

For the first time that morning, Howard Unruh seemed to be in a hurry. He trotted lightly back toward the apartment where he lived, vaulted the fence, and ran inside. The thin wail of police sirens was heard. Unruh had barely climbed the stairs when the first police car arrived at the intersection. The time was 9:32 a.m. Only twelve minutes had passed since life on the street had first been interrupted in its normal routine! Soon the entire area swarmed with law enforcement officials.

The news spread quickly and, at the office of the Camden *Courier-Post*, city editor Phillip Buxton had a hunch that he felt compelled to follow. He had heard the killer's identification reported over the police radio and had quickly snatched up the Camden telephone listings to look for a name. When he had located the only possibility, the editor dialed the number, hoping that the deranged killer would answer the phone.

Barricaded in his apartment, Howard Unruh still acted unconcerned. Even while the bullets of the police tore through the plaster walls, he calmly answered the phone. The story of this incredible telephone interview was carried on the front page of the *Courier-Post*.

"Hello," Unruh said into the receiver. His voice was calm.

"Is this Howard?" Buxton asked.

"Yes, this is Howard," the man answered with his usual courtesy. "What is the last name of the party you want?"

"Unruh."

"Who are you and what do you want?"

"I'm a friend," Buxton said, trying to win his confidence, "and I want to know what they're doing to you."

"Well, they haven't done anything to me, yet, but I'm doing plenty to them." He sounded as if he might have been describing a shopping trip.

"How many have you killed?"

"I don't know yet – I haven't counted 'em, but it looks like a pretty good score."

"Why are you killing people?"

"I don't know. I can't answer that yet – I am too busy. I'll have to talk to you later." He hung up.

Unruh was indeed very busy. The police had begun heaving tear gas through the shattered windows, and, almost immediately, the killer lost interest in returning their small-arms fire. He could have retaliated with the tear gas he also carried, but instead he chose to give himself up. Fifty guns were trained on Howard Unruh as he walked out of the back door with his hands in the air. He was frisked and handcuffed immediately.

"What's the matter with you?" someone demanded as they led him away. "You a psycho?"

"I'm no psycho," Unruh replied calmly. "I have a good mind."

Howard Unruh was never brought to trial. A team of over twenty specialists were unanimous in their determination that he was insane. Not many people wanted the twenty-eight-year-old man on the loose, however, and it is doubtful that he will ever leave the New Jersey State Mental Hospital at Trenton.

During one interrogation he told psychiatrists: "I'd have killed a thousand if I'd had bullets enough." Fortunately, Howard Unruh had run out of ammunition.

Brad Steiger

A Mixed Bag

As in the previous volume, *Murder in the 1930s*, I conclude with some shorter accounts of cases that deserve at least a mention.

Although I have avoided political murders in this "Murder File", the assassination of Leon Trotsky deserves to be the exception, since it is one of the few murders of this period which is also a "historical event". This account is from the *Encyclopedia of Murder*, as are all but one of the others that follow.

The brief account of Bruno Lüdke is included because Lüdke was undoubtedly one of the major German sex killers of the 20th century; if his confession to eighty-five murders is accurate, then he is *the* major German sex killer. But since he was summarily executed without trial, no full account of his crimes survives.

I include the unsolved case of the Texarkana Moonlight Murderer because, together with the Black Dahlia case, it may be regarded as *the* unsolved sex crime of the 1940s.

The odd case of Ley and Smith is included in the *Notable British Trials* and must inevitably figure in any list of British crimes of the period.

The classic British murder mystery of the 1940s is undoubtedly the Lower Quinton "Witchcraft" murder. I was torn between whether to include the account by Fabian of the Yard, or the chapter from *Perfect Murder* by Bernard Taylor and Stephen Knight; however, space was running out, and this short account is by Rowan Wilson, from a book on unsolved murders I co-authored with my sons Damon and Rowan.

Finally, we end as we began, with a typical American sex murder of the forties. Like most sex killers, Charles Floyd was an inadequate personality. And, like so many sex killers, he began simply as a voyeur, watching girls undress through uncurtained windows. Twenty years later, a far more intelligent killer, Ted Bundy, would begin his career of crime in the same way – catching a casual glimpse of a girl removing her clothes, and then turning voyeurism into a "project", which ended – inevitably – by breaking into houses.

From the point of view of the history of crime, the lesson of the 1940s seems to be that the Second World War served as a catalyst, leaving no doubt that the Age of Sex Crime – which began so hesitantly in the last quarter of the 19th century – had finally come to stay.

The Assassination of Leon Trotsky

In the afternoon of 20 August 1940 exiled Russian Communist leader Leon Trotsky received a visit from a man known to him as Frank Jacson, 26, journalist, whose mistress, Sylvia Ageloff, was a devoted supporter of Trotsky's political creed. Few people gained admittance to the Mexican fortress (a villa in Coyoacan, a suburb of Mexico City) where the 61-year-old revolutionary lived, still regarded as a deviationist and potential menace by Russian dictator Stalin and his satellites. An abortive attempt on Trotsky's life had been made on 24 May, when twenty men, disguised as policemen, had gained admittance to the villa (through the gullibility or possible collusion of secretary Robert Sheldon Hart, a 23-year-old American, found days afterwards shot dead in a bed of quicklime), had machine-gunned Trotsky's bedroom and thrown incendiary bombs as their target and his wife Natalia cowered under the bed. Four days after this incident Frank Jacson paid the first of many visits, and on this hot August day Natalia Trotsky expressed amazement that her guest should be carrying a raincoat. Left alone with Trotsky (Jacson said he wished to consult him concerning an article draft) the younger man produced from the raincoat pockets a fourteen-inch dagger, a .45 automatic pistol, and an ice pick, which he rammed into Trotsky's head. Jacson, bludgeoned by guards summoned by Trotsky's screams ("Who made you do it? The Soviet Secret Police?"), was taken into custody muttering, "They've got something on me. They are keeping my mother as a prisoner." Trotsky died next day, his brain ($3^1/2$ lb. in weight) having been pierced to a depth of three inches. In Jacson's pocket was a letter expressing disillusionment with Trotsky, who, he said, was only motivated by the desire for personal revenge and who had instructed him to assassinate Stalin. He was sentenced to Mexico's ultimate penalty, twenty years' imprisonment; he proved a model prisoner, teaching illiterates to read, setting up a prison electrical repair shop (employing twenty-six men), and even taking a beautiful Mexican woman, Roquelia Mendoza, as his common-law wife, a practice permissible in Mexico prisons.

This assassin's true identity remains in doubt. He had been introduced to Sylvia Ageloff in Paris in 1938 as Jacques Mornard, a Belgian reporter; he joined her afterwards in New York as Frank Jacson, explaining that he had used a forged passport in order to avoid the Belgian call-up. Jacson-Mornard himself said he was Jacques Vandendreschd, born in Teheran, son of that country's Belgian ambassador, but this story was found to be false. As he could speak a Barcelona dialect, one investigator looked up Madrid police fingerprint files on Civil War political prisoners, and found that Jacson-Mornard's prints tallied with those of anti-Franco fighter Ramon Mercades del Rio, born 1914, whose mother had been a member of the Barcelona Communist Party and later an agent of the Russian Secret Police, fleeing to Moscow with some of her children in 1937 after Spanish forces were routed.

On his release from jail on 6 May 1960, Jacson-Mornard had a passport issued to him by Czecho-Slovakia, and was last seen in Havana.

Bruno Lüdke

Lüdke was born in 1909; he was definitely mentally defective, in the same way as Earle Nelson. He began his murders at the age of 18. During the war he found it easy to kill. He was arrested for a sexual assault and sterilized by order of Himmler's SS. He was a petty thief (like Kürten) and a sadist who enjoyed torturing animals and (on one occasion) running down a woman with his horse-drawn delivery van. (He worked as a laundry roundsman.)

On 29 January 1943, a 51-year-old woman, Frieda Rösner, was found strangled on the outskirts of a wood near Berlin where she had been collecting fuel. Kriminal Kommissar Franz, in charge of the case, examined all the known criminals in Köpenick, the nearby village. These included Lüdke, who lived at 32 Grüne Trift. When he was asked if he had known the murdered woman, Lüdke admitted that he had, and that he had last seen her in the woods. Asked if he had killed her, he sprang at his interrogator and had to be overpowered; he then admitted he was the murderer, and added that under Paragraph 51 (concerning mental defectives) he could not be indicted for the crime. Lüdke went on to confess to killing eighty-five women throughout Germany since 1928. His normal method was strangulation or stabbing with a knife, and although he stole their belongings, rape was the chief motive. Franz investigated the murders and after a year, reported that it seemed to be true that Lüdke was responsible for all the crimes he confessed to. But it is also true that local police chiefs blamed all their unsolved murders on Lüdke, the ideal scapegoat.

Lüdke believed that he could never be indicted because he was insane. In fact, the embarrassment of various police forces who had arrested innocent men for Lüdke's crimes led to the case being hushed up and treated as a State secret. Lüdke was sent to a hospital in Vienna where he was a guinea-pig for various experiments, and one of the injections killed him on 8 April 1944.

The Texarkana Moonlight Murderer

On the night of 20 February 1946 a young couple were seated in their car near Texarkana, Texas, listening to the radio, when the door was swung open, and the man was struck on the head with a revolver. The girl was also knocked unconscious as she attempted to run away, and was raped. It was daylight when the man regained consciousness, carried his fiancée to the car, and drove to the nearest house for assistance. Six men were arrested almost immediately, following the description given of the attacker by the young couple, and tyre-tracks were noticed close to the spot where the assault had taken place. However, no positive evidence could be obtained, and the men were released. Towns within two hundred miles of the Texas-Arkansas border were alerted to be on the lookout for the criminal.

A month later, on 24 March, Richard Griffin and Polly Anne Moore, a 24-year-old salesman and his 19-year-old girl-friend, parked their car only a mile away from the spot where the previous couple had been assaulted. Griffin was shot through the head; the girl was shot twice, mutilated with a sharp knife, and sexually assaulted. Evidence showed that Griffin had been murdered two hours or so before the girl. Tyreprints near the murder site were identical with those found near the scene of the previous assault. The bullets came from a .32 revolver.

On both occasions a bright full moon had simplified the sex-maniac's search for victims.

Again, many suspects were arrested and released.

On 13 April a 15-year-old girl, Betty Jo Booker, had been playing a saxophone at a local dance. She left the dance after midnight with her boy-friend, 17-year-old Paul Martin. The next morning, both bodies were found a mile away from the car. The youth had been shot in the back three times. The girl had evidently been dragged away from the car, and was shot and mutilated about four hours after the death of her boy-friend. She had been tortured for some time before she was killed; she was also raped.

Scores of suspects were interviewed, and all available police in Texas and Arkansas were used on the case, without result. The newspapers headlined the unknown killer, and a "reign of terror" began in the area of the murders.

On 3 May 1946, again on the night of a full moon, a wealthy farmer, Virgil Starks, was shot as he sat reading a newspaper at ten-thirty. His wife, rushing into the room, was also shot. She managed to run to the house of a neighbour, A.V. Prater, and gave the alarm. This crime had occurred within the state of Arkansas.

Evidence showed that the murderer had killed Virgil Starks with a .22 rifle, and had entered the house immediately after Mrs Starks ran for help. His intention was probably to assault the housewife in his usual manner; the familiar tyre-tracks were found near the house. Mrs Starks recovered from her wounds a few weeks later.

Measures for discovering the criminal were on the enormous scale that is usual in such cases. Hundreds of men were interviewed in towns for a hundred miles around. All military personnel were investigated. A detective with a dummy dressed like a woman sat in a car for night after night in the murder area, but the murderer ignored the bait.

After the murder of Virgil Starks, the crimes stopped. In 1954 a man confessed to being the killer, but careful investigation revealed that this was impossible.

There seems one likely explanation of the sudden cessation of the murders. A few days after the death of Virgil Starks, a man committed suicide by leaping under a train near Texarkana. His description fitted that of the murderer; he was obviously not the hobo type; but he was unknown in the vicinity. His identity was never established. But at the same time that he committed suicide a small car was found burning in a heavily wooded area near the site of the murders. It was definitely a case of deliberate arson, but the tyres had been destroyed, and the ground was too hard to show tracks. It seems remotely possible that the murderer was a Jekyll and Hyde character who was affected by the full moon, and who may have committed suicide in a fit of remorse.

Ley and Smith

If I had more space, I would have liked to include an account of another of Simpson's classic cases, the Chalkpit Murder. As it is, a brief summary will have to suffice.

The case is a curious one; Thomas Ley was certainly insane, and developed a strange obsession about Mudie; he then hired Smith to murder him. But the obsession had no relation whatever to reality.

The career of Thomas Ley had been in many ways remarkable; in New South Wales he had once been the Hon. Thomas Ley, Minister for Justice, but a charge of bribery, and two suspicious deaths – business associates of Ley who were in his way at the time of death – brought his political career to an end. Ley was a grossly fat man, whose fortune had been made by many dubiously legal activities. He returned to England in 1929.

A few weeks after he returned to England, Mrs Maggie Brook followed him; she was a widow of a Perth J.P., and had been 40 when she met Ley in 1922. She became his mistress, and it was because of Ley's jealousy of her that the murder was committed.

Mrs Brook had a daughter, who married a man named Barron and went to live in Wimbledon. When the daughter was ill in hospital, Ley suggested to Mrs Brook that she should go and look after her son-in-law. This was in May 1946. On 12 June 1946, at 10 p.m., Ley telephoned Mrs Brook and accused her of having sexual relations with her son-in-law. (Mrs Brook was 66!) At two-thirty in the morning he arrived in a car and insisted that Mrs Brook return with him to his house in Knightsbridge Court.

There is no explaining Ley's strange jealousy obsession about Mrs Brook – they had ceased to have sexual intercourse ten years before. But there can be no doubt of his madness. He went to Mrs Brook's landlady in Wimbledon and declared that Mrs Brook had asked him to take her away because she was being pestered by the men in the house.

He asked the names of the male lodgers, and Mrs Evans (the landlady) gave them. They included John Mudie, a 35-year-old barman and a decent young man who had only once ever spoken to Mrs Brook. Mrs Evans assured Ley that it was unlikely Mudie had slept with Mrs Brook. Later, Ley called again, saying he wanted to apologize to Mudie. Mrs Evans gave him Mudie's new address at Reigate, where he had become a barman.

Ley moved into a new property at 5 Beaufort Gardens. One day Mrs Brook's son-in-law received a phone call asking him to have tea with Mrs Brook at Beaufort Gardens. He was suspicious and checked with Mrs Brook, who knew nothing about the invitation. Barron was lucky, for Ley was waiting for him at Beaufort Gardens with hired thugs, who might very probably have killed him as Mudie was later killed.

After this failure Ley turned his attention to Mudie, and on 19 June tried a curious trick to find out if Mudie was associating with Mrs Brook. He sent some cheques to Mrs Brook care of Mudie; Mrs Brook's counter-signature was needed on them. Naturally, Mudie had no idea where Mrs Brook was, and returned the cheques to the firm directed by Ley and Mrs Brook. Ley then had his solicitors write to Mudie demanding the return of the cheques, and finally went to see Mudie himself; Mudie satisfied Ley that the cheques had been returned and, after confirming this, Ley apologized. The reasons for his conduct are mysterious.

Ley now contacted John William Buckingham, a car-hirer, and invited Buckingham to a meeting. At this meeting, attended by Ley, Buckingham, and John Lawrence Smith, a joiner, Buckingham was told that Mudie was a black-mailer who must be decoyed to London and forced to sign a pledge not to bother Mrs Brook and her daughter again. A friend of Buckingham's, a Mrs Bruce, was also brought into the conspiracy. Her job was to go to the Reigate Hill Hotel and make Mudie's acquaintance. Smith hired a car, a Ford 8, number FGP 101, and on Wednesday 27 November 1946 drove down to a chalk pit situated on the Slines Road, leading from the main Croydon – Westerham road to Woldingham in Surrey. At about four-forty on this date, two labourers saw Smith standing on the edge of the chalk pit; when he saw them he ran away to the car, which was parked behind some trees, and drove off fast; they noticed the 101 in the number of the car, and also its make.

Mrs Bruce made Mudie's acquaintance according to plan, posing as a wealthy lady, and invited him to come and mix cocktails at a party to be given by her in London. Mudie accepted. On 28 November Mrs Bruce and Buckingham's son went to Reigate to pick up Mudie, and drove him to Beaufort Gardens, where Mrs Bruce let him in by a side door. She then closed the door and went off with Buckingham junior; this was the last she saw of Mudie. For this service she received £30. She had, of course, no idea that Mudie was to be murdered.

Inside the house, Smith and Buckingham pounced on Mudie and threw a blanket over his head, then tied him up with some clothes-line which Buckingham had bought. Buckingham was then given £200 – thirty of which were for Mrs Bruce – and told to go, and not to contact Ley again. (A few days later he was told that Mudie had signed the agreement, and had left the country with £500 given him by Ley.)

Now either Ley or Smith, or both, administered a brutal beating up to Mudie – probably Ley, in view of his motives. Then one of them strangled Mudie and the body was taken out to the chalk pit and dumped.

Two days later, on 30 November, the body was discovered by Mr Walter Coombs. A rope was tied around the throat, and there was signs of violent blows on the head, chest, and stomach. He was soon identified as Mudie, and among his possessions at the hotel were letters relating to his dealings with Ley. The police soon had Ley, Smith, and Buckingham under arrest and charged Ley and Smith with murder. Buckingham had gone to Scotland Yard of his own accord on 14 December, two weeks after discovery of the body, and made a statement.

Smith was an evasive witness who made a bad impression. He declared that he had left Mudie bound and gagged and alone in the house with Ley. He admitted his indifference to Mudie's fate, but claimed he did not believe Ley intended to murder him.

The trial opened on 19 March 1947 at the Old Bailey before Lord Goddard, Lord Chief Justice. Mr Anthony Hawke and Mr Henry Elam prosecuted; Sir Walter Monckton led Ley's defence, and Mr Derek Curtis Bennett defended Smith. Both pleaded not guilty, but Ley simply disclaimed all knowledge of Mudie. This was stupid, and it gave Ley's counsel an extremely difficult task.

An interesting witness for the defence was an ex-convict named Robert Cruikshank, who had been in Australia in 1929 (and so may have known Ley) and who was living in Switzerland at the time of the murder. But Cruikshank claimed that he had flown to England on the afternoon of the murder on some smuggling venture, and had a few hours to kill before flying back the same night. He decided to call on Ley, whom he claimed he did not know, hoping that Ley, as a rich Australian, might help him to get back to Australia. He also claimed that at 8 p.m. he found the house in darkness, and decided that it might be worth burgling. He let himself into the basement, and saw a man tied into a chair. His lighter failed at that moment, but he went to the man and pulled on the ropes. However, he abandoned any intention of freeing the man and made off. The whole point of Cruikshank's evidence seemed to be that he *might* have strangled the man by pulling on the ropes. Lord Goddard asked if he meant to confess to killing the man, and Cruikshank replied that it was only a possibility. In his summing up, Lord Goddard made no bones about the possibility that Cruikshank had been bribed to confuse the prosecution with a possibility that Mudie had died accidentally.

Both Ley and Smith were sentenced to death, but on May 5, after an examination by three specialists, Ley was declared insane and moved to Broadmoor. A month later he died of a seizure. Since it would have been hardly fair to reprieve the master and not the man, Smith's sentence was also commuted to penal servitude for life.

The Lower Quinton Witchcraft Murder

Charles Walton was practically retired from labouring by the spring of 1945. He had worked on the local farms all his life and now, in his seventy-fourth year, was afflicted with crippling rheumatism. Despite this he still insisted on doing some work around farmer Albert Potter's farm when the weather allowed him.

St Valentine's Day, 14 February 1945, was a clear and sunny day in Lower Quinton when Charles Walton took up his walking stick and made for Meon Hill on Potter's farm to do some hedge cutting. Walton lived with his niece Edith who had a war job in a nearby factory. When she got home at 6 o'clock that evening, her uncle had not returned. Normally he was back from work around 4. Edith was anxious, worried that he had fallen and, unable to stand up, was lying out in the open in the approaching darkness.

Co-opting a neighbour to help her search, Edith made for Potter's farm. Accompanied by the farmer, Edith and her neighbour hunted through the fields by torchlight. Their shouts brought no reply. Edith was beginning to fear for her uncle's life. Suddenly, in the beam of the torch, they saw a body. Charles Walton was pinned to the ground with his own pitchfork. Edith, stunned with shock, returned to her cottage escorted by the neighbour while Potter remained with the body.

Only when the police arrived with spotlights did it become clear how violently Walton had been butchered. His throat was slashed with his own hand scythe, which had been left jutting from the wound. His arms were criss-crossed with cuts where he had evidently tried to defend himself. The pitchfork that fixed him to the ground took two policemen to remove – Potter had tried and failed. Cut into the wrinkled skin of Walton's neck and chest was a cross.

Superintendent Robert Fabian, known as Fabian of the Yard, one of Britain's most celebrated detectives, took over the case after local police failed to uncover any leads. A tin watch had been removed from the corpse, and Fabian enlisted the help of the Royal Engineers equipped with mine detectors to search the surrounding countryside for it. Meanwhile constables took statements from the village's 493 inhabitants.

The crime should have been easy to solve. The murderer must have been someone with a grudge against Walton. In a small community, such a motive would be difficult to hide. This was the rational view. The terrible violence of the attack and the superstitious silence of the locals suggested a more ritualistic cause for Walton's death.

The pinning of a witch to the ground in order to destroy her power is a ritual dating from Anglo-Saxon times. The villagers tacitly implied that this is what happened to Walton. In 1875 a man called John Haywood had murdered an old lady named Ann Turner because he believed her to be a witch who was persecuting him. In his statement to the court he said that it was common knowledge that most of the misfortunes suffered by the local community were inflicted by a small coven of witches. He had merely taken his revenge. He had stabbed her with a pitchfork and cut a cross into her neck.

Fabian uncovered only one other lead. A villager had made a statement to the effect that a POW from the nearby camp was seen wiping blood from his hands in a ditch on the day of the killing. The camp inmates were all searched and an Italian was found to have bloodstains on his coat. He refused to answer questions. The coat was sent, along with other samples taken from villagers, to the forensic lab. The Royal Engineers were despatched to search the ditch. They found metal. It was not however the tin watch, but a rabbit snare. The blood on the coat also proved to be that of a rabbit. The POW had declined to talk because he was scared that he would be punished for poaching.

There the investigation ended – it remained one of Fabian's few total failures. But in their book *Perfect Murder*, Bernard Taylor and Stephen Knight claim to have learned the solution to the mystery. In "The Mysterious Death of Charles Walton", Knight alleges that Fabian was certain of the identity of the killer, but simply lacked the evidence to prosecute. The murderer, Knight says, was Farmer Potter himself. His motive had nothing to do with ridding the countryside of a witch, but was purely financial. Walton was an obsessive saver, and he had lent Potter a large sum when Potter was on the brink of ruin. The money became due; Potter was unable to pay it back, and on that St Valentine's Day, he chose a violent solution to his problem. Potter may not have intended to kill Charles Walton when he went to talk to him about the debt – or to ask for an extension. Perhaps Walton threatened him with court action, or flourished the receipt under his nose. Whatever the reason, Potter killed the frail old man, then mutilated the body to suggest a witchcraft connection.

Knight's evidence for this theory tends to centre upon Potter's conflicting statements to police and the ease with which he found Walton's body in the dark that February evening. His attempts to pull the pitchfork from Walton's chest were, according to the theory, attempts to cover his fingerprints from the time of the murder.

Whether or not Potter killed Walton, the aspect of the story that intrigues is the idea of a well hidden group of Satan worshippers at the heart of a seemingly tranquil English village life. Even if Potter did kill Charles Walton and mark the body with pagan symbolism, where did he learn the pagan symbolism? It would seem that the more comfortable, greed-based explanation of Charles Walton's murder merely leads to more questions.

Rowan Wilson

Charles Floyd

No full account of Floyd's case history has been given; his first victim may have been Mrs William C. Brown, the 20-year-old wife of a Tulsa truck-driver, strangled and raped in her flat at 825 North Main Street on 10 July 1942. She was pregnant and only six days away from delivering the child when she was murdered; the unborn baby was also killed.

Less than six months later, 6-year-old Clara Stewart and her daughter, Mrs Georgina Green, were battered to death and raped in their apartment, again on the north side of the city. Mrs Green's husband was in the army. All three victims were redheads.

Two and a half years went by before the next attack, on 15 May 1945. Panta Lou Liles, the redheaded wife of a sailor, returning to her ground-floor room at 501 Cheyenne Street, undressed without drawing the curtains. The "peeping Tom" outside watched her undress, waited until she was asleep, and clambered over the windowsill into the room. He knocked the girl unconcious before she woke up, and went on to batter her to death. He then wrapped her head in a sheet, and raped her. Several hours later he was still in the room when Mrs Liles" room-mate, a night nurse, rang up to wake the girl in time to be at her work at a nearby aircraft plant. A man's voice answered; and the nurse called the police.

A man named Henry Owens was arrested on suspicion; he was known to be weak-minded, and had been booked before on a charge of molesting women. A lie-detector test was inconclusive; although the graph jumped when Owens was asked about the murders, it seemed possible that he might be deluding himself by a kind of wishful thinking. The lie-detector operator told of an interesting case, when a lunatic who claimed he was Napoleon was given a test. When asked if he was Napoleon, he denied it, but the detector showed he was lying!

While Owens was still in custody, the murderer had another outburst, this time wounding three girls and killing a fourth. This was on 1 July 1948. The murderer broke into the flat of a woman on North Cheyenne Street, and attacked the woman and two children who were sleeping in the flat – her daughter and a friend, aged respectively 12 and 14. The woman was knocked unconscious and an "unnatural sex act" committed on her. The two children were knocked unconscious and partly undressed, but the killer was disturbed by a neighbour who had been roused by screams and escaped by the back door before he could complete the assault. Two blocks away, at 11 East Cameron Street, the killer found another redhead, Ruth Norton, whom he bludgeoned while she was still asleep and then raped. Ruth Norton died of her injuries. The killer had apparently forced his way in by cutting a hole in the back door – a method reminiscent of the New Orleans Axe Man.

A description of the murderer came from a woman who

had been awakened by the barking of a dog on the night of the Ruth Norton murder. She had seen a man standing outside and flashing a torch; he was more than six feet tall and looked like a truck-driver.

The police began a careful check on all trucking companies in Tulsa, and finally discovered that a tall man named Charles Floyd had left his job on the day after the murder of Ruth Norton; Floyd was known to have a passion for redheads. It took some time to find Floyd, but he was finally arrested a year and a half after his last murder. Floyd seemed to be tired and confused, but he was able to supply details that would be known only to the murderer. He admitted to being an inveterate "peeping Tom" who had killed when the sexual excitement became too overpowering.

In some ways, the case fails to conform to the usual pattern of the sexual murderer, whose crimes tend to become more and more frequent. After the three murders in 1942, two and a half years elapsed before the next, then a period of three years.

It has at least one feature worth commenting on. From Floyd's confession, it emerged that he was in the habit of watching Panta Lou Liles undressing through her window. In a sense, therefore, the girl was partly to blame for not drawing her curtains. One of the causes of the increase in sexual crime is certainly the increase in stimulation.